Where Ladybugs Go to Die

KIRSTEN GALE

For my parents, my husband, my children, and my dearest friends—your love, strength, and unwavering belief lit the path that brought this story to life.

Prologue

Black Sheep

A sinister smile curled across his face as he stared into the fire, warming his hands over the red-hot burn barrel. The night air bit at his skin as he stripped down to black boxer briefs. The crackling flames and rustling leaves were the only sounds while his blood-soaked clothes shriveled to ash.

Adrenaline, a frantic hummingbird, thrummed in his veins. He wanted to laugh out loud, unhinged, but he was only a few yards into the trees in his backyard. He couldn't risk drawing attention.

Shivering, he crouched beside the last of the animals he'd caught. A tabby cat purred and rubbed against his leg, trusting, unaware. He grabbed it by the neck and slammed it to the frozen ground. It hissed, claws lashing out. The scream came when he drove a serrated hunting knife deep into its belly, twisting. Then he split it open. Blood soaked its fur as he dug through soft, yielding flesh.

His hands, as tools, ripped and sorted the organs with care, a grotesque routine he'd perfected. He imagined it was human flesh beneath his fingers, and his mouth watered. But for now, the cat would do. It dulled the hunger.

Killing cats was a ritual, but hunting, stalking, cornering, and conquering them satisfied a deeper hunger. He dreamed of grander prey, human prey, and tonight, he was closer than ever. A secret he had kept flawlessly since he was six. Sometimes, he dumped the bodies in a river or buried them miles from home. However, burning them was quicker, cleaner, and final.

Years of planning and precision had led him to this moment. He was ready, his mind and body sharpened. The plan was foolproof. If everything went as calculated, no one would ever know.

The nursery rhymes never left him. He despised their sing-song echoes. However, as he grew, he began to hear secrets in the verses—meanings others overlooked. In that darkness, he discovered purpose.

Her sins had stolen the only thing that ever mattered to him, leaving him hollow and frayed at the edges. Now, it was time to collect the debt.

He tossed the cat's remains into the barrel, watching the flames devour it. The fire blazed high, orange light dancing in his eyes as it licked at the cat's fur. The stench of burning hair and flesh filled his nose, but instead of recoiling, he calmed. His heart slowed.

> *"Baa, Baa, Black Sheep, have you any wool?*
> *Yes, sir, yes, sir, three bags full.*
> *One for the girl who cried in the dark,*
> *One for the boy who bore the mark,*
> *And one for the mother with lies on her tongue*
> *Now all the sheep are gone but one."*

In his twisted mind, the rhyme was his creed. He was the Black Sheep, the outcast marked by a past he couldn't escape. The girl who cried in the dark was the innocent daughter of the woman who had destroyed him. She wove a web of deceit that cost him everything. The three bags of wool symbolized the lives he intended to claim, each representing a piece of his vengeance.

A sharp gust tore through the night, flinging the screen door open with a creak that shattered the silence. He reached for the blunt-nosed shovel resting against a tree and hurled dirt onto the fire. It hissed in defiance. Turning away from the smoldering barrel, fury surged within him. He muttered a curse, gripping the shovel tighter, each step toward the house a vow of erasure.

He would silence the person who ruined his life and the cursed legacy she bore.

He was Satan.

1

Alexis

"Mom, I can take care of myself. You've been dating since I was eight. I'm seventeen now. Why are you acting worried?" I rolled my eyes—she couldn't see, but still. Her concern was an act. We both knew it.

Outside, the scent of ocean salt and blooming jasmine drifted in through the cracked kitchen window. The low hum of evening rush hour traffic from the Pacific Coast Highway murmured in the distance, mingling with the distant crash of waves. Sunlight filtered through the blinds, casting golden slatted shadows across the tile floor, warm and beautiful, yet it didn't reach us.

"I know, baby."

I cringed. I hated it when she called me that.

"I just worry about you sometimes, Alexis." Her voice was soft, as if she were navigating a minefield. "I never see you with any friends, and you seem lonely. You know, if you want, you're welcome to invite someone over while I'm out. Perhaps even a boy." She forced a smile, her lips twitching, uncertain as if she were trying to bridge a gap too wide to cross.

I shifted, my sneakers scuffing the worn linoleum, the sound sharp in the quiet. My dark hair slipped into my eyes, and I swiped it back with a quick, restless hand, my fingers trembling slightly.

"Mom, I really don't want to go into this right now." The words came out clipped, my throat tight as if each syllable had to claw its way free. I glanced out the window, where the Pacific roiled under a pinkish-orange sky, waves crashing like they could swallow my frustration whole.

"Honey, I'm just looking out for you." She stepped closer, her lavender perfume sharp against the salty air, her hand hovering as if she might reach for me but thought better of it. "Exploring multiple relationships now can help you discover who you are and build confidence for a meaningful partnership later on."

I nearly choked on the word "exploring." My mind flashed to sex ed class, where we learned about STDs and how the risk skyrockets with multiple partners. Did she not understand that? Had she ever experienced something like that herself? A shudder ran through me. I squeezed my eyes shut, taking a deep breath to avoid snapping at her.

"Mom," I warned again. "You know how I feel about this. I'm seventeen and have plenty of time to worry about sex after I graduate." Besides, I didn't want to become like her; I wanted to have morals. I couldn't believe I was having this conversation with her again. She knew it bothered me that she used her body to get men, but she still brought it up.

The phone vibrated as Mom prepared, her reflection a blend of shine and shade. "B, not right now. No, you don't need to come to Ventura," she snapped, her tone sharp. "I'm going out tonight. You know that." She ended the call, her gaze shifting to me. "Someone I knew in Gold Beach. She constantly interferes." I frowned. B? Another hidden truth trailed behind her.

As I rose from the couch, I leaned down to grab the remote and switched off the television—so much for an enjoyable evening. I hadn't even glanced at her after she emerged from the bathroom. She was heading out for one of her numerous dates, having spent an eternity in there. She could and often did spend hours getting ready. I often wondered where she met all these guys. Occasionally, she'd bring them home, while other times, she wouldn't return until morning. Yet, there were instances when she'd leave with one man but come back with another. She believed I was naïve and unaware of her actions, but she was mistaken. It had become her game.

She stood by the bathroom door, her gold-chained clutch draped over her shoulder, when I glanced up at her. Her glossy, ebony hair was fashioned in a loose French twist, and she donned her iconic first-date black sleeveless cocktail dress. She was very selective about her clothing for these occasions, classifying her dresses as first, second, or third-date options. I had seen this particular dress more than any other since she rarely dated a guy more than once.

Whenever she portrayed the 'perfect' mother role, I questioned whether she had some type of multiple personality disorder. The only comforting aspect was that I had become adept at recognizing her mood swings.

"So, what's his name this time, Mom?" She was always pushing me, trying to make me like her. I wasn't. I wanted my first time to mean something. Maybe that was naive, but I'd rather be alone than end up like her. Most people kept their distance anyway; no one wanted their kid around the "whore's daughter."

"His name is William Thompson. He's an accountant, and I knew him when we lived in Gold Beach," she said with a dreamy, far-off look on her face.

We had left my father, Luke, in Oregon. The weather was cold there, yet it was beautiful in its own way, at least from what I could recall from when I was five.

I groaned as I closed my eyes and asked, "What do you mean you knew him?"

"Don't have an attitude, Alexis," she scolded. "He was a school friend of your dad's. They grew up together, and when your dad and I were still together, we would go out with him and his wife, B. Well, now his ex-wife. They got divorced not long after your dad and I did."

I rolled my eyes. "Yeah, and I bet that's why B was meddling because she heard you're going out with her ex-husband," I muttered, barely hiding my annoyance.

Nicole's cheeks turned crimson as she struck the door with her fist, making her flawless face twitch with discomfort. "You watch your tone, young lady!" she retorted, jabbing a shaky finger in my direction. "You can't speak to me that way, especially regarding matters you know nothing about!"

My stomach knotted, and I opened my mouth to respond, but the sudden chime of the doorbell cut through the tension. I froze, grateful for the distraction, then hurried to the door before she could speak again.

I straightened my bulky, too-hot sweater set for May and shoved my hands in my hair, giving it a good rumpling to try to look less attractive. I opened it and assessed her date. He wasn't bad looking. He was tall, over six feet, with olive skin, dark, curly black hair, and brown eyes. I felt a bit intimidated as he towered over my five-foot frame.

"Oh, sorry,—uh, I'm looking for Nicole Roberts?" He glanced past me. Hearing her maiden name sounded weird.

"No, this is the right place. Nicole's my mom."

"Oh, wow. Alexis?" His eyes widened, too familiar. How did he know my name? His gaze lingered, unsettled me, like he recognized someone else in me. A chill ran down my back.

He extended his hand, eager to shake mine. Instead, I occupied my hands by tugging my zipped-up hoodie up to hide my messy hair. Thankfully, he caught on and withdrew his hand, placing it in the front pocket of his gray pinstripe slacks.

"Yeah." That was all I could manage to say before I heard Nicole coming out of the bathroom. I turned to look at her.

"Alexis, why didn't you invite him in?" she whined. Mr. Creepy spoke up before I could answer.

"Nicole, don't be upset with her. I thought I'd gotten the wrong house. You never mentioned you had custody of Alexis." He looked back at me and raised his eyebrows. "You've grown up just like I pictured." He officially became creepier.

So much for looking less attractive. I hated the parade of men she brought into our home.

"Alexis, I." She paused, her gaze softening, revealing the mother she might have been. But just as swiftly as it appeared, that warmth vanished, returning to her customary sharp demeanor. "Just don't mess this up for me. Good night, Alexis," she shouted back.

Ignoring her, I slammed the door shut. Why did she always get angry with me? I wasn't the creepy one trying to flirt with her daughter. Honestly, I couldn't understand why he would even consider it. I was just ordinary me, with dull green eyes and frizzy auburn hair. I had a petite frame and lacked curves, just plain boring. Plus, I was short. Way too short.

I plopped down on the cozy sofa and turned the television back on, excited to see my favorite cooking show. I wished I were there, as I loved to cook and knew I'd outperform the competing chefs. I listened well, had a good memory, cooked efficiently, and took constructive criticism well.

My junior year ended, and I was thrilled to earn straight A's, even in gym class. At barely five feet, my long legs powered me in running, a newfound love, and I excelled on the track team. Next year, I will join the varsity team and plan to train throughout the summer. Running, like reading or cooking, lets my mind escape from negative thoughts, though I often feel alone. I begged Nicole for a dog, but she refused, calling them filthy. I told her I was lonely, but she laughed, saying I had her like that was enough.

Life was tough, and Nicole blamed me for her failed relationships, calling me her baggage. Her dates groped me, and fighting them off only angered her more. I'd retreat to my locked room, claiming homework. Their touches, never my lips, left a lingering feeling of violation. Nicole never stopped them, saying I provoked them. After a bad date, she'd slap me, accusing me of flirting. Her insecurities fueled this, and it was getting under my skin. I just wanted her to see me.

While she never physically harmed me, she also failed to shield me. Her intense OCD required perfection: immaculate cupboards, perfectly aligned towels, straight vacuum lines, no dirt, and no shoes allowed indoors. She resembled the husband from "Sleeping with the Enemy."

My thoughts drifted away from the cooking show, and I soon fell into a dreamless sleep.

2

Black Sheep

He had watched Nicole for months, lurking just out of sight. Her string of men disgusted him. But it was her daughter who haunted him—innocent but already marked by her mother's sins. He would make them both pay, one step at a time.

Her smile as another man entered was a mockery. She was filth. But he wasn't focused on her anymore—he wanted her gone.

The time had come.

The knob was unlocked, as always. He slipped inside, moving from shadow to shadow. His steps were cautious—he knew which floorboards creaked. He waited in the pantry, listening for Nicole to say her goodbyes.

When Nicole's door closed, he moved to the girl on the couch. She needed to stay asleep. He slid the needle into her neck. She jolted, but the sedative worked fast. No scream, no struggle. Not yet. Ladybug's part would come later.

He turned then, moving with practiced ease down the hallway. Nicole's door creaked open beneath his gloved hand.

She was at her vanity, putting a wedding band on her finger, when she saw his reflection behind her in the mirror. Her eyes widened. "You?" She breathed, a flash of recognition, then fear. "How did you?"

"I always knew you'd end like this, Nicole," he whispered, his voice smooth yet bitter. "You took everything from me. Now I'm returning the favor."

She barely had time to rise before he surged forward, pressing a cloth to her mouth. Her limbs flailed, but it was too late—the chloroform did its work. Her body went slack in his arms.

Her ring finger, the one she'd used to swear her wedding vows to every man who promised her love but never stayed, was the key. Like the wife in "Peter, Peter, Pumpkin Eater," she couldn't be kept, not by promises, not by love. It was the final symbol of everything she had done wrong. She couldn't even keep her promises, not to her daughter, not to anyone.

He placed the severed finger into a carved pumpkin shell, its jagged grin leering like Peter's fabled pumpkin, a hollowed-out prison for a wayward soul. It was a mockery of everything Halloween was supposed to represent: innocence, childhood joy twisted into something grotesque. From his coat pocket, he scattered a handful of raw pumpkin seeds across the floor, tiny, slimy echoes of what had been carved away. Each seed was a taunt, a nod to Peter's futile attempt to trap what could never be contained. A trail, a signature. A reminder that something had been gutted, emptied. Left hollow.

Blood was everywhere: smeared across the sheets, spattered on the walls, and dripping in deliberate arcs. It wasn't just a crime scene; it was a canvas, a performance, a message. He spent hours drawing blood from her as it mixed with his own concoction into a metal bucket. The authorities would be baffled by the volume of blood from one severed finger. He painted it with care, knowing the sheer amount would scream one thing to the authorities: she was dead.

Before he left, he returned to the couch where Ladybug slept, peaceful, sedated, and unaware. He crouched beside her, his presence soft and steady, brushing two fingers gently across her cheek. She leaned into the warmth of his touch, letting out a soft sigh—a fleeting moment of comfort, like a whispered promise. Blood from Nicole smeared heavily against her skin, a crimson stroke beneath her eye. A mark. A memory she wouldn't understand yet. She was no cat, no simple kill. Ladybug, you'll be my greatest hunt.

He whispered the nursery rhyme one last time as he hoisted the heavy duffle bag, Nicole's body folded neatly inside, limbs bound, head tilted as if still listening, and then slipped back into the shadows of the night, heading for the marina.

> *"Peter, Peter, pumpkin eater,*
> *Had a wife, but couldn't keep her;*
> *Put her in a pumpkin shell,*
> *And there he kept her very well."*

He chose the rhyme for her intentionally. "Peter, Peter, Pumpkin Eater" wasn't just about a man and his wife. It was about possession. It was about locking something away when you couldn't control it. Nicole had never been loyal to anyone. Not to her husband. Not to her lovers. Not to her daughter. Not even to him.

She wore the mask of a mother but never fulfilled the role. She chose vanity, validation, and empty men over family. She devoured love like candy— sweet, disposable, and meaningless.

So, he made her the wife who couldn't be kept. And then he placed her in her own version of the pumpkin shell. A mockery of motherhood.

To him, it wasn't just a rhyme; it represented a judgment. It served as a lesson for those who believed they could evade the consequences of their actions. The mother had failed in every sense of the word.

Ladybug would wake soon; her story was just beginning.

3

Alexis

The slam of the front door jolted me awake. I blinked, heart pounding. Nicole and some guy stood in the doorway, half in shadow.

I didn't move, just tried to melt into the couch. Their kisses, the rustle of clothes—I held my breath. They stumbled to her bedroom and shut the door. Relief, then blackness. I drifted back to sleep, but in the dream, a man whispered:

> *"Peter, Peter, pumpkin eater,*
> *Had a wife and couldn't keep her!*
> *He put her in a pumpkin shell,*
> *And there he kept her very well."*

He chanted repeatedly. Each time, his abrasive voice sounded increasingly spine-chilling. My limbs thrashed about, twisting the blanket around my legs as I willed the voice to leave me alone, struggling hard to pull myself out of slumber. My body felt heavy, as if a strange fog had settled over my mind, dragging me deeper into a sleep I couldn't escape. Sticky, hot sweat covered my skin. No matter what I tried, I was trapped in this dreadful nightmare.

As my mind counted, the voice repeated the rhyme ten more times, each repetition becoming more distorted. Then, as if I had pressed stop on the video, silence enveloped me. My body gradually calmed and relaxed, leading me into a deep sleep. Thankfully, no dreams came that time.

Upon waking up the next morning, my eyes were blurry, and my limbs felt heavy. For the life of me, I couldn't figure out why I had heard a man's voice repeating the same nursery rhyme over and over. Was it a dream or more like a nightmare? I groaned and rubbed the back of my achy neck.

I knew the rhyme well because before my parents divorced and we still lived in Gold Beach, Nicole used to tell me all kinds of nursery rhymes before bed. "Peter, Peter, Pumpkin Eater" was one of them. Ever since we moved to California, Nicole had stopped telling them to me, so I hadn't heard them in years. It was bizarre hearing it now after all this time. I never knew why she stopped, but I would never bring it up. She hated it when I questioned her, and I was afraid of making her mad, scared of getting slapped, and fearful of being blamed for one more thing. She wasn't 'Mom' anymore.

Chill air prickled my face. I stretched, rubbing sleep from my eyes, and felt something sticky. My hands came away crimson.

Blood. Everywhere. Smeared across my face.

I shot up from the couch, breath hitching, hands trembling as I wiped the blood on my shorts.

"Mom?"

No answer.

Red footprints stained the carpet, leading from her room to the front door. Pumpkin seeds were scattered in the blood. I picked one up, wiped my bloody fingers on my shorts, then took a step toward her room. I shut my eyes and breathed in. The stench—metallic, rotten—made me gag.

I forced the bile down my throat, fingers gripping the door handle. My mind battled. *Open it! Don't!* My hands trembled. *Open it, don't. Call 911.* Face the horror waiting beyond.

Bloody footprints and crimson-soaked pumpkin seeds flashed through my mind, their slick surface sparkling under the flickering light, urging me to open the door. The coppery scent of blood stung my nose, sharp and metallic, blending with the faint sweetness of rotting pumpkin flesh. She might be bleeding out, desperately needing help. I nodded, my resolve hardening like ice in my veins, and grabbed the handle, its cold metal biting into my palm. Hesitation gripped me, a heavy weight in my chest, but it vanished as I pushed the door open. It crashed against the wall with a jarring thud, the sound echoing like a gunshot in my ears. My eyes widened, stinging from the cloying cloud of Nicole's shattered perfume bottle on the floor, its floral scent battling the foul, rancid odor of decay. A photo of us from happier times lay splattered with blood, Nicole's smile warped, her eyes seemingly following me. I couldn't look away as I sank to my knees, the hardwood bruising my skin, dread whispering in my ear like a cold breath. Was it her blood or something worse?

Nicole's bedspread was soaked in gore, the metallic stench curling in my throat. Feathers and pumpkin seeds clung everywhere, glued by blood. I brushed them off, repulsed by their soft, sticky touch. The air was thick and bitter. As I stood, the floor groaned beneath me, echoing my pulse. But what made my skin crawl most was the pumpkin at the center of the bed—a grotesque centerpiece, its jagged grin leering in the dim light.

I froze when I noticed the deep, ragged slash marks carved into the mattress as if something had clawed its way through, the torn fabric rough under my trembling fingertips.

Forcing myself away from her bed, I turned, the air thick with the sour stink of fear, and decided to get the phone from the kitchen. My socked feet slipped on the blood-slick floor, each step seeping into my skin. In the kitchen, I noticed my calm demeanor, a strange numbness tingling through my body, my skin prickling as if dusted with frost. Shock? Disoriented, unease bubbled up inside me, a sour churn in my gut, but I brushed it aside as I mechanically called 911, the phone's plastic cool against my ear.

"911, what's the address of the emergency?" The voice crackled, sharp and distant.

"There's blood everywhere. I don't know where my mom is, but there's blood." I looked down at my hands, sticky with drying blood, their tacky warmth coating my skin. "I have blood on my hands and my face." Panic surged, a bitter taste flooding my mouth. I realized what I was saying must not have sounded good.

"Settle down, ma'am. We have traced your location. If you wait a minute, I'll send an officer and an ambulance out." She paused, and my breathing quickened, a rasping sound in my throat. "Ma'am, stay on the line; someone will arrive shortly." Another pause. "Ma'am, are you still there? Are you hurt?"

"Yes, I mean yes, I'm still here, but I'm not hurt," I choked out, my voice raw and scraping my throat. Tears streamed down my face, hot and salty, dripping onto my white tank top. The tears washed the blood from my cheeks, staining my shirt red, the fabric clinging damply to my skin. For a brief second, I wondered. Why is blood only on my face?

While the dispatcher rattled off questions, their words buzzed like distant bees, and I answered without really hearing, my voice detached, my mind elsewhere. I drifted back toward the room, drawn like a moth to a flame, and the air grew heavier with the sickly, sweet stench of pumpkin and blood. As I neared the bed, I noticed something about the pumpkin that I hadn't seen before: the top could come off, its rough edge scraping my palm as I brushed against it. My chest constricted, my breath was shallow, and the air tasting of dust and decay. I knew I shouldn't touch it. Every instinct screamed for me to walk away, a warning resonating like a low hum in my bones. Yet still, I wondered if there was something inside.

The pumpkin's base was scratched up, jagged lines spelling "put her in a shell." The rhyme wasn't random.

On the lid: "open me," carved deep and uneven.

My hands shook as I lifted the lid.

Inside sat a severed, bloodied finger, my mother's wedding ring still on it. A note, blood-stained, read:

Peter, Peter, pumpkin eater,
had a wife, but couldn't keep her.
The gold ring gleamed, cold and familiar.

A wave of nausea soured my mouth as the air grew colder, prickling my skin. A memory flickered, Nicole's voice, soft and warm, reading "Peter, Peter" before bed, her hand stroking my hair, the scent of her lavender lotion enveloping me. Once a comfort, the rhyme now echoed like a mocking curse. Was this a message for me? I stumbled back, the floor tilting, and noticed Dad's old fishing knife on the counter, its wooden handle smooth and familiar, untouched by blood. Why was it here? Had he visited without telling me? The faint buzz of a distant appliance hummed in the surreal silence, grounding me as regret and dread churned in my gut.

My stomach twisted with a sharp pang, the taste of bile lingering. Was the rhyme a clue, not just a taunt? What linked the rhyme to her? Was I to blame? The questions buzzed like static, my skin prickling with sweat.

Was she still alive?

How could she be when there was so much blood and part of her body lay inside the pumpkin, its pulpy interior slick against my trembling fingers?

My stomach churned. My knees buckled, and I collapsed against the kitchen counter, the cold tile biting through my jeans. The room spun, walls tilting inward as if to crush me. This can't be happening. Nicole's voice sliced through the haze, sharp and accusing: *"You'll never be enough, Alexis."* I felt the sting of her slap again that night; she'd caught me sneaking out, her hand leaving a mark that lingered for hours. Now, her blood stained my hands, and the guilt clawed at me. Had I pushed her away, left her exposed to this? The thought was irrational, a splinter burrowing deeper with every breath. I pressed my palms to my eyes, trying to block out the rhyme looping in my skull: "Peter, Peter, pumpkin eater…" It wasn't just a taunt—it was a mirror, reflecting every failure I'd buried. Tears mixed with the blood on my face, warm and bitter, and for a fleeting second, I wanted to vanish, to melt into the floor and escape. But I couldn't. Not yet. Not until I understood who'd done this and why they'd chosen her.

I couldn't hold back. Bile rose and splattered on the blood-stained floor. A scream ripped from my throat, raw and helpless, as sirens wailed closer. I screamed again when the cops burst in, again when a paramedic's voice faded to static, and once more as a needle bit my arm, coolness spreading, darkness closing in. Just before it all went quiet, I heard the rhyme, "And there he kept her very well."

4

Alexis

"Breaking News: Alleged Homicide in Ventura. Local woman's body hasn't been located . . ."

I wanted my dad. I needed him. They might have considered him a primary suspect, but I didn't; I could not believe that. Not him. He was a detective. My dad. He'd always been calm and patient, even when things got messy with Nicole. I had never once seen him angry and had never heard him raise his voice at either of us.

Still, the authorities wouldn't let me leave California until I provided a formal witness statement, and they managed to contact him. It felt like I was being punished for something I hadn't done. The Department of Child and Family Services stepped in and placed me in temporary foster care pending guardian verification. Since I wasn't eighteen, I had no say in the matter. For four long days, I pleaded with them to reach out to him. At first, they said they couldn't get in touch, which didn't sit right with me. He was a detective. Detectives don't just vanish.

On the fourth day, they informed me he was finally en route. He had been on his annual deep-sea fishing trip in Baja. I wasn't surprised; he always took that trip like clockwork. However, this time... I truly needed him more than ever.

We weren't exactly close, not in a way that mattered. I spent summers with him until high school and called him once or twice a month. Our conversations were surface level, mostly updates, small talk, nothing heavy. I never told him how Nicole screamed, how she made me feel worthless, or about the men. Why would I? He wasn't around enough to fix it, and part of me always believed he didn't really want me.

Still, I used to wish quietly and secretly that I could have lived with him instead. But I knew that wasn't realistic. He was always on the go, taking jobs across Curry County to make ends meet. Gold Beach wasn't exactly overflowing with crime; he did what he had to do, and I wasn't old enough to be on my own.

The irony? I had already been raising myself. Nicole was present in the body, but that was it.

The only thing I liked about the foster home was its location on the beach, just like my place with Nicole. I spent hours there, my toes digging into the wet sand, letting the ocean wind wrap around me. There was something cathartic and grounding about it. I'd stare at the waves and imagine a life I'd only read about in books, one where people loved you back, where someone held you close and meant it, where you mattered.

But that kind of real, steady, unconditional love felt like fiction, beautiful, unreachable fiction. My life didn't resemble a storybook; it looked like a mess. Still, that's what dreams were for, right? A place to escape when the truth was too ugly to face.

Inside, the Fisher house felt like a different planet. Not just because of how clean it was or the way the windows were always cracked open to let the salt air drift in, but also because there wasn't a single spot inside that held fear. No angry silences, no slammed doors, and no pretending everything was fine when it wasn't.

They had two other foster kids: Jamie, who was ten and turned everything into a magic trick, and Olivia, a quiet thirteen-year-old with a chipped tooth and a laugh that seemed seldom used.

I wasn't sure who I was in this world. In mine, I was the girl who tiptoed, who braced herself before speaking, and who read the room as if it could detonate at any moment. I was the watcher, the adjuster, the one who knew when to be invisible.

But here, invisibility wasn't needed. Not even possible.

One night, I found myself at the kitchen table with them. I hadn't meant to join. I had just wandered in, drawn by the smell of cinnamon and something sweeter I couldn't name. Jamie was showing Olivia how to make a penny disappear behind his ear. She giggled, eyes wide, as if it were the best trick in the world. Jim poured glasses of milk. Lori pulled cinnamon rolls from the oven and placed them in the center as if they were some kind of sacred offering.

"Thursday nights are for sugar and second chances," she said, smiling as if it weren't just a line.

I didn't say anything; I just sat there, watching. When Lori slid a plate in front of me without asking, and Jamie offered me the last roll without hesitation, something cracked inside me.

It wasn't much. Just a flicker. A warmth I didn't know how to embrace. A glimpse of something I'd never had but always wanted.

I wasn't part of their story, not really. But for a second, I could pretend.

And there were still so many questions I couldn't stop mulling over in my mind. Why Nicole? Was it William? Did he kill her?

I remembered finding a letter in Nicole's drawer, signed "W.T.," promising to "make things right." It felt off, but I never confronted her about it.

Dad? *No.* Could I have done something to stop it? Why was I still alive?

That last one clung to me, cold and sharp. The thought that maybe... maybe whoever did this wasn't finished.

And that... twisted my stomach with a sensation colder than fear. A feeling close to dread.

A knock at the bedroom door pulled me out of my spiral of self-pity. Lori Fisher, my foster mom, appeared almost unreal in her beauty. Her fiery red hair flared like a warning against her pale skin, but today, it was her husband, Jim, who caught my eye. He stood behind her silently, clutching a newspaper with Nicole's face on it, *Ventura Homicide: No Body Found.* His knuckles were white, as if he were angry or scared. Why was he so shaken? Had he known her, perhaps crossed paths in Gold Beach?

I might've considered staying if I hadn't had a father, someone I still believed could piece things back together. But I didn't belong here. I needed to go home... or at least, to what was left of it.

"Alexis, your dad's here," Lori said softly, her smile laced with sympathy that tightened my chest.

I sprang off the bed and bolted down the hallway, only to freeze as I entered the living room.
He was rising from the couch.

My dad.

I'm not sure what I expected, but time had not been kind to him. His hair, once just like mine, was now streaked with more gray than I recalled.

"I was on that fishing trip," he said, his voice steady yet rushed. "Baja, like every year. The problem is, I went alone this time; no one to vouch for me till I got back." His eyes flicked away as if he were hiding something, and my stomach twisted. Had he really been gone, or was he closer to Ventura than he admitted? The lines around his eyes had deepened, crow's feet carved by years I hadn't been part of. He still looked like my father with his quiet strength… but the years we'd lost clung to him like shadows.

Tears blurred my vision before I could even speak. We'd missed so much. In an instant, the space between us vanished. He rushed to me, wrapping me in a hug that made me believe the world might be okay again.

"Sweetheart, I'm so sorry you had to go through all of that alone," he whispered into my hair. "I didn't get the message until yesterday. I was out of town. First flight I could get. You must be wrecked. I stopped by the Ventura PD before coming here and had to clear my name. They walked me through the case file, took my statement, and sent me to the lab for processing."

It struck me as odd how his words spilled out so quickly, so unfiltered. I couldn't remember him ever rambling before.

My brows pulled together as I registered what he'd said. "Wait… the lab? Why did you have to go there?"

"They had to swab for DNA and run a blood panel."

My stomach tightened. "Why?"

"To eliminate me as a person of interest," he said gently. "They recovered forensic evidence of your mother's ring, cataloged under chain of custody, so I was one of the primary suspects since I gave her that ring. Me and that Thompson guy."

My throat closed. "So… you're cleared then?"

He nodded. "Pending final lab results, yeah. My prints and DNA were already in the system from my badge, Curry County Sheriff's database, so they expedited the comparison."

He gave me a small, weary smile and pressed a kiss to the top of my head. It didn't erase the ache in my chest.

"What about William Thompson?"

"I don't know yet," he admitted, his voice dropping lower. "All they told me is they found your DNA, your mother's… and an unidentified trace sample still at the state lab." His eyes flicked away from mine as he rubbed the back of his neck.

The sting of the needle haunted my arm, throbbing anew, its ugly, swollen bruise purple-black like my neck, echoing the killer's syringe that silenced Nicole, a ghostly prick connecting me to her blood-soaked fate.

I exhaled shakily. "Daddy… I want to go home."

His face stiffened. "I can't take you back there."

The words struck harder than I expected. For a moment, it felt like rejection all over again, as if I were being cast off.

"You don't want me," I said quietly, barely able to hear myself.

"No, no, sweetheart. Don't think that." His arms tightened around me as if he were trying to anchor us both. "Of course I want you."

"Then why can't I go with you?"

"Because your house is still an active crime scene," he said softly as if that explained everything.

But it didn't. Not to me.

"No," I whispered, shaking my head. "I want to go with you. I want to be home with you."

His gaze locked with mine, and I saw moisture gathering in the corners of his eyes. A flicker of pain, he tried to blink away.

"Please… take me home, Daddy. I don't want to be here. I can't be here. I need you."

His hug was tight, almost desperate, but when he pulled back, his eyes flicked away, a shadow crossing his face. "Let's get you home," he said, but his smile didn't reach his eyes.

My heart thudded as I stood in the cramped living room, the scent of Lori's lavender candles fading like a memory. Even though I'd been with them for less than a week, a tinge of attachment tugged at me, making the goodbye heavier. Saying farewell to my foster parents, each word caught in my throat. Lori, my foster mom, hugged me tightly, her soft sweater warm against my cheek, whispering, "You're always welcome back," her voice cracking. I wondered if she meant it. Jamie, my foster dad, pressed a worn penny into my palm, saying, "For luck," his eyes glistening with hope. I closed my fingers around it, its metallic tang sharp, feeling gratitude and guilt for this man who believed in me. Ruffling his hair, I forced a smile, swallowing tears. This goodbye was another unraveling, and as I stepped toward the door, the penny heavy in my hand, I wondered if I could still believe in luck.

5

Alexis

I had nothing but the clothes from the foster home when we got into the taxi. My dad offered to request Ventura PD clearance to access the scene, still marked by blood spatter, but I couldn't face it and politely declined. We would buy what I needed in Medford. He fidgeted, adjusting his seatbelt twice, then a third time, his fingers twitching with restless precision until it clicked perfectly. His jaw tightened, eyes darting to the strap, checking its alignment as if being a fraction off would unravel everything. It was a ritual I had seen before his need for control in a world that felt too chaotic, a silent echo of the years we had spent apart.

Most of my old clothes belonged to Nicole, anyway. Right now, I wasn't sure how I felt about wearing pieces of her like armor or ghosts.

Maybe it was my subconscious attempting to split my life into two: the one that ended in that house and the one waiting for me in Oregon. Either way, my mother would never fully leave me. She'd always be there, stitched into my memory, my blood, my scars. I'd carry her forever, whether I wanted to or not.

As the taxi swerved methodically, no relief came, only the weight of grief, with closure remaining a distant, unreachable shadow. Closure wasn't possible yet. Not until they found the rest of her body… and apprehended the person who killed her.

I leaned my head against the window, focusing on the clouds drifting by like tufts of cotton. The sky was soft, too soft. I wanted to crawl into it, disappear inside the haze, and sleep until my bones stopped aching from the inside out. I couldn't remember the last time I had slept without nightmares clawing through my head.

Just as my eyes started to droop, my dad spoke. "You know... if you ever want to talk, I'm here."

I turned slowly toward him, studying his face. "I know, Dad. It's just... hard." I hesitated, then let the words fall. "Sometimes it feels like she's not really gone. Like she's just on a trip or off somewhere, and she'll come back." I swallowed the lump in my throat. "Growing up with her, her being gone wasn't unusual. She was always out. But this time... It's different. I know she's gone. I saw it. I felt it. But my heart and my head aren't syncing up." I stared down at my lap, watching my fingers twist and untwist. "She was always distant... but this is another kind of absence."

He reached over, took my restless hands in his, and held them still. His eyes searched mine. "Your mom... she wasn't always easy to love," he said, staring out the window. His voice was low, as if he were talking to himself. "She had a way of making you feel like you weren't enough." I shifted uncomfortably, unsure how to respond. He looked at me, his eyes hard. "But you're nothing like her, Alexis. Don't ever think you are. I know your relationship with your mom wasn't easy." His voice was careful, as if assessing the weight of every word, and I sensed he was holding back.

I froze. My stomach tightened. I never told him what it was really like living with her, how cruel she could be, the way her boyfriends looked at me, and the things she ignored. I didn't want him to know. Not yet.

"I talked to her more than you think," he continued. "She said things about you that... didn't sit right with me. I got the sense she saw you as a competition more than a daughter. Like you threatened her somehow, and… one day, I'll tell you everything that happened between us. But for now, please just know I'm here. If you ever want to talk, if you have questions about anything, I'll listen."

A threat. Is that how she saw me?

I didn't answer, not aloud. But I believed him. For the first time in a long time, I felt like someone saw me, even though I wasn't ready to speak the truth.

I nodded slightly to let him know I heard him, and I offered a small smile.

The rest of the trip passed in a blur, the steady buzz of the taxi's engine fading into a hazy hum as I drifted in and out of a restless half-sleep, the weight of Nicole's absence pressing against my chest. We approached LAX for our flight to Medford, Oregon, and the terminal greeted us with a chaotic symphony of rolling suitcases, muffled announcements, and the shuffle of hurried travelers. I trailed behind Dad, my eyes heavy with exhaustion, the penny from Jamie still clutched in my pocket, its edges digging into my palm. Then I felt a prickling sensation, like a thread tugging at the edge of my awareness. Across the crowded terminal, a man in a dark coat stood motionless near a row of seats, his gaze locked on me. His eyes were sharp, unblinking, cutting through the bustle with an intensity that made my pulse stutter. A glint of silver flashed at his wrist as he shifted, and I caught a faint scar curving near his jaw, barely visible in the fluorescent light. His stare stirred the same dread I'd felt staring at the pumpkin as if he knew what I'd found and what I'd lost. I stopped, caught in the weight of his gaze, the noise around me dimming to a distant buzz. When I blinked and looked again, he'd vanished, swallowed by the sea of people, but the chill of his presence lingered, coiling tight beneath my skin, a warning I couldn't shake.

I tried to shake it off, chalking it up to fatigue or an overactive imagination, but the unease clung to me as I turned to find Dad. He'd stepped a few paces away, his phone pressed to his ear, his broad shoulders hunched as if shielding the call from the world. His voice was low and clipped, carrying an urgency that sharpened my senses. "Yes, she's with me. No, not yet." He glanced over his shoulder, his eyes meeting mine for a fleeting second before he turned away, his face a mask, calm on the surface but with something flickering beneath, something unreadable. His free hand tightened around the phone, knuckles whitening, and the air between us seemed to thicken, heavy with questions I couldn't voice. The stranger's stare still echoed in my mind, and now Dad's hushed words tangled with it, weaving a thread of tension that pulled tighter with every passing second.

As we descended into Medford, the skies were gray, and a steady rain tapped against the windows. That was not surprising, according to my dad, who spoke as if I had never been here before. But the weather felt right. Gloom for gloom.

Instead of driving the two hundred miles to Gold Beach, we decided to board a smaller plane. Thanks to Dad's badge from the Curry County Sheriff's Office, he coordinated with a local charter for expedited transport under law enforcement priority. The pilot was ready to wait until we were prepared.

Arriving in Gold Beach early in the morning after a sleepless night, I felt heavy and numb on the surreal private flight with my dad and our overflowing Walmart haul of new clothes, bedding, and decorations for my new room as he theatrically tried to overwrite the past.

When I tried to argue about the phone and the laptop, saying it was too much, he replied, "Get used to it. I've got a lot of making up to do."

I stopped arguing.

But a voice in the back of my mind whispered that gifts don't fix ghosts. And love, when bought too easily, begins to feel like a bribe.

I told him the laptop was enough. He argued that the phone was necessary since he didn't have a landline, insisting it was more for him than for me.

Excuses.

Maybe he meant them. Maybe he didn't.

But something about the way his jaw clenched every time I looked at him too long made me feel like I wasn't the only one haunted.

6

Alexis

Stepping off the plane, the briny ocean air struck me, evoking a fleeting memory of warmth. Unlike California's heat, the breeze bit with a chill, yet with Dad's steady presence beside me, it stirred a fragile echo of the elusive comfort of home.

Not perfect. Not healing. But it's something I could hold on to.

I stopped in my tracks, furrowing my brows at the black Crown Victoria parked alone in the airport lot. With our luggage in tow, I took in the car's old-school frame. It had to be from the '70s. Definitely a '78 Ford LTD Crown Vic, 351 Windsor V8 under the hood, all torque and no finesse. I knew cars like Nicole knew her men as they dragged us like trophies to car shows. Guess they were her 'type'. Muscle cars, muscle men. The chrome trim screamed vintage, but those aftermarket tint jobs were pure cop; nobody else had blacked-out windows like that. It was pushing antique status. The windows were tinted so dark they looked painted.

"Seriously? This is your car?" I scanned the mostly empty lot. Yep, it had to be. It looked like something a mob boss would step out of.

Propping up my rolling suitcase, I watched Dad pop the trunk and toss his luggage inside. He turned toward me, hand out, waiting for my bags.

I stared at him, then at the car. "Dad, isn't it a little on the nose to drive a 'black detective car'?" I said, trying not to grin. I mean, a Crown Vic's practically a badge on wheels. I bet it's got the Police Interceptor package, too, with that heavy-duty suspension.

He pointed a finger at me, his shaggy, salt-and-pepper hair falling into his eyes. "There's nothing cliché about my car." He chuckled.

He was trying not to smile. I decided to go for the kill. "Come on. Let me guess, 1978?"

His jaw dropped. Bingo. He shook his head, grabbed my luggage, and tossed it into the trunk with a smirk. "Good guess. And yeah, it's a '78."

It wasn't a guess. I knew that car inside and out, thanks to years of tagging along to car shows with Nicole's ever-changing lineup of boyfriends. Those guys loved their classic Chevelles, Mustangs, and even a '69 Camaro SS once. I could spot a Holley carburetor from ten yards away.

Inside, I took a quick look around the interior. Not bad. Leather seats are in a deep maroon. Upgraded stereo with a CD player. Clean, maybe too clean. The dash shone as if it had just been hit with a can of Armor All. Even the floors displayed neat vacuum lines. My stomach sank. Did Dad have OCD? And worse… was it genetic?

I shoved the thought aside as Dad started the engine. The V8 rumbled like a beast, delivering four hundred horsepower thanks to a rebuilt block. No wonder he kept this relic running. "You know they make newer models, right?" I asked, throwing him a sideways look. Like a Dodge Charger SRT, 6.4-liter HEMI modern muscle with better fuel injection.

He shot a glance, feigning offense with sly charm, then adjusted the mirrors with eerie precision, each angle meticulously set. "I forgot how much you love giving your old man grief," he said, straightening the dashboard's pens, "But I haven't forgotten how ticklish you are."

He wiggled his fingers, and my eyes widened. "Okay, okay! I surrender," I said, hands raised.

Before pulling out, he asked, "Want to grab breakfast? There's nothing at the house unless you count whatever's growing in my fridge, which I'll scrub spotless later."

I snorted. "How about we hit the grocery store? I'll cook. Maybe even make you my devil's food cake with cream cheese filling and chocolate buttercream."

He turned onto Ellensburg Avenue. "That's a better plan than I had."

Minutes later, we pulled into Ray's Food Place, smaller than California's sprawling markets but adequate. Inside, Dad thrust the cart at me, his pace relentless, eyes scanning the shelves with a predator's focus. His OCD was in overdrive. Cereal boxes were aligned alphabetically, soup cans stacked with military precision, bread standing upright, and eggs cradled like fragile relics. He paused to adjust a can's label, fingers twitching until it faced perfectly forward, then rechecked the cart's symmetry, his jaw tight. Something felt off; his eerie precision chilled me more than the cold wafting from the juice section.

"Dad," I called. No response.

He muttered, "Pulp-free. Where's the pulp-free?"

"Dad!" I raised my voice, sharper than I had expected.

He snapped his head toward me, dropping a juice can that landed with a dull clunk. Grimacing, he swapped it for a pristine can, carefully aligning it in the cart before meeting my gaze. "Sorry, Alexis. What do you need?"

I glanced at the cart's orderly contents, plenty to work with. Before I could respond, a voice called, "Luke?"

Dad turned, his obsessive edge softened as he approached a couple at the end of the aisle. I maneuvered the heavy cart aside and followed. He slung an arm over my shoulder, a rare warmth. "Alexis, meet our neighbors, Dr. Finn and Tami."

I cleared my throat, easing the tension. "Nice to meet you. You're our neighbors?"

"Sort of," Dr. Finn said. "Two miles out on Saunders Creek."

I nodded, polite but unfamiliar with the name.

Tami stepped closer and whispered into Dad's ear as if I couldn't hear. Her chestnut waves caught the light, and her motherly smile stirred an ache in my chest. "Nicole had a knack for…" She faltered, her smile fading. "Not that I'd wish that on anyone." Her words hung heavy, hinting at old grudges. Had Nicole crossed her?

Dr. Finn, striking with sharp eyes and auburn hair like mine, shook my hand firmly. His gaze lingered as if he recognized something familiar. "Nicole was… unforgettable, I'm sorry for your loss," he said, his tight smile masking something deeper. Tami's glance at him was sharp, almost accusatory. Did he know Nicole too well?

Tami's tone brightened. "Luke, how's Becca doing?"

Dad's arm stiffened before it dropped. "She's good. Last I heard, consulting on a custody case for the Pistol River DA."

Tami's eyes widened. "The double homicide? Oh, sweetie, I'm sorry." She looked at me, visibly mortified.

"It's fine," I said quickly, waving it off, although my throat tightened.

Dr. Finn frowned. "It's not fine. What you've been through… it'll catch up." He touched my shoulder gently; I flinched. He pulled back, studying me, but stayed silent.

Dad cut in, nodding at their chaotic cart. "Throwing a party?"

Tami beamed. "Our boys are coming home. Come for dinner next week. Alexis should meet them."

Dad hesitated, his fingers tapping the cart handle rhythmically with a nervous tic. "Duty roster's packed with a new case backlog, but we'll figure it out."

Dr. Finn smiled. "Alexis, you're always welcome at the hospital."

We said goodbye and went to check out. We then stopped at Dan's Ace Hardware. Dad suggested a room makeover, so I picked teal, black, and white paint to match my new bedspread. I'd never painted before, but I felt a stir of anticipation, a faint hope for renewal.

Once we were back in the car, we followed the Rogue River along Highway 101. Dad hadn't said much since we left the store. I gazed out the window before breaking the silence.

"So… who's Becca?"

The car jerked slightly. "She's my… girlfriend," he said as if he wasn't sure.

"That's great, Dad. How long?"

"Nine months."

I glanced over. His hands clamped tight on the wheel.

"Does she make you happy?"

"Very."

"Then I'm happy." I patted his arm. "You deserve that."

And I meant it. Plus, she was a woman; hopefully, I wouldn't have to worry about her making an advance.

We pulled into the driveway on Jack's Landing Road, the LTD's rumble fading as Dad turned off the engine. The brown brick house loomed, both familiar and strange, its green metal roof catching the Oregon drizzle. I shifted uneasy, a prickling fresh start, same ghosts. Dad grabbed our bags.

"House looks amazing," I said, glancing toward the backyard that sprawled into the shadows, the tire swing creaking as it swayed, chains rattling in the breeze. Fog wreathed the trees, thick and spectral, blurring the edges of the property. The air carried damp earth and salt, the ocean's whisper threading through the pines. "Oh my God, you kept the tire swing... and the tree house?"

Dad smiled. "Of course. I didn't know if you'd ever come back, but I didn't want you to be upset if I got rid of them." His eyes glistened. "They reminded me of you." He glanced at the back fence. "Stay clear of Kessler's place, sweetheart," he said, his voice low, nodding toward the neighbor's overgrown lot, where shadows pooled under gnarled trees. "Old guy's harmless but keeps to himself. Watches too much." His eyes flicked away as if he'd said more than he intended. I squinted through the drizzle, Kessler's fence appearing like a dark scar against the overcast sky. His lot was a jungle of shadows, overgrown weeds, rusted tools, a place where secrets could fester. A sharp clang rang from his garage, metal on concrete, and my pulse quickened. What's he hiding? Maybe he was harmless, but the prickling on my neck screamed otherwise.

My throat tightened as I imagined eyes in the dark, like Nicole's men, their hands too close. "Watches?" I asked, gripping my backpack, my heart racing faster.

Dad shrugged, forcing a smile. "Just small-town quirks. Come on, let's get inside." He walked toward the door, but I lingered, scanning Kessler's fence as a chill settled deep, whispering trouble.

As we ate our omelets, Dad's phone buzzed. He glanced at it, his face tightening. "Work," he muttered, but I saw the name Becca. He silenced it and avoided my gaze. I brushed it aside and went to my room.

I spent the rest of the day organizing my room, surrounded by pink walls and a bedspread that felt like relics from a childhood I'd long outgrown. The entire place looked as if the Pink Panther had mauled it, a chaotic mess of faded memories. Painting could wait. I unpacked my things and tried to fit my suitcase into the closet, but it wouldn't slide in all the way, stubbornly catching on to something.

Frustrated, I dragged a chair over and climbed up, only to bump my head against the bulb hanging from the ceiling. There, on the shelf above, sat a black box that was dusty and forgotten. I took it down, my curiosity piqued and carefully opened it.

Inside was a weathered copy of "Children's Classic Nursery Rhymes." The book felt strangely heavy in my hands, its leather cover cracked and worn as if it had absorbed years of secrets. I traced the faded gold lettering, a shiver crawling up my spine. These were the same rhymes Nicole used to read to me, her voice soft and warm, offering a rare glimpse of the mother I'd lost long before she died. But now, the pages seemed tainted, the once-innocent verses twisted by something dark and unseen. I flipped through them, the paper brittle beneath my fingers, and a faint scent of dust and decay rose from the binding. Why was this here? My chest tightened as I recalled the pumpkin, the rhyme, the blood. This wasn't a coincidence; it was a message.

My fingers brushed over 'Peter, Peter'; pleasant memories hit me like a wave. Mom and I were on the bed, giggling over rhymes, while Dad leaned in the doorway. We were happy. She was perfect. Everything was perfect.

What changed?

7

Alexis

The next day, I connected my laptop and got the wireless internet working properly. I was grateful that Dad had already set it up at his home. I've searched online and studied the right painting techniques. I also found an impressive yet simple pattern that would look fantastic on my walls.

I closed my eyes, and a memory washed over me: Gold Beach, where I was barely four, curled up in Mom's lap. She smelled like lavender, her voice soft as she read 'Humpty Dumpty' from that old rhyme book. "You're my little egg," she whispered, kissing my forehead. "I'll never let you fall." Her smile was genuine, before the men, before the anger. I opened my eyes, the memory turning bitter. When had she stopped meaning it?

Last night, before I retreated to my room for the night, I reflected on the memories I had earlier that day with my dad. The wrinkles around his eyes deepened with concern. He didn't share his thoughts on the matter but assured me he would notify the Ventura PD detective squad for the follow-up on the case. I felt relieved but silently wondered why he hadn't asked me any more questions. I brushed it off as he gave me a brief hug and a kiss on the cheek, and then I went to bed.

After a rare night of unbroken sleep, I stood in the center of my bedroom, my hair tangled in a messy bun, and white paint streaked across my skin from head to toe. In a futile attempt to erase Nicole's blood-soaked memory, I had coated the walls, desperate to bury her ghost. The cracked window let in a cool, crisp breeze that rustled the plastic floor covering while sunlight glinted off the wet paint, flooding the room with a brightness that stung my eyes. It felt pure and untainted, a fragile hope for a new life, yet the ache in my chest whispered that I'd never outrun her shadow.

I stepped outside for air; the backyard was quiet except for a low mutter coming from the fence. Mr. Kessler, the creepy neighbor Dad mentioned, was there, shoveling dirt in his yard. "Gotta clean up messes," he grumbled, glancing my way. His eyes were cold. I hurried back inside, my pulse racing.

Across the street, Kessler's garage housed a '66 Pontiac GTO, its Tri-Power carbs gleaming under the hood. That beast, a true muscle car legend, could accelerate from 0 to 60 in under six seconds. Had he driven it to California and back, covering his tracks?

I grabbed the tattered nursery rhyme book and started flipping through it, stopping at 'Peter, Peter.' The killer chose it for Nicole. Each verse felt like a judgment. I searched up the nursery rhyme on the internet, asking for the deeper meaning. What popped up shocked me as it was so spot on: infidelity, containment. It explained the rhyme and why her ring finger was in the pumpkin.

My suspicions were valid. This was someone she knew. I researched further. One version was about how Peter put a chastity belt on his wife or stuffed her in a pumpkin shell and even worse figuring out how to kill her. Another part explained the pumpkin shell represented pregnancy.

The killer wasn't treating this as a childhood rhyme, they were using it as steps to murder Nicole.

My stomach churned. This was hitting too close to home.

Who would do this?

Forensic reports Dad mentioned noted high-velocity blood spatter in her room, suggesting a blade rather than a gun. Was Kessler's shovel hiding that weapon? Was he Peter? Would he strike again? Did he know my mom?

Everyone was a suspect.

A folded paper slipped from the book's pages, yellowed and crisp. I unfolded it, my heart racing. Scrawled in jagged ink was a single line: "Ladybug, Ladybug, fly away home, your house is on fire…". The words sent chills down my spine, too vivid for the book's age. I glanced at the tire swing swaying in the breeze and clutched the paper tighter. Could it be Nicole? Dad?

My browsing was interrupted when my cell phone rang. I didn't even need to check the caller's identity because, first, only one person had my number, and second, I had set his ringtone to the theme music of 'COPS.'

Before I responded, I started bobbing my head and singing. Feeling any joy felt wrong. I shook my head as strands of hair fell from my loose bun, and I flipped my phone open. "Hey, Dad."

"Hey, sweetheart, have the paint fumes gotten to you?" he chuckled, and I could picture the smile on his face.

"Yeah, Dad, it's the paint fumes." I rolled my eyes and managed a small laugh. "What's up?"

"Can't a dad just call up his only daughter on her first day alone to see if she's okay?"

"Of course you can, but you know all too well that I can take care of myself." I walked over to the window, looked toward the backyard, and watched the tire swing sway slightly in the breeze. It beckoned me. "I think you're sweet for calling, but really, Dad, what's going on?"

"Okay, okay, you caught me. I can't figure out how you can still read me like a book." I heard a police radio squawk in the background. "I just got off the phone with the Ventura PD Major Crimes Unit, and they asked me a few questions about... Nicole."

I closed my eyes and hoped that what he told me would be good news. Did they find her killer? Did they locate her body?

"So, what did they say?" I asked, clearing my throat as it suddenly felt raw and dry.

"Well... they said they combed through every inch of the house, even her car. Latent prints are trace evidence, all logged under the chain of custody. Nothing conclusive yet," he said, then paused, keeping the rest of the details to himself. I wasn't sure I was ready to hear more anyway. "They wanted to know what they should do with the car. It's sitting in the impound lot right now. They'll put it up for auction if you don't claim it. And the house...it was paid off. So technically, it's yours if you want it."

It was overwhelming to absorb everything all at once. That house had been a part of my life for as long as I could remember, every memory, good and bad, woven into its walls. And the car, a silver Pontiac G6, that she had scraped and saved for, penny by penny, to pay it off completely. The same money she never spent on the things I needed, like a decent pair of track shoes or, for crying out loud, a new bra.

"Sweetheart?"

My eyes snapped back open, and I realized I hadn't answered, "Dad, isn't it too soon for all that?" My heart felt like I had drunk an energy drink fast and erratic, like it wanted to leap out of my chest.

"Well…they also mentioned that the amount of blood at the scene was too much. The chances of her being alive are very slim."

"So, there's still a chance she can be alive then." My voice cracked as the tears fought to escape. "I want to wait a little longer, please."

"Okay," he said after a beat. "We'll wait." But the way he said it, soft, uncertain, told me he didn't believe it. Not really.

I glanced at the tire swing through the window, its sway hypnotic. A thump echoed as my phone slipped, my eyes widening. A barefoot figure in a black cocktail dress stood beside it, gently pushing. Her ebony hair whipped across her face, hiding her features. My mother. How was she here?

I shoved the window open, shouting, "Mom!" Her head snapped toward me, the wind sweeping her hair away. Her eyes were dim, violet-shadowed, lifeless, her skin pale, a sickly purple. She looked like a corpse, her missing ring finger waving faintly, pointing to the forest as if it were a warning.

A memory flickered, sharp and warm: I was four, curled in Nicole's lap on that same tire swing, Gold Beach's ocean breeze tickling my nose. Her lavender scent enveloped me as she read "Humpty Dumpty" from the nursery rhyme book, her voice soft. "You're my little egg," she whispered, kissing my forehead. "I'll never let you fall." Her smile was real, her crooked hands gentle, before the men, before the anger.

The vision shattered the memory. A sob tore from my chest, tears streaming. "Mom!" I screamed and squeezed my eyes close. When I opened them, it was just the swing. She had vanished, my mind twisting grief into something I could almost touch.

But she vanished, her form dissolving like a cruel trick. I collapsed, gripping the penny from Jamie, exhaustion overtaking me, Nicole's lavender fading into the rhyme's echo.

I took the penny from my desk, wishing that luck would seep in as I gripped it tighter, and then I collapsed onto the ground. My body shook with sobs until exhaustion overcame me, and I fell asleep.

8

Alexis

I woke up on the worn brown couch, a plaid blanket tucked under my chin, with a faint nursery rhyme echoing in my mind. Voices murmured in the house, beckoning me toward my bedroom. I froze in the doorway. A striking man stood on a stepladder, his bronzed muscles flexing under a tight white tank top as he peeled blue painter's tape from the freshly painted walls. Dad was working across the room on another ladder.

On my desk, the nursery rhyme book lay open to "Peter, Peter, Pumpkin Eater."

"Sweetheart, you're awake," Dad said, climbing down.

My gaze shifted from him to the man, who turned toward me with a warm smile. His eyes briefly flicked to the book on my desk before meeting mine, a hint of curiosity in his expression.

"How long did I sleep?" I asked, smoothing my tangled hair.

"About six hours," Dad replied, glancing at the man. "Right?"

He nodded, his gaze now fully on me. "Yeah, about that."

A flutter stirred in my stomach. There was something magnetic about him, the way he carried himself with quiet confidence. I couldn't help but feel drawn to him, even as questions lingered in my mind.

"Nathan's helping with the painting," Dad added. "He's a friend from work."

So, he does have a name; something familiar tugged at my mind. I managed a smile, my curiosity piqued. "Can I talk to you, Dad?" I asked, my voice steady.

We stepped into the hall. I glanced back, and Nathan was watching me, a faint smile on his lips. There was an intensity in his eyes that made my heart skip a beat, but I couldn't quite place what it meant.

In the hall, I turned to Dad, keeping my voice low. "Who's Nathan? How do you know him? Do I know him?"

Dad gave me a reassuring smile. "He's my partner's son from work. Good guy, always willing to lend a hand and watches over my place when I'm gone. He was a year ahead of you when you were in kindergarten."

The memory was faint, a quiet boy with hollow eyes walking beside me in the dark, saying nothing but somehow making me feel less alone. I nodded, but my thoughts snagged on Nathan's glance at the nursery rhyme book. It was probably nothing, just a passing look, but it nagged at me. "He was looking at the book on my desk," I said, testing Dad's reaction.

Dad glanced back toward the bedroom. "The nursery rhyme book? Yeah, it's been there since you were little. Your mom used to read it to you."

A pang hit me at the mention of Mom, *Nicole*, but I pressed on. "I know, but… it was open to 'Peter, Peter, Pumpkin Eater.' That's the rhyme from…" I hesitated, not wanting to dig too deep into the memory.

Dad's look became serious briefly before softening again. "It's just a coincidence, sweetheart. Nathan probably noticed the door was open. Are you going to explain why I hurried home only to find you lying on the floor?"

"Later, when it's just us." He didn't push, and I was thankful for that small mercy.

I wasn't completely convinced, but I decided to drop it. Perhaps I was overanalyzing. We returned to the bedroom, where Nathan was carefully peeling the final strip of painter's tape, his actions fluid and intentional. He didn't glance at the book again, which eased some of my discomfort.

As Dad climbed back up his ladder, Nathan stepped down, wiping his hands on a rag. He turned to me, that warm smile returning. "Feeling better?"

I let out a small laugh, still self-conscious about my messy hair. "Yeah, thanks. And thanks for helping with the painting."

"No problem," he said, his tone easy. "It's looking good, right?" He raised his thick eyebrows, and I wondered if they would resemble a caterpillar if he scrunched them together.

He turned to see me staring. My face flushed, and I glanced around the room, taking in the fresh paint. "Yeah, it does. I like the color."

Nathan's gaze locked onto mine, and for a moment, the air felt charged, like a thread of something unspoken stretched between us. "So, what are your plans now that you're here in Gold Beach?" he asked, breaking the silence.

I shrugged, trying to act cool, unsure of my capability. "Not sure yet. Probably just settle in, maybe explore a bit since I haven't been here since I was little."

His face brightened, and he leaned casually against the ladder, his gaze steady. "I could show you around if you want. There are some great spots nearby, hidden trails, and quiet beaches. You'd like it."

My cheeks warmed again, and that flutter in my stomach grew stronger. "That sounds nice," I said, surprised at how easily the words came out.

Nathan's smile widened as he took out his phone. "Let me get your number. I'll text you later, and we can set something up."

We exchanged numbers, and as he slipped his phone back into his pocket, his eyes lingered on mine a little longer than necessary. There was an intensity there searching, almost that sent a thrill through me. It wasn't unsettling, though; it drew me in, making me want to unravel whatever lay behind it.

"Looking forward to it," he said, his voice low, before turning back to finish up.

I stood there, watching him work, my mind flickering between confusion and curiosity. There was something about Nathan, his calm presence, the way he didn't force a conversation that held my attention longer than I expected. Was he the sad little boy from school? I wasn't sure. My heart didn't race; it tightened. Everything felt too raw and too recent to trust easily. Still, a quiet part of me wondered who he was now and why that mattered. I didn't lean into the feeling. I hovered near it, cautious and unsure but not completely willing to look away.

9

Black Sheep

The harbor reeked of salt and decay—a grim comfort—as he hunched at the stern of his boat, cloaked in shadow behind the Port Hole Café. Through the café's grimy windows, he spotted Detective Harper, Becca, and his Ladybug. Her real name was too soft, too human to cross his lips. The rhyme looped in his mind: "Ladybug, Ladybug, fly away home…"

Gossip clung to this town like mold on old wood. At diners, gas stations, and docks, whispers swirled around Nicole's murder and her shattered daughter. Each mention of Ladybug stoked the fire in his chest, a rage sharpened by hunger. Killing Nicole, his first human hunt, hadn't satisfied him. It cracked open something deeper—a craving for another pulse to chase.

He raised his binoculars, and her face snapped into focus. Her emerald eyes, heavy with grief, stared past the glass, locking onto something unseen. For a heartbeat, he froze, hidden in the harbor's murk as the sun spilled out on the horizon.

She looked lost, adrift between her father and Becca. His grip tightened, knuckles white. Why did her pain twist within him? Why did he care?

Fury boiled over. He tossed the binoculars into the water; the clatter was swallowed by the waves. He paced the deck, tugging at his hair. In days, his plan would unfold—clean, precise, final. Yet here he was, unraveling over her. The thrill of the hunt already eclipsed that of Nicole's.

Boots thudding, he leaped onto the dock and strode toward town. The ache gnawed, insatiable. For now, a cat would do.

10

Alexis

Stress was like a gargoyle perched on my chest, squeezing the air from my lungs the morning after dinner with Dad and Becca. Meeting her had been overwhelming, to say the least. She had beautiful blonde curls framing a warm smile that seemed to light up the Port Hole Café last night. I could see why Dad cared for her, but her voice grated like arsenic-laced honey, too sweet, leaving a bitter twist in my gut. Something felt off about her. The more I replayed the evening, the more I noticed Dad's strange behavior: his eyes lingered on her, and his laughter came too quickly, almost forced, as if he were playing a role. They included me in the conversation, asking about school, California, and my plans. But their body language told a different story. They leaned toward each other, brushed hands, and moved in sync as if I were an outsider in their private world.

Then there was Becca's reaction when Dad mentioned Nicole. Her voice turned clipped. "She was… complicated," she said. "Some secrets are better left buried." The words landed heavily, sharp and cryptic, lingering in the silence that followed.

I attempted to rationalize it. They're a couple, I told myself. It's normal. But doubt slithered in, cold and insistent. Had Dad always been like this, even before Becca? Or was I imagining things, haunted by my past? Images of Nicole's boyfriends flashed through my mind, Nicole's men, with their initial charm, car shows, drag races, and empty promises of family. That charm never lasted. I shuddered, the hair on my arms prickling.

Later, after Dad stepped out to take a call, Becca and I were alone at the table. That's when it happened.

"So," she said, folding her napkin just a bit too precisely. "How are you really doing?"

I didn't respond immediately. I didn't trust her tone, warm on the surface, but something pulsed beneath it, as if she were trying to seem more maternal than she had a right to.

"I'm fine," I said.

"You don't look fine." She smiled as if that were comforting. It wasn't.

"I've had better weeks," I said, my voice flatter than I intended.

She sipped her water slowly. "Nicole... your mom. I talked to her the day it happened."

I froze. "What?"

Becca blinked like she hadn't meant to say it. "It wasn't a big deal. Just a short conversation. She was upset and said some confusing things. I figured she was just spiraling again. I didn't think."

"Spiraling?" I repeated, my voice sharp.

Becca set her glass down gently. "She had a history, Alexis. You know that."

I stared at her, my pulse pounding in my ears. She was the 'B', the one Mom talked to before she died.

She shrugged too casually. "It doesn't matter."

"It matters to me."

Her smile faltered just slightly. "I'm sorry. I didn't want to upset you."

But I was already upset, already spiraling, already wondering why the hell Becca Shaw, the woman now sitting across from me like a polished porcelain doll, had been close enough to my mother to receive that call and never mentioned a word until now.

Dad returned before I could press her. The moment evaporated, neatly tucked behind the smile she wore too well.

Pushing the unease aside, I yanked my hair into a high ponytail, the motion sharp and grounding. I needed to think, to breathe. California's beaches had always been my escape, with gritty sand between my toes and waves crashing in a rhythm that drowned out the world. I hadn't been to a beach since before Nicole was murdered; the pumpkin on her bed and that bloody rhyme "Peter, Peter…pumpkin eater" burned into my memory.

Gold Beach wasn't Ventura, but it was close enough. I needed it today. In the kitchen, the front door creaked open. "You here?" Dad's voice called, rougher than usual.

"Yeah, Dad," I answered, slipping on my white Keds and grabbing a light jacket. July in Oregon felt off, cool, and gray, vastly different from California's relentless heat.

He appeared with a suit jacket draped over his arm, his face paler than the dawn outside, brow furrowed as if he'd aged overnight. "I know it was my day off, and we were going to look for a car for you, but I need to head to the office for a couple of hours."

"Is everything okay?" I asked, noticing the haunting strain in his eyes.

His gaze locked with mine, a fleeting smirk curling his lips, gone like an ember in drizzle. "Just a case dragging on, no progress, and I need it done." He paused, voice low, "Maybe this new lead will crack it. Someone close to your mom."

I had my doubts. The vague lead seemed like another unraveling thread, reminiscent of the cryptic notes in Dad's desk reports. "Can you drop me at the beach on your way?"

"Sure," he said, adjusting his tie. "But first, tell me about the other day when you were painting your room."

I sighed as I stepped toward his Ford LTD parked out front. The black beast's chrome was scuffed, and its V8 growled low as we climbed in, with tinted windows that hid the world. "I'll tell you on the way."

As we pulled out, Dad cleared his throat. "Well?"

"Alright, alright," I said, my voice tight. I recalled the vision of Nicole's figure by the tire swing and the cold dread that followed. He listened, his knuckles white on the wheel, remaining silent even after I finished.

We were nearly at the beach when he spoke, his tone soft yet firm. "I want you to talk to Dr. Finn."

"Dad, there's nothing wrong. I'm only tired, haven't been sleeping well." I folded my arms, huffing as I angled toward the passenger door. It was a childish move, but the irritation burned within me. Visions weren't real; they were just stress, not ghosts.

He reached over, squeezing my shoulder gently. I flinched, startled that he hadn't touched me since that awkward hug at the foster home in California. His eyes widened, reflecting my surprise, and he dropped his hand back to the wheel, the car's rumble breaking the silence.

"Just think about it," he said, almost pleading.

I nodded. I'd think about it. But I was already thinking. Too much.

All of it was Dad's evasiveness, Becca's polished smiles, and the strange, tangled tension that laced every conversation. The way they looked at each other when they thought I wasn't watching.

The way no one mentioned certain things, as if they had rehearsed what to say and what to leave out.

Or were they hiding something more?

Something about Becca gnawed at me, chewed at the edge of memory, too slick to hold onto yet too loud to ignore. I needed to know more about her; about the connection no one was discussing. Only one person came to mind: Kaitlyn Martin. Fortunately, I had her phone number memorized.

We weren't close, not really, but she was the only person from Gold Beach who stayed in touch after I left a few birthday texts, occasional memes, the kind of low-effort friendship that still felt genuine. So, I pulled out my phone and sent a message.

Hey, this is Alexis; this is my new number. I have a question for you.

No typing bubble yet, but it was out there. A breadcrumb dropped. Now I had to wait.

11

Alexis

After Dad dropped me off at the beach, I wandered down the shoreline until I found a quiet patch of sand where the wind didn't whip so hard. I sat with my arms wrapped around my knees, just like I used to when I was a kid on the back porch, waiting for Nicole to unlock the bathroom door, whether she was crying or, worse, screaming.

The waves thundered in the distance, but my thoughts were louder.

Something wasn't right. And I wasn't crazy for feeling it.

There was more to my mom's disappearance. Or death. And I was determined to figure it out.

Slipping off my Keds, I sank my toes into the cool sand, chasing the calm I'd once found in California's waves. The wind whipped my ponytail, raising goosebumps on my sore neck as I closed my eyes, but the ocean's rhythm couldn't quiet my thoughts today. They kept circling with the book's rhymes flickering like a warning I couldn't shake.

I hated dwelling on things and despised letting them fester. But lately, everything felt wrong: Dad, Becca, this town. Whispers about Nicole's murder followed me from the diner to the gas station, rumors about her "secrets" from a clerk. The nagging sense that something wasn't right grew louder with every step, like the hum of an engine running too hot. I wrapped my jacket tighter, but the chill wasn't just the Oregon air; it was the shadow of that pumpkin, those seeds, and the finger I'd never unsee. The sensation of eyes on me crept beneath my skin, and if there was one thing I trusted, it was my instincts.

A sudden burst of laughter snapped me out of it.

I looked up to see a young woman and her family spread out on the sand— blankets, cooler, folding chairs—the entire small-town weekend setup. A little boy threw a football that just missed their dog, who barked as if it were part of the fun.

Weird, she kind of looks like Kaitlyn.

"Alexis?" she called, I jumped. "I was just texting you back." She shaded her eyes with one hand.

"No way. Kaitlyn?" I chuckled in disbelief.

She jogged over, all long legs and effortless confidence. Her cheer hoodie was zipped halfway up over her uniform, displaying the Wildcats logo boldly against the blue and gold, with her hair pulled back into a glossy golden high ponytail. She looked exactly like someone who belonged here.

She pulled me into a hug. "Hey it's so good to see you... I'm really sorry about your mom," she said, her voice dropping a little. "People are being jerks, but they're always like that here. Give 'em something twisted, and they'll run wild with it."

"I noticed. I feel they know more about me than I do," I muttered, my gaze drifting back to the water.

Kaitlyn sighed and rubbed her arms. "This town is poison sometimes. I swear, the minute I graduate, I'm out. Eugene or UCLA if I can swing it."

"You're thinking LA?"

She shrugged. "I've been talking to a few programs. Suppose the cheer scholarship pans out, maybe. Honestly, I just want out. Too many memories here and not all the good kind."

I nodded, and for a moment, we stood there in silence, listening to the waves and the laughter behind her.

"I know this probably isn't the best time," she said, softer, "but if you ever want to hang out, vent, or literally just sit and ignore each other, I'm around."

"Thanks," I said, and I meant it even if I didn't know how to handle kindness anymore.

She offered me a tight smile, but just before she turned to leave, I found myself blurting, "Hey, do you know anything about Becca Shaw?"

Kaitlyn's brows lifted. "Uh, Becca? You mean, like, your dad's Becca?"

"Yeah. Her."

Kaitlyn hesitated. "I mean… yeah, sort of. She used to be married to William Thompson."

My stomach dropped.

"She was?" I asked, trying to keep my voice steady.

"Totally. Like, years ago. Everyone in town knew they were a thing. It got messy, though, with some drama and a divorce, then she just kind of faded for a while. Didn't think she'd end up with your dad, though."

"Yeah," I said slowly as the memory of Nicole mentioning Becca being William Thompson's ex came to the forefront. I pushed that day to the back of my memory. "Neither did I."

Kaitlyn tilted her head, clearly noticing my shift. "Why?"

I shook my head. "Just something I remembered. Thanks."

She shot me one more curious glance before jogging back to her family, calling out for her brother to stop throwing the football so close to the dog.

I watched her go, my pulse pounding.

Becca. William. Nicole

They were more connected than anyone was admitting. And I was finished pretending I didn't feel it.

12

Black Sheep

Crouched behind jagged boulders on the beach, he watched her with a predator's intensity, his eyes cold and unyielding. Her sun-kissed skin shimmered in the fading light—every feature sharpened into a lure that twisted in his gut. The hunt was everything, he thought, savoring the pulse of anticipation. She was no mere cat, no fleeting kill. Chasing her quickened his blood and sharpened his edge. His blood-smeared fingers clutched the cat's limp neck, craving to tangle in her glossy hair, to feel its silk, then tighten until her breath ceased.

His tongue flicked over cracked lips, tasting salt and obsession. Her crimson lips haunted him; salt and cherries, he imagined, forbidden and maddening. She was Nicole's daughter, the seed of a woman he'd loathed, yet her beauty clawed at him, threatening his control. Last night, he'd been too close, watching her sleep through her window, the rhyme looping in his mind: "Ladybug, Ladybug, fly away home…" That closeness was a mistake, a dangerous thrill that nearly broke his plan.

He clenched his teeth, pulse hammering. The chase is sweeter than the kill, he mused, each step bringing her closer to my trap. If he lingered, the rage, the want, would unravel him. Not yet, he hissed, slipping back into the trees. He needed distance, focus, and another kill to quiet the fire. The rhyme would guide him, as it always had.

13

Alexis

The sun hung low over Gold Beach, painting the waves with streaks of orange and gold. I'd been walking for what felt like ages, barefoot, with the cool sand squishing between my toes. My flip-flops dangled from one hand, and my phone remained silent in my pocket. No texts from Dad, no updates about Nicole's case, and an unsent text to Kaitlyn. Just me and the ocean's steady roar, loud enough to nearly drown out the ache in my chest. Nearly.

I wasn't paying much attention to anything beyond the horizon when I saw some guy running along the shore, maybe fifty yards ahead. He was fast, his strides long and easy, dark hair catching the fading light. I squinted, trying to place him, but my brain was too foggy with everything else: Nicole, the move, that stupid nursery rhyme note Dad wouldn't explain. I shook my head and kept walking, kicking at a clump of seaweed.

Then he turned, not completely, just enough to glance back as if checking for something behind him. That's when it happened. He didn't see me, didn't slow down, and before I could dodge, he crashed into me.

I yelped, stumbling backward as my flip-flops flew from my hand. My arms flailed, grasping at nothing, and I landed hard on my butt, sand spraying around me. The tide lapped at my ankles, cold and sudden, soaking the hem of my jeans. For a moment, I just sat there, stunned, my heart pounding against my ribs.

"Oh crap, I'm so sorry!" His voice cut through the haze, breathless and panicked. "Are you okay?"

I blinked up at him, my breath hitching. He was closer now, crouched a few feet away, one hand hovering as if unsure whether to help or back off. His hair was a mess of dark curls, damp with sweat or ocean spray, and his eyes, bright blue, were locked onto mine. My stomach did a weird flip, and I couldn't tell if it was from the fall or… him.

"Uh…" I opened my mouth, but my voice cracked, barely a whisper. Great, Alexis. Super smooth. I cleared my throat, brushing sand off my Metallica tank top, suddenly hyper-aware of how I must look, hair tangled, cheeks probably red from the wind. "Yeah. I'm fine. I think."

He exhaled, a small laugh escaping, and stood up, brushing the sand off his knees. "I didn't see you. I swear I'm not usually this clumsy." His grin was lopsided and sheepish, and it made my chest tighten in a way I wasn't ready for.

I scrambled to my feet, wincing as the wet sand clung to my legs. "It's… whatever," I mumbled, avoiding his gaze. My flip-flops were half-buried a few steps away, and I shuffled over to grab them, buying time to figure out what to say. Why am I so nervous? He's just some guy. A really good-looking guy, sure, but still.

"You sure you're okay?" he asked, trailing slightly behind me, his voice softer now. "You hit the ground pretty hard."

I straightened up, clutching my flip-flops like a shield, and finally met his eyes again. Big mistake. They were too blue, too intense, and I felt my face heat up. "I've survived worse," I said, trying to sound casual, maybe even cool. It came out sharper than I intended, and I cringed internally. Nice going. Scare him off, why don't you?

He didn't seem scared, though. He tilted his head, studying me, and that grin crept back. "Tough, huh? I like that."

My heart stuttered. Is he flirting? No way. He's just being nice. Right? I shifted my weight, the sand moving beneath me, and tucked a strand of hair behind my ear. "Not really. Just... used to falling, I guess."

He laughed a genuine laugh, full of warmth and ease, and it made me want to smile, even though I resisted it. "I'm Asher, by the way. Asher Finn."

"Alexis," I said, quieter than I intended. "Harper. Alexis Harper." I bit my lip, wondering if he would recognize the name of Detective Harper's daughter, the new girl with the dead mom. But his expression didn't change; it just remained open and curious.

"Cool name," he said, nodding as if it were a fact. "You're not from around here, are you?"

I hesitated, the question poking at something raw. "No. Just moved. My dad's..." I trailed off, not sure how much to say. "He's working a case."

Asher nodded as if it made sense and didn't press further. Instead, he looked down at the beach and then back at me. "So, what's a city girl doing out here, anyway? Besides getting run over by me."

I snorted, surprised by my own laugh, and it eased some of the tension in my shoulders. "Just walking. Thinking. You know, exciting stuff." I kicked at the sand again, watching it scatter. "What about you? Why were you sprinting like that?"

"Football," he said with a shrug. "Just graduated. Trying to stay in shape before college." He jokingly flexed his arm, and I rolled my eyes, but I couldn't stop the tiny grin tugging at my lips.

"Show-off," I muttered, crossing my arms. But I was looking at him now, really looking at his faded red board shorts, the way his shoulders were broad yet not bulky, and the freckles dusting his nose. My stomach fluttered again, and I hated how obvious it probably was.

"Maybe a little," he admitted, smirking. "Gotta impress somebody, right?"

"Oh, yeah? Who?" I shot back, raised an eyebrow, my voice teasing before I could stop it. Am I flirting? Oh God, I'm flirting. Am I doing it right?

He moved a step closer, just one, but it was enough to make my pulse race. "Maybe you," he said, his tone casual but his eyes steady, holding mine.

I froze, my breath catching. The waves crashed louder, or maybe it was just my heartbeat. I wanted to say something clever, something flirty, but all I managed was, "Well, you're off to a great start, knocking me over."

He laughed again, this time louder, and rubbed the back of his neck, looking almost… shy. "Okay, fair. I owe you one. How about I walk with you? Make sure no one else takes you out?"

I chewed my lip, torn between wanting to say yes and fearing I'd embarrass myself. "You don't have to," I said, but it came off weak, like I didn't mean it.

"I want to," he said simply, and that was that.

We began walking side by side, the space between us small but electric. The sun sank lower, the air cooling, and I could smell the salt and seaweed—sharp and alive. Neither of us spoke for a minute, and the silence wasn't awkward. It simply existed, letting me feel everything. The way his arm brushed mine accidentally once, and I didn't pull away. The way I kept sneaking glances at him, hoping he wouldn't notice.

I cleared my throat, breaking the silence, "What do you want to study in college?"

Asher pointed to the kids playing frisbee on the beach. "I used to dream of coaching, you know? Kids like me need someone to believe in them. But Dad's got me on this Princeton path, doctor, fixer, like him."

Kids like him?

I didn't press. "You can't 'fix' people. They have to be open to change. I should know." I gave him a small, reassuring smile as I chewed on my thumbnail.

"Exactly! So," he said, locking his hands on the back of his head, making his biceps tighten, "you like music?" He nodded at my tank top. "Metallica's old-school. Good taste."

"Yeah," I said a little too quickly. "My mom," I stopped, the word catching in my throat. I swallowed hard and tried again. "I grew up with it. You into music?"

"More of a classic rock guy," he said. "Zeppelin, Stones. That kind of thing."

"Zeppelin's solid," I agreed, relaxing a bit. "Kashmir's my favorite."

"No way," he said, turning to me with his eyes lighting up. "That's mine too."

I smiled, truly smiled for the first time all day, and he smiled back; it felt like something clicked. Not big, not loud, just... right.

We kept talking about music, about the beach, about nothing important, but it felt important, nonetheless. The sun sank lower, painting the sky in streaks of orange and pink, and a chilly breeze swept over the beach, tugging at my hair. I pulled my phone from my pocket, no messages from Dad, just the time staring back at me: 6:47 p.m. I'd lost track of how long we'd been sitting here, talking. "I should probably head back," my voice came out softer than I intended, as if I wasn't ready to leave.

Asher looked up from the sand, where he had been idly tracing patterns with a stick. His eyes flicked to the horizon and then back to me. "Yeah, it's getting late." He paused, brushing the sand off his hands. "How'd you get here? Walk?"

"Dad dropped me off earlier," I said, shoving my phone back into my pocket. "He was supposed to pick me up, but…" I didn't finish. Dad's reliability was a coin toss these days.

"Or," Asher cut in, a small, lopsided smile tugging at his lips, "I could give you a ride. My car's just up by the lot."

I blinked, taken by surprise. "You don't have to. I can just call him."

"It's no trouble," he said, standing and offering me a hand. "We're neighbors, right? It's basically on my way."

I hesitated, then took his hand, allowing him to pull me up. His grip was warm and steady, but I let it go a bit too quickly, my stomach flipping in that annoying way again. It's just a ride, Alexis. Chill. "Okay," I said, forcing a casual tone. "Thanks."

We walked side by side toward the parking lot, the sound of the waves fading behind us. My flip-flops slapped against the sand, and I kept stealing glances at him, his sharp jawline, and the way the wind tousled his hair. He caught me once, and I snapped my eyes forward, my cheeks burning. Real subtle.

When we reached the lot, I stopped abruptly. There it was, parked under a flickering streetlight: a black Shelby GT500, its sleek lines and chrome accents shimmering like something out of a dream. "That's yours?" I asked, my voice betraying me with a mix of shock and admiration.

Asher grinned, a flicker of pride in his eyes. "Yep. 2008 collector's edition."

"No way," I said, stepping closer. This was a monster: a 5.4-liter supercharged V8, going from zero to sixty in under 4.5 seconds. "How'd you even get this?"

"Graduation gift," he said, unlocking the passenger door and holding it open for me. "Dad's friend owed him big time."

I slid into the leather seat, brushing my fingers on the dashboard. "Some friend," I muttered, taking in the polished interior, black leather, a faint whiff of saltwater and car wax. It felt alive, even sitting still.

Asher climbed in beside me, and the engine roared to life with a deep, throaty rumble that vibrated through my bones. He glanced over, catching my wide-eyed stare. "You like it?"

"It's insane," I said honestly, settling back as he merged onto the coastal road. The power hummed beneath us, steady yet coiled, as if it were waiting to break free.

For a minute, we drove in silence, the ocean a dark blur outside my window. It wasn't awkward, though, just easy, as if we didn't need to force anything. Still, I couldn't help myself. "So, what'd your dad do to score this favor?" I asked, half-joking.

His smile flickered, and his hands tightened on the wheel for a split second. "Something big," he said, his tone dipping into something heavier. He didn't elaborate, and the shift made me wonder what he wasn't saying. But then he shook it off and glanced at me. "You know cars, huh?"

"A little," I said, shrugging. "Mom's boyfriends were obsessed with drag racing and car shows. I picked up some stuff."

"That's cool," he said, nodding. "Ever been to a race?"

"A few," I replied, flashes of memory hitting me, screaming engines, Nicole's laughter, guys who never lasted. I pushed it down. "Nothing like this, though."

He softly laughed. "Maybe I'll take you some time. Show you what she can really do."

My pulse jumped. Sometimes. Like this wasn't just a one-off. "Yeah," I said a little too quickly. "That'd be cool."

The rest of the drive slipped by, the Shelby's growl filling the quiet stretches. When we pulled into my driveway, the porch light glowed softly and yellow. I unbuckled, suddenly hyper-aware of how close we were to the car's tight space. "Thanks for the ride," I said, my hand on the door.

"Anytime," he replied, his eyes locking with mine. The air felt thick and charged, and for a moment, I thought he might say something different. Then he smiled, breaking the tension. "See you around, Alexis."

"See you," I managed, slipping out. I stood there as he drove away, the taillights fading into the night, my heart still thudding.

Inside, the house was silent except for the faint scent of pizza lingering in the air. Dad must've ordered dinner. I drifted over to the kitchen table, where a newspaper lay open, its headline screaming up at me: "William Thompson, Person of Interest in Nicole Roberts Murder, Freed After Alibi Verified."

My breath caught. I snatched it up, scanning the text: "Businessman William Thompson faced scrutiny in the brutal slaying of Nicole Roberts. After interrogation, his alibi was held, securing his release." Ice slid down my spine. I had felt it on the beach like someone was watching from the shadows.

Nicole's killer remained at large, and the pieces were slipping further apart.

14

Black Sheep

The storm rolled in after midnight, lightning splitting the sky like a warning, and rain battered the earth in frantic bursts. Nature concealed its steps. God turned away His gaze.

The gates of Our Lady of Sorrows Church sagged on rusted hinges. No one bothered to lock the doors. Who would dare harm women of God? *I would,* he thought, a thrill pulsing through him. *The hunt is my sacrament.*

He glided through the abbey halls like smoke; their names and prayers etched in his mind. He knew where they would kneel, their devotion serving as his map. Nine nuns that night, each christened "Mary" for the Holy Mother, each marked in his black book with a single word: Contrary. One had known Nicole, having tried to save her youth from ruin. Her failure was a debt, and he was here to collect.

They never saw his face, never heard his approach, only the soft, sinister chime of silver bells pinned to their chests as they fell, arterial spray painting the stone in crimson arcs. Each kill sharpens me, he mused; Nicole's blood was just the spark. These nuns stoke the fire, but Ladybug will be the blaze.

By dawn, the rain had settled. A pale sun rose, bewildered, over the blood-slick earth. The nuns knelt in the courtyard, three perfect rows of three, hands folded, habits clinging like sodden shrouds. Silver bells jingled faintly in the breeze. Their heads, severed with surgical precision to rest atop their necks, tilted forward in mock prayer, a grotesque parody of reverence. Crimson seeped from ragged seams, pooling on the stone. Their mouths, stuffed with cockle shells, oozed blood down distended jaws.

No struggle. No defensive wounds. As if they'd willingly rooted themselves in his garden of death, their necks gaping like wilted blooms. Carved beneath their knees:

"Mary, Mary, quite contrary,
How does your garden grow?
With silver bells and cockle shells,
And pretty maids all in a row."

Priests wailed. Sisters wept. Reporters swarmed like locusts, cameras flashing on the carnage. He stood among the onlookers, concealed by a hooded coat, separated only by the yellow police tape snapping in the wind. Red and blue squad car lights danced across the stained-glass windows, a stark contrast to the deeper red crusting on his nails from hours earlier.

He stood motionless, hands in his pockets, inhaling the chaos like incense, the coppery tang of slaughter lingering on his breath. *This is my art,* he thought, *the hunt's masterpiece; each kill a step closer to her.* His foot tapped the asphalt, softly humming the rhyme, a scowl veiling his surging satisfaction as his pulse raced with the gore's beauty.

A little girl tugged her mother's hand, pointing. "Mommy, he smells like flowers and smoke." His lips curled beneath the hood, revealing a blood-flecked smile. Children always noticed what others missed.

The idea had taken root in obsession. "Mary, Mary, Quite Contrary," a nursery rhyme, a queen, a martyr was his muse. Bloody Mary burned heretics, and he hunted his. Nicole's sin sprouted this garden, he reflected, her failure to be saved and her poison seeping into Ladybug. The rhyme marked his taunt for the nun who couldn't redeem Nicole and the eight others who shared her name, complicit in their faith's futility.

In the church's wine cellar, his altar, he'd taken them one by one. A strike behind the ear with his hunting knife's blunt handle cracked skulls like eggshells. Bound. Gagged. Their muffled screams formed a choir, dragged below where God wouldn't listen. He whispered the rhyme as he worked, testing his "silver bells" thumbscrews forged from cruelty and honed on cats' squeals and spilling entrails. The cockle shells, jagged and theatrical, sliced tongues for show.

A new chainsaw, his modern guillotine, roared through their necks, blood and bone spraying his face, warm and intimate. He savored the hunt's climax; each kill fueled his craving for the next. Rats skittered from the walls, gnawing at sinew. Let them feast.

His phone buzzed with a message from Spider: "Stick to the plan. No deviations." He scowled but nodded, then returned to his boat, his mind drifting. Ladybug waits, he thought, the true prize of the hunt; her chase fueled the fire that Nicole's death ignited.

He pictured her face when the news broke: "Massacre at Our Lady of Sorrows Church. Nuns Beheaded, Dismembered." The thought warmed his blood, a pulse of ecstasy. She'd know it was him. She had to know. This garden was for her.

15

Alexis

I'm a stick figure on a blood-smeared chalkboard, hollow and trapped. A carved pumpkin oozes blood on a table, its jagged grin mocking my trembling grasp. Across from it, Nicole's silhouette weeps crimson, her mournful smile cutting deep. A word bubble scrawls: Ladybug, fly away. I'm sorry. Above, nursery rhymes scratch faintly bells, shells, a whisper of dread. A shadow lingers, hands rough with ash and reeking of decay.

My eyes flew open, heart racing. I pulled the covers up, breath uneven. Ladybug, fly away. Not my name a taunt, sharp as the killer's knife. Stumbling to the closet, I grabbed the nursery rhyme book, its pages fragile. A new mark caught my eye: "Mary, Mary, quite contrary," a ladybug sticker pressed beside it. My pulse quickened. Had it always been there, or was someone in my room?

A loud noise shattered the silence, urgent, from the yard. I rushed to the window, peering through the dawn fog. An old, beat-up truck idled across the street, its dark-tinted windows glinting and engine growling low. My breath hitched. The truck looked familiar. I bolted out of my room, shoved my feet into sneakers, and yanked the door open. But the truck's tires screeched as it sped off into the mist, its taillights fading.

I sank onto the porch, gripping the book heavy in my hand. Another clue, or a trap? I hugged my knee, trying to calm my nerves, but the truck's shadow lingered. It was just a truck and I was wound tight from my nightmare.

I wasn't losing it. Last week, Nicole's silhouette was by the tire swing. Her perfume, sharp and fleeting, felt too vivid. These dreams, though, cut deeper, clawing at truths I couldn't reach. Gold Beach, a new life; my mother's savage death could shatter anyone. But I'd endured her cruelty, her men, her lies. I wouldn't break now. I'd find the truth, no matter the cost.

I returned to my room, grabbed my journal, and lay back in bed. My hand shook as I recorded images from my dream: bells, shells, predator, rhymes. Since last night, after learning about William Thompson's alibi, I became fixated on the rhyme that haunted my childhood.

I closed my eyes once more, recalling the last time I saw Nicole alive, her distracted smile, her voice sharp as she argued with Becca on the phone. My chest ached with a throbbing longing for a better goodbye, for words I never said: *I love you.* Tears slipped past my ears, soaking my pillow as I blinked them away, the house's silence pressing in like a warning.

Then, the mattress dipped beside me. I tensed, fight-or-flight kicking in, ready to bolt until something rough and slimy grazed my cheek. I yelped, flinging my eyes open, only to freeze. Staring back was the cutest face I had ever seen. A long, light-brown snout twitched softly, warm brown eyes brimming with curiosity, and tall black ears perked like sentinels, a German Shepherd pup with gangly legs and oversized paws. I burst into giggles that shook my chest, surprising me with their lightness. He looked like the Big Bad Wolf from "Little Red Riding Hood" if the wolf were adorable and more likely to lick you to death than eat you.

"Hey there, puppy," I murmured, scratching behind its velvety ears. Its tail thumped, and I laughed again, the dreams and the heaviness lifting for a moment.

He perked up at my voice and leaped off the bed, bolting from the room like a furry rocket. Startled yet curious, I threw off the covers and chased him, my bare feet slapping against the cold wooden floor. When I reached the front door, it stood wide open, the Oregon wind rustling the pines outside. I paused at the threshold, watching the pup bound toward Dad and Nathan, who were unloading grocery bags from the trunk of Dad's car. The old Ford's black paint gleamed faintly in the afternoon light; a beast as weathered as Dad himself.

"Nathan!" I called, raising my voice over the wind. "Is this your dog?"

Nathan looked up, his gaze flickering over my tank top and shorts before settling on my face with a lopsided grin. "Nope."

I frowned as I stepped onto the porch, the boards creaking beneath my weight. "Then where'd he come from? Is he a stray?"

I turned to Dad, raising an eyebrow in silent inquiry. He paused, scratching his head, a nervous tic I had noticed more often since we left California. He gave me an unreadable look as if he were weighing his words, not shocked that I was weighing his.

"Sweetheart, he's yours." His voice was softer than usual.

My eyes widened. "Wait, what? You got me a dog?" Another gift?

"Yep," he replied, shrugging as he and Nathan walked toward the house, the pup happily trotting at their heels, its tail wagging like a metronome.

I pressed my lips together, emotions swirling: joy, confusion, and a pang of something heavier. "Why?" I asked, quieter now. Dad stopped mid-step, turning to face me. "I mean… It's not that I don't want a dog... whatever," I said, shaking my head in disbelief. "It's just that Nicole never let me have a goldfish, let alone a whole dog."

Dad's expression darkened, his jaw tightening like it had when he read the police report about William Thompson's alibi. "Well, I'm not your mother," he said, his tone sharp, cutting through the air.

The words hit like a slap, and I blinked, startled by the sharpness in his voice. Nicole's rules her control had always created a barrier between us, but hearing Dad dismiss her so coldly hurt more than I anticipated.

He walked past me into the house, leaving me rooted on the porch. I looked at Nathan, who bent down, his voice low. "He's had a long day." Then he followed Dad inside, grocery bags rustling.

Day? I glanced at the clock in the foyer as I stepped back inside: 4:45 p.m., Monday. My brows furrowed. I had slept for over twenty hours since yesterday's beach trip with Asher. No wonder I felt so tired.

In the kitchen, Dad and Nathan put away groceries, the pup weaving between their legs. I would've helped, but Dad's mood and cryptic jab about Nicole irritated me, coiling tight with the unease I'd felt since dinner with Becca at the Port Hole Café. I sank to the floor in the doorway, and the dog padded over, flopping down beside me with a contented sigh. I scratched his belly, and his warmth eased the knot in my chest.

"Where'd he come from?" I asked, glancing up.

Nathan paused, kneeling to pet the pup, his hand brushing against mine repeatedly, sending a flush of heat across my skin. He cleared his throat and pulled back. "He's a gift from my dad and me. We breed German Shepherds, and his mom was Dad's old police partner in the K9 unit, retired now."

Dad pulled out a chair, its screech across the tile jarring, and sat down, elbows on his knees, hands tugging at his hair. "Sweetheart, I thought since I'm gone a lot, it'd be nice for you to have company, someone to watch out for you."

I knelt beside the puppy, my fingers sinking into his soft fur. He looked up at me with wide, trusting eyes, his tail wagging tentatively as if he sensed the weight of the moment. A small smile tugged at my lips despite the tension in the air. "You need a name," I murmured, more to myself than to Dad. Something strong, something that feels like safety. My mind drifted to the stories I'd loved as a kid, tales of rangers protecting the wild, always watchful and always there. "Ranger," I whispered, testing the word. It felt right, like a promise. "You'll be my Ranger."

I looked up at Dad, aware that he was watching me closely. His hands were buried in his hair, pulling harder as if trying to hold himself together. "What's going on, Dad?" I asked, my voice steady but laced with concern. "There's something you're not telling me."

Abruptly, he stood and stormed to the backyard. I wasn't going to let him dodge this, not after that tone, not after the way he'd brushed off Nicole's memory. My stomach churned, little pincers of dread snipping at me, whispering that whatever he was hiding concerned me. I followed the pup at my heels, and we sat on the swings, the same ones where I'd seen Nicole's ghost. I shook off the chill, focusing on Dad.

"Dad?" I touched his forearm, my voice gentle but firm.

He looked up, noticing my concern, and sighed.

I swallowed, worry lodged in my throat.

"We heard at the station about murders Saturday night in Santa Barbara." He paused, his eyes distant. "At first, it was just another report; we get them daily. But something caught my ear." He stopped, his jaw tight, showing no sign of continuing.

"Well, what?" I pressed, glancing at Nathan on the porch, sitting in a white plastic chair with the pup at his feet. He gave me a tight smile, respecting our space, but his presence steadied me. I turned back to Dad.

His hands gripped the swing's chains, knuckles white. His face turned toward me, but his gaze was lost in the trees, where I'd imagined Nicole's shadow days ago. "Dad, if you're worried about your job, don't be. Whatever you say stays between us."

"I'm not worried about my job," he said, his voice low. "I'm worried about what this means for Nicole's case." His cryptic tone sparked agitation, much like when Becca's honeyed words had cloaked something sour.

I huffed, my patience wearing thin. "Just tell me."

"Let me show you." He stood up, led me inside, and flipped on the TV and took it to the YouTube channel. The screen lit up, and my head spun as the news anchor's voice cut through the air.

Breaking news from Santa Barbara: police are investigating a gruesome scene found early this morning at Our Lady of Sorrows Catholic Church...The authorities believe they may have a serial killer at large...The Rhyme Reaper...

The air vanished from the room.

Rhyme Reaper?

"Nine victims... nuns... arranged in the courtyard in perfect rows..."

Rows.

"Silver bells pinned to their chests..."

No, no.

I stumbled back, my knees hitting the couch. I collapsed onto it, my hands shaking and my eyes fixed on the screen.

"Cockle shells were found in their mouths. Etched into the stone beneath them: How does your garden grow?'

The nursery rhyme echoed in my head, a record stuck on repeat: "Mary, Mary, quite contrary, how does your garden grow? With silver bells and cockle shells, and pretty maids all in a row..."

My lungs seized, gasps clawing at my throat. Colors danced and melted, kaleidoscope vision blurring the room. The pup barked, sharp and frantic, as voices tried to reach me, muffled like cotton stuffed in my ears.

So many questions, but no answers. The rhyme was him, the same vicious, soulless monster who had turned Santa Barbara's church into a graveyard. Nicole's killer is out there, and he isn't finished.

Lost at sea, my head and stomach churned like a canoe tossed in a storm, desperate for calm. Someone was carrying me, with arms strong yet gentle. Through my haze, I glimpsed the windshield of Dad's car, its familiar dashboard gleaming under the streetlights. Dad stood outside, talking on his phone and gesturing wildly. Nathan approached, said something softly, and then walked away, his silhouette fading into the dusk.

Exhaustion pinned me down; heavier than the twenty hours I had slept the day before. Breathing was a struggle, each breath shallow and ragged. My eyes drifted shut, and a voice crept in, the same one from the night Nicole died, reciting rhymes she had read to me as a child. It twisted, sinister now, a taunt from the dark.

My lungs protested as I woke, gulping air. My hand flew to my chest, patting hard as if I could force the breath to stay. The unfamiliar room sent panic spiking through the white walls and soft lamplight until Dad and Dr. Finn stepped into view. I was on a couch, not mine, in what had to be Finn's house; the pup curled at my feet, whining softly, bringing me the warmth I didn't know I needed.

Dad knelt, hands on my shoulders, his face etched with worry. "Sweetheart, focus on your breathing."

I couldn't. The rhymes, the pumpkin, the finger, the bells, and the shells choked me. He pressed on, his voice steady. "Come on, please. If you don't, Dr. Finn will give you something to calm you, and it'll knock you out again."

Sleep. No, I couldn't go back there, not with that voice waiting. Nightmares had claws, and I'd had enough. I shook my head, gasping, "No." As I pulled Ranger up onto my chest, his soft fur brushed against my fingers, and I felt my racing heart begin to slow.

"Alright, no sleep," Dad said, nodding. "Just calm down." He breathed in and out, his cheeks puffing up like a pufferfish, almost comical. I latched onto it, mimicking him, and slowly, painfully, my breathing steadied. Yet my body remained tense, a coiled spring of fear.

Dr. Finn took tentative steps, sitting closer than I preferred on the edge of the couch. "Angel, your dad and I think it's time we sit down. Between doctor and patient, let's talk about what's happening."

"Angel?" The word jarred me, too familiar, like something Nicole might have called me. Why did he use it? I knew he meant well, but his closeness and calm felt like a trap. Was anyone really who they seemed?

Dad noticed my hesitation; his eyes were pleading. "Please, sweetheart. Let Dr. Finn help."

The thought of yesterday's newspaper, William Thompson's alibi, was another dead end. The world felt like a puzzle with missing pieces, and the killer held them all. That news report, those nuns, wasn't random. It was a message, maybe for me.

Denial wasn't working anymore. Dad's distress, the pup's worried nudge against my hand, and the echo of "How does your garden grow?" felt overwhelming. I nodded, my voice small but certain. "Okay, I'll talk."

16

Alexis

"How are you feeling?" Dr. Finn's voice was calm and steady, like the hum of a finely tuned engine, yet it did little to ease the irritation creeping beneath my skin.

"Fine," I muttered, shifting in the leather chair. It clung to my legs, making my shorts and tank top feel like a mistake. The small office was warm, and the chair's grip intensified my discomfort.

Dr. Finn tilted his head, his eyes searching mine. I knew he didn't believe me. "Have you been sleeping well?"

"What do you think?" I snapped, then caught myself. He wasn't blind; those dark circles under my eyes shouted. "Sorry," I added, softer now, guilt prickling like sand in my shoes from the beach yesterday.

"No need to stress," he replied calmly. "Have you gotten used to living with your dad?"

"I think so." Short answers, I figured, might help me leave this room faster, which felt like a trap.

"Do you miss your mother?"

Dr. Finn's question: *Do I miss her?* Burned like salt in a cut. I shifted, the leather chair sticking to my thighs, and my shorts too thin for this heat. "I don't know," I said, my voice cracking, eyes on the floor. Did I miss Nicole's lavender hugs or her cold stare when I begged her to stop them? My chest tightened, a memory clawing up—her boyfriend's Mustang idling outside, his hand sliding up my skirt when I was twelve, her laughter from the kitchen, *"Loosen up, Alexis."* She knew.

Dr. Finn leaned forward, his fingertips steepled, his calm unnerving as he observed too much. "What's that look like, Alexis? Something specific?"

I sat in Dr. Finn's office, my hands twisting in my lap as if they had a mind of their own. The words didn't want to emerge, but they did anyway, spilling out like word vomit, messy and fast. I didn't want to share any of it. I wanted to keep it buried where it couldn't expose me. But it was too hard to hold in any longer. It was either talk or explode.

"I keep seeing things, Dr. Finn. Things that aren't there." My voice cracked, and I hated it sounding so small. "It's my mom. She's sitting there, reading to me, 'Mary, Mary, quite contrary,' but her smile… it twists into something awful, like she's laughing at me. And there's this pumpkin, grinning, just like the one they found her finger in."

I swallowed; my throat was so dry it hurt. "It used to just be nightmares, but now it's during the day when I'm awake. I can't tell what's real anymore."

Dr. Finn leaned forward, his eyes soft but steady, as if he wasn't freaked out by what I'd just said. "Alexis, what you're describing sounds incredibly vivid and distressing. It's not uncommon for trauma to show up like this. When something overwhelming happens, like what you went through with your mom, your mind can create intense images or sounds as a way to process it. They're called hallucinations, and they can feel completely real, even though they're not happening right now."

I stared at him, my heart thumping so loudly I could hear it. "So, it's because of her? Because of… what happened?"

He nodded, calm as ever. "Yes. Your brain is wrestling with something huge, something no one should have to face. Hallucinations can happen to people after trauma. It's a way your mind copes, even if it feels like it's doing the opposite."

I bit my lip hard, trying to figure out what that meant for me. "Does that mean I'm losing it? Like I'm crazy?"

Dr. Finn shook his head immediately, firm yet kind. "No, Alexis. You're not crazy. You're a survivor. Your mind's just reacting to something unbearable, and that doesn't make you weak or broken."

Survivor. That word hit me like a punch, but a good one. I let out a shaky breath I didn't even know I'd been holding. "But it's so real. Like she's right there, watching me."

"I get that," he said, his voice gentle. "And it's scary because it feels so real. But there are ways we can work on this together, ways to help you feel more in control when it happens."

I frowned, curious despite myself. "Like what?"

"Things like mindfulness, grounding techniques, stuff to bring you back to the moment. We can also talk through the hallucinations when they come up. It's about finding what works for you."

I wasn't completely convinced but knowing there was a plan helped ease the knot in my chest just a little. "Okay," I said quietly. "I'll give it a shot."

Dr. Finn's pen paused, and something shifted. "That rhyme... It's heavy for you. Why 'Mary, Mary'?"

I averted my eyes and saw a file on his desk labeled "Nicole Roberts." It peeked out but was quickly covered. "Just old records," he muttered, but his hands shook.

My skin crawled; the nursery rhymes felt like a trap he had set. His tone was too careful, as if he knew more about Nicole's secrets, which resided in his files. I could use this time to learn more about her and see if her secrets were linked with the killer.

I moved on, my nails digging into my palms, grounding me. "It's what she read to me before... everything." Before the men and the cars, before she turned away. I glared, daring him to push. "You called me Angel earlier. Why? She did, sometimes, when no one was around." My voice shook, resentful of the softness.

He froze for just a second, then scribbled, avoiding my eyes. "A reflex, I guess. Sounds like she left a lot unsaid." His dodge stung, like Dad's silence about her dates. Was Dr. Finn hiding something from her past, mine?

I paced the room, the air thick and suffocating, my confession spilling out in a rush as Ranger padded softly beside me, a steady shadow at my heels.

"She let them touch me," I choked, tears burning, blurring Dr. Finn. "Her boyfriends. Stephen... pinned me, hand over my mouth. She ignored it." My knees buckled, and I hit the floor, sobs escaping, and Ranger's soft whine cut through the haze as he pressed his warm body against my side, his head resting on my trembling leg. "She knew and let it happen." Dr. Finn froze, eyes glistening, jaw tight, his silence heavy with unspoken grief.

He left me crumpled and silent, offering a tight smile that provided a touch of comfort.

Dr. Finn stood and crossed to his desk, pulling out a black prescription pad, his jaw tight as he scribbled. "I'm giving these to your dad to fill," he said through clenched teeth, his calm fraying. "One for anxiety, one for sleep. You must take both. Lack of sleep fuels anxiety. Please, Alexis, take them. I'd like to see you every two weeks. We could've gone longer today, but you've been through enough. Next time, we'll pick up from here."

Dr. Finn gave me a small, warm smile. "You're stronger than you think, Alexis. We'll figure this out, one step at a time."

For the first time in forever, I felt this tiny spark, like maybe I wasn't doomed to fall apart. Maybe if I could trust him to be in my corner, I could face the ghosts and not let them win.

That's how it went down: me spilling my guts, Dr. Finn making sense of it, and me clinging to a shred of hope by the end.

17

Alexis

Standing at the base of the stairs in Finn's house, I overheard Dad's voice, tinged with guilt. "This is my fault. If I'd raised her, Nicole would still be alive, and my baby girl wouldn't be going through this heartache."

His words cut sharper than the news of the nun's massacre. He wasn't to blame. How could he stop the killer? I couldn't let him bear that weight.

I marched over, wrapping my arms around his waist and hugging him tightly. Tears surged, with sobs wracking my body. I was exhausted from crying and feeling fragile, but Dad's guilt stung more than Nicole's loss.

His hands hovered over me in the Finns' living room, eyes shadowed with secrets. He muttered to Dr. Finn, "Ronny's poking into her case again," bitterly, as if he hated the name.

I'd heard it in his tense calls since Ronny wasn't on the force anymore, but he wouldn't let it go. Was he hiding something about Nicole's death? The air thickened, the killer's rhyme echoing in my mind.

"Are you alright?" he asked, guiding me to the couch. I wiped my face, feeling nausea rise, and my head throbbed, noticing Dr. Finn, Tami, and Asher watching. Dr. Finn shifted, tapping a ladybug keychain on the table, oddly nervous. Their concern grew thicker in the room, fog whispering rhymes outside.

I clapped a hand over my mouth. "I'm gonna throw up. Where's the bathroom?"

"Through there," Tami said, looking concerned, and pointed down the hall. "Last door on the right." I bolted before she finished, dropping to my knees in the bathroom and heaving until my stomach was empty, dry heaves wracking my body.

I flushed and plopped down on the closed seat and began looking at the bookmarked website. Since the news assume this was a serial killer I figured I needed to try and understand him through the rhymes. I scrolled through and found "Mary, Mary".

The rhyme symbolized growth and preservation. I remember going to church when I was little, but once my parents divorced, Nicole stopped going. Did Nicole go to church before I was born? Did she need that sense of control? Or sins that she needed cleansing of? Was this even about her?

I always begged to go. I believed in God. I couldn't shake the feeling that this killer was playing God.

I put my phone in my pocket and stood at the sink. I splashed cold water on my face, sweat and tears mixing. I looked up and jumped when the mirror revealed not just me but another girl with thin, jet-black hair cropped to her chin. Her piercing blue eyes bored into mine as if they could see every secret I'd locked away. She didn't speak; she just stared, unblinking, freaking me out.

"Um… hello?" I waved a hand. She blinked, smiled faintly, and shook her head.

"Sorry," she said, extending her hand. "You must be Alexis. I'm Sadie."

I shook her hand; her grip was firm but kind. "Hi, nice to meet you. Are you Tami and Keith's daughter?"

She laughed, a bright sound that eased the tension. "No, their niece. Tami and my mom, Kate, are sisters, but I live here now."

Her face shadowed briefly, a sadness I recognized. "I'm here to escape… things like her, Nicole." She glanced at the floor as if Nicole's name burned. Did she know something? "My mom's… not well." Her smile faltered.

Escape. I got that. Not wanting to linger, I said, "I'd better get back. They're probably worried." She followed as I stepped outside.

"You okay?" she asked, her voice soft.

"Yes… no… I don't know. Stress, I think." I glanced back, offering her a small smile.

"If you need to talk, I'm here. What grade will you be in this fall?"

"Senior."

"Great, me too," she said, her grin infectious.

In the front room, Tami asked, "Are you alright?" The question was becoming my shadow.

"I will be," I said, forcing a sad smile.

"Aunt Tami, Alexis is a senior too," Sadie said, excitedly brightening the room.

I scanned the faces, stopping at Asher. His brows were furrowed, his lips pouting, but his face lit up when our eyes met. A smile broke through like sunlight after a storm. My pulse quickened, recalling how he had looked at me yesterday, open, honest, not like Nicole's men with their flashy cars and emptier promises.

"Sweetheart?" Dad's voice pulled me back. He still looked wrecked; guilt etched deep into his features.

I'd ask about Ronny later; I had to know. I wished to wipe it away. "I'm okay," I said, my voice now gentler.

"I gotta get to work," he said, standing and looking embarrassed. "The station needs me."

"Sorry, Dad. I kept you," I said with guilt in my voice, referencing his long shifts and my collapse. "Can you drop me home, or I can walk?"

He looked at me like I'd suggested swimming to California. "You're not walking alone. Besides, the Finns and I think you should stay here this weekend."

"Weekend?" I blinked, time slipping away like the sand on that beach.

"I'm on call, long shift," he said, grabbing his suit jacket off the couch. "Asher'll take you home to grab clothes and whatever you need."

I nodded, too tired to argue. If staying here eased Dad's mind, I would do it. His worry was a burden I couldn't bear, especially after hearing him blame himself.

Dad left, and Tami approached, her maternal warmth contrasting with Nicole's sharp edges. "Alexis, if you need anything, tea, a blanket, someone to listen, we're here." Her eyes, soft yet searching, reminded me of the school counselor who'd tried to "fix" me. I managed a tight smile, unsure how to accept kindness that felt so foreign.

In Asher's Shelby, the silence was thick; the engine rumbled, the only sound as we hit the main road. Yesterday, he'd been all smiles, teasing about football and cars, maybe even flirting. Now, he was quiet, his bulk filling the driver's seat, muscles tensed as he gripped the wheel. It grated on me, the shift to closed-off rejection.

"So, Asher," I said, leaning closer, "your Shelby's got a 4.6-liter V8, right?" A lie, I knew it was 5.4, supercharged, raw power to spark a reaction and pierce the silence.

He whipped his head toward me, eyes sharp. "4.6? Nah, it's 5.4, supercharged. But you knew that." I grinned, his remark breaking the silence.

"Ever floored her to the max?"

He chuckled, his eyes flicking to the road. "Guess her top speed?"

"Okay," I said, fighting a grin. "Hundred fifty-five miles per hour, zero to sixty in four point five seconds." I'd overheard it at a car show Nicole dragged me to, where some guy bragged about his Mustang to impress her.

After meeting Asher, every detail about Shelby stuck with me, like the rhymes I couldn't shake. But then he veered off the road, braking hard enough that I clutched the seat, my fingers pressing into the leather. He gazed down at his lap, shaking his head.

"Asher, what the hell?" My voice was sharp; my heart raced from the jolt.

"You can't say stuff like that," he said, his voice low and almost pained.

"What?" I laughed, puzzled, thinking it was about the car.

He killed the engine and turned to face me, his ice-blue eyes intense, just like yesterday on the beach. "I think you're smart, funny, pretty… no, stunning." His words hit like a wave, unexpected and cold. My brows shot up, heat creeping into my cheeks. "But when you talk about cars and sports, it's sexy, and it makes me like you more, but I shouldn't." He closed his eyes, and jaw tight.

"Why?" I asked, curiosity outweighing caution. My life was a wreck. I wasn't ready for feelings, not with Asher's easy charm or Nathan's quiet grins pulling at me. They were distractions, bright spots in a storm, but merely distractions.

"I'm leaving for college, Princeton, in the fall," he said, voice heavy. "Starting something now… It's not fair… and…"

I cut him off; his clarity was sharp. "Asher, my life's too messy for that. I just met you. I'm not looking for a relationship;

there are too many ghosts." I thought of Nicole's men, their cars revving outside, their hands too close. "I just need a friend. I've never had a loyal one, and that's what I need most."

He smiled, relief softening his expression, and reached for my hand. I pulled back, instincts kicking in, and his brow furrowed. He noticed but didn't push. "Friend," he said, nodding. "I can do that."

"Great." I bounced in my seat, feeling lighter now.

"You know," he added, starting the car, "Sadie'd be a good friend, too."

"I think so," I said, picturing her bright laugh and her weird comment about Nicole. The car's growl filled the quiet as we drove, easing the tension. I gave directions, but he just laughed.

At the house, I bolted out. "Be right back," I called, sprinting inside. I tossed clothes, my toothbrush, and the pup's new collar into my gym bag, pausing at the kitchen table where yesterday's newspaper still lay: *William Thompson Released*. A chill ran through me, the rhyme flickering: "Peter, Peter…."

Throughout town, whispers circulated that he was seen near Gold Beach, free yet creeping. My fingers trembled as I tore off the headline and pocketed it, something to check later. The rhymes weren't just in my head; they were clues, taunts, and pieces of a puzzle I had to solve. I grabbed my bag, heart pounding, and ran back to the car, the air outside too still, like the calm before a storm.

Back at the car, Asher said, "Mom and Dad called, need me to grab pizzas. Do you want to come, or should I drop you off at their place?"

I smiled. "I'll come, friend." He grinned as he pulled onto the road, the V8's rumble a steady pulse.

My phone vibrated against my leg. I pulled it out, frowning at a text from an unknown number. As I opened it, I froze at a photo of a ladybug, wings spread, vivid against a dark leaf, with the words: Ladybug, ladybug, fly away home… Pretty, but wrong, like a taunt.

"Something wrong?" Asher asked, glancing over.

"It's from an unknown number." I held up the phone, and his eyes flicked from the road.

"A ladybug?" His brow furrowed in confusion, but the words sent a shiver down my spine: "Ladybug, ladybug, fly away home…"

I forwarded it to Dad, the rhyme looping louder, its cadence synced with my pulse. The ladybug wasn't random. Someone was watching, playing a game I didn't understand.

I glanced at Asher, who was focused on the road, oblivious to the dread coiling in my chest. "Asher, have you ever heard of killers leaving… messages?" I asked, my voice barely steady.

He frowned, his eyes focused ahead. "Like what? Rhymes at the crime scene?"

My left eye twitched. Did he know something?

"Yeah, but… personal. Pictures, texts." I held my breath, hoping he would laugh it off.

He shrugged, his grip tightening. "Not that I know. Why? You think that ladybugs are from him?"

"I don't know," I lied, staring at the photo. The wings seemed to pulse, a warning. The Finns' house, Sadie's sad eyes, and Asher's steady presence meant they were safe for now. But the rhymes were closing in, and I couldn't shake the feeling that I was next.

18

Alexis

Awkward.

The Finns' dining room felt like a stage, every clink of silverware too loud. Asher's knee brushed mine under the table, his warmth steady, but my eyes flicked to Sadie, her fork trembling. Dr. Finn and Tami exchanged glances, their smiles tight. The silence grew heavy, my stomach knotting. Nicole's dinners were never this quiet, always sharp with her venom.

Sadie's voice was barely above a whisper as her eyes flitted to the window. "Nicole knew bad people," she declared, her tone sharp. I held my breath, the air heavy at the table. She paused as though her words had betrayed her, and Tami's fork clattered against her plate. "Just... something Mom mentioned," Sadie stammered, retreating into herself, yet her fear loomed as thick as the fog over Gold Beach.

Dr. Finn cleared his throat and shifted the topic, but my heart raced. Bad people? The shadow of the killer loomed over me, his nursery rhymes mocking. I excused myself for some air, but Asher's concerned gaze trailed me to the kitchen. "Thanks for dinner. I need some, yeah," I replied.

Sadie caught me by the sink, her fingers cold on my wrist. "Alexis, I didn't mean to scare you," she whispered, eyes wide, glancing back at the dining room. "Mom said Nicole's guys were trouble and dangerous. Be careful, okay?" Her voice trembled, a shadow crossing her face, fear, or something heavier? I nodded, my throat tight, her warning echoing the Reaper's rhymes. She slipped back to the table, leaving me unsteady. How did her mom know mine?

The guest room was too tidy: blue walls, soft bedding, and a faint rose scent that felt foreign to me. Sleep pulled me under, but a nightmare awaited. I stood in Gold Beach's forest, fog curling around me. Nicole faced me, the lavender scent sharp, her eyes pleading. "Bad people, Alexis," she whispered, her voice cracking. Shadows loomed men with cruel smiles and hands rough with ash. A nursery rhyme book fell open to "Ladybug, Ladybug," with red ink circling the words: Fly away home. The men chanted it, closing in as Nicole dissolved.

A twig snapped outside, jerking me awake, my heart hammering. I crept to the back door barefoot, the fog swallowing the Finns' yard. The rush of the Rogue River hummed, Ladybug, Ladybug… My skin prickled. A pine's bark glinted, carved with a ladybug, wings spread, fresh. My fingers traced it. "I'll find you," I whispered, the Rhyme Reaper's game tightening.

Walking back to the house, the image of the carved ladybug lingered in my mind. I was reminded of Dr. Finn's advice to find something that would ground me during moments when my sight couldn't be trusted. Baking felt safer. Sweets gave me the control I needed.

In Tami's kitchen, cool tiles underfoot, I mixed eclair dough, flour dusting my AC/DC shirt. Unlike Nicole's sparse kitchen, where I baked to forget, Tami's "Make yourself at home" gave me strength. As I opened the recipe book to check for other recipes, a familiar ladybug sticker caught my eye, its wings jagged, a taunt left for me. My breath hitched as my fingers traced it, my resolve hardening. Each stir of the dough was a vow: I'd hunt the killer.

The oven's warmth anchored me, eclairs rising as I whispered to the shadows, "You won't win."

19

Alexis

Sweat dripped down my neck, soaking my shirt as I whirled through the kitchen, a frantic dance between the mixer, oven, fridge, and pantry. Flour dusted the floor, eggs cracked and stuck to my feet, a mess I embraced, unlike the blood in my dreams. The air grew dense, sweet with sugar, pricking with unseen eyes, like on the beach, a stranger's gaze too near, heavy with danger.

I shook it off, blaming exhaustion. That ladybug carved in the pine last night, its wings jagged like a warning, then the sticker, stuck in my mind. The Rhyme Reaper's game taunted me. I'd figure it out for Dad, just like I swore by the tree line. A faint whisper, "Ladybug, Ladybug," curled through the kitchen, or maybe it was the hum of the fridge. My skin crawled, but I kept moving.

Chocolate-iced eclairs, strawberry crepes with whipped cream, coffee cake, double chocolate cherry muffins, every counter brimmed with sweet scents that were overwhelming, nearly suffocating, like the dread Dr. Finn's voice stirred in therapy.

Dodging the clock, I saw the sunrise glow through the windows, four hours gone, baking through the night, wired, as if the house's silence urged me to block out "Peter, Peter…"

Pulling the last muffins from the oven, I placed them on a cooling rack. A hand snatched one over my shoulder, and I jumped, causing the tin to slip. It burned my bare foot, pain lancing up my leg like a knife's sting. I yelped, gasping at the red mark blooming, muffins scattered like dream pages.

Two tall boys loomed, toned, their stillness eerie. The Finns' entry photos flashed perfect smiles, but here, they felt like threats, echoes of William Thompson's glare the last person I saw with Nicole. My pulse spiked, the rhyme whispering: "Had a wife and couldn't keep her..."

Fear and irritation from their silence, I moved closer to the fridge, haunted by Tami's caught voice and Dr. Finn's clenched grip on that pen at dinner. The cold metal of the fridge bit into my spine, grounding me, but not enough.

"You're not Sadie," the bigger one said, his voice low and playful.

My eyes narrowed. "Really, I'm not?" With sarcasm as my shield, I placed a hand on my chest.

The smaller one snorted. "No, definitely not."

They smiled, their teeth gleaming, and I exhaled. Asher's brothers, not killers. The photos clicked: the Finn brothers, blue eyes like Asher's, on the beach.

"And you boys aren't burglars," I smirked, easing the knot in my stomach.

They laughed, warming the room. I took some ice, wrapped it in a towel, and sat on a barstool, pressing it against my foot.

"Well, if you're not burglars, who are you?" I asked.

"I'm Cooper; this is Tanner," the bigger one said, pointing toward his brother.

"Asher's brothers," I nodded, the ice soothing the burn.

"And who are you?" Tanner asked, arms crossed and muscles flexing.

Before I could respond, Asher's voice interrupted.

95

"What the crap?" he said, standing in the doorway, sniffing, his eyes wide. "Did I hear you scream? What are you doing? What's that amazing smell?"

Giggling, I said, "Breakfast."

"For an army?" he asked, amusement warming me.

"I couldn't sleep or run, so I baked," I shrugged, glancing at the counters. "Guess I got carried away."

He gave a curious glance while standing between his brothers.

"You think?" he said.

"It's obvious you two know each other," Tanner said, waggling his brows. "So, Asher, introduce us to your friend."

Asher shifted uneasily, so I jumped in.

"I'm Alexis Harper," I said, trying to brush the flour from my shirt.

Silence crashed heavily. The brothers exchanged glances; they knew. About Nicole, the pumpkin, maybe more. My stomach twisted.

Cooper grabbed an eclair, smirking. "Alexis, you baked enough for a *Jurassic Park* sequel, dinosaurs included. Seriously, you're out here feeding the whole Gold Beach T-Rex population." He winked and punched Tanner in the arm.

I giggled.

"Right," Tanner agreed, laughing and grabbing a crepe. "Plane snacks are junk, not enough for a growing man." He winked, and I smiled, their confidence drawing me back.

Tanner and Asher walked back into the kitchen, piling more baked goods onto their plates. Cooper sat at the table, trying to hide a worn sketchbook on his lap while eating his éclair.

I hopped over, wincing at the pain from the burn. "Do you draw?" I asked.

His voice was quiet, "Don't laugh, but... I draw stuff sometimes. Nobody knows, not even Ash or Tan. This one's from before Mom and Dad got me a house; the swing's all busted. Keeps showing up in my head, like it's trying to tell me something."

I leaned closer, studying the sketch. "It's... real. Like you're holding onto it. Why hide it?"

He shrugged, smiling but eyes distant. "Big bad Cooper can't be caught doodling, right? 'Sides, it's just ghost stuff we can't shake," he paused, closing the book. "Have you ever drawn to forget? Or just bake?"

"Baking's my escape. But... maybe I'll try drawing. If you show me more sometime."

Cooper grins, genuine. "Deal. But only if you keep it secret. Don't need Tanner writing poems about my 'tortured soul.'" He stood, curling up the sketch book, then grabbed more eclairs.

"Hey, you okay?" Asher asked, now beside me, his voice deep. "Sorry if they scared you. Forgot to mention they were coming."

My breath caught at his proximity, evoking the memory of the beach.

"It's fine. I'm going to change," I said, pointing to my flour-dusted shirt and shorts as I felt my foot throb.

"You've got flour on your face, too," he said, his thumb brushing my cheek.

I recoiled, instincts heightened; as his brows furrowed, he noticed it.

"Sorry," I muttered, bolting.

After a shower, I came back in jeans and a tee, feeling cleaner but still a bit raw. Asher noticed me, his smile catching the attention of Sadie, Cooper, and Tanner.

"Alexis, you've met the rest of 'The Trips,'" Sadie said, crumbs from her muffin lingering on her lips.

"The what?" I asked, puzzled.

"The triplets. The Trips," she said, as if it were apparent.

I smiled.

"Still not following," I said.

She rolled her eyes.

"Asher, Cooper, and Tanner are triplets. Geez, I didn't realize you were so dense," she said.

The boys grinned, their eyes sparkling with amusement.

"Triplets, huh?" I asked, noting how their ice-blue gazes mirrored Asher's.

Sadie licked her fingers, nodding. "Yup, that's the deal," she said.

How is it that all of them are this buff and handsome?

A discord of laughter filled the room.

"Did I say that aloud?" I blurted, my cheeks burning as I feared I'd voiced their charm.

"Oh, yeah," Cooper teased, smirking. "Buff and handsome, right?"

"You're enjoying this," I shot back, settling next to Asher and Sadie.

Their warmth eased my embarrassment. Unlike Nicole's transient men with empty promises, these friends felt reliable.

"Glad you're here," Cooper added. "Summer's gonna spark."

Tanner leaned back, his eyes on me as I picked at my muffin. "You didn't sleep, did you?" he says softly, surprising her. "Sadie gets that look, too haunted. Whatever's eating you, Alexis, I see it." He glanced at Sadie, his jaw tightening, hinting at his worry. "We got you, both of you."

I smiled as friendship bloomed, a quiet vow.

Breakfast was vibrant, nothing like dinner's chill. Asher's teasing, Sadie's chatter, and the Trips' laughter brought it to life, and they raved about my food, too. Eclairs vanished, muffins crumbled, and crepes disappeared with satisfied moans. I had only cooked for Nicole and Dad, rejecting her pleas for dinners with men, making hollow vows, unworthy of my effort. Cooking and running were my pride, and doubts about my skill faded as the Finns inhaled every bite, unlike the silence when I had shown Dad the closet's rhyme book.

I started cleaning, flour and eggs creating familiar chaos, but Tami's hand stopped me, her rosewater scent too perfect, like the voice that caught me last night, hiding something. I had to figure it out, keep Dad safe from whatever had carved that ladybug.

"Honey, after that work and delicious food, everyone else will clean while you eat," she said, brushing hair from my face with a tender touch that stung my eyes.

Nicole's harshness lingered, but Tami's warmth flowed freely, almost too perfect. She noticed my tears, smiled silently, and walked over to the sink.

Asher sat beside me, his forearms resting on the island. "We're playing video games later. Wanna join?"

I pushed food around my plate, dodging his eyes. "Not great at games. Thought I'd run,"

He nudged me, sparking a grin of delight. "Play, and I'll run with you tonight. Think you can keep up?"

I laughed. "You should worry about keeping up," I teased, sealing the games and a run, a sliver of normalcy.

Video games with the Trips were wild, loud, competitive chaos that I craved. Was this what it felt like to have siblings? They were flawless, no surprise there, but I held my own, enjoying sports games. Tennis against Asher was a blast. I won, and his scowl at losing to a "beginner girl" made me laugh like I hadn't since California's tracks.

Sadie and Tanner's closeness jolted me as I watched them snuggling on the couch, her "bad people" mutter from dinner ringing in my ears. Did she know more about Nicole, the Rhyme Reaper? Cousins didn't act like that, did they?

"They're cute, huh?" Cooper said, sinking beside me.

"If you're into that," I said, uneasy, tugging at my hair.

"Love's clearly the best," he joked, laughing as I cringed.

"Cooper, quit messin'," Sadie snapped. "No blood relation, ya'll."

She glared, wrist flicking.

"Asher and Cooper give us crap," Tanner said, kissing her cheek.

"It's just wrong," Asher teased, handing me lemonade. "I grew up with her as a cousin, then last year, we found out that we were adopted. Their relief? Priceless."

Adopted? Dad hadn't mentioned that.

"Not as priceless as our parents' faces when you said you'd dated for six months," Cooper added, sparking laughter I didn't share.

Asher saw, leaning close. "Had to be there," he said, arm behind me, warmth steadying me.

20

Alexis

The evening air was chilled, with Rogue River fog swirling over the forest floor, where green trees stood against the brown earth, creating a dreamlike and soothing scene. Running usually calmed me, but nightmares of pumpkins, insects, and rhymes haunted my thoughts.

I wasn't just chasing peace anymore—I was chasing answers.

My mother's name was scrawled on the file in Dr. Finn's office. Nicole Harper, underlined twice in blue ink, pulsed, taunting me to read what was inside. Dr. Finn's calm, dismissive behavior rang alarm bells in my head, just as annoying as the school bell.

I couldn't stop thinking about it. Did he intend for me to see it? Was it a slip or bait?

Whatever it was, it worked. I felt a pull I couldn't explain, like that file was whispering something just out of reach.

Tonight, I started forming a plan.

Sneak in. Get the file. Get out.

"Murder Victim's Daughter Helps FBI Catch the Rhyme Reaper," I imagined, the headline bold and heroic. But even the fantasy felt heavy, chilling me like Nicole's lavender scent, faint, cloying, and inescapable.

"So, I didn't know you ran," Asher said, jogging beside me and snapping me back.

"Lots you don't know," I said, smiling, my foot straining under the ache from this morning. "Love it. Ran track in California."

"Really?"

I chuckled. "Surprised?"

"No," he said fast. "I ran track, too."

"Thought you played football." I glanced over and saw his bicep flex. He noticed and smiled.

"Did both." His arm brushed against mine, a spark reminiscent of the beach.

"If Nic-, Mom hadn't..." I cleared my throat, avoiding her name. "Was set for varsity, but that's gone."

He stopped, and so did I. "Hey," he said, rubbing my arm. Oddly, I didn't flinch. "Join the team here. Gold Beach High is small, so there's no JV. You're varsity good, I bet."

"You think?" Doubt weighed on me.

He nodded. "Try it."

I grinned, teased, and darted off. "Not fair, cheater!" he yelled, chasing after me.

My lungs burned as his steps drew near. He was faster; we both knew it. Arms wrapped around my waist as we collided to the ground, Asher pinning me. Panic surged through me, light-headed, gasping, eyes wide.

"Get... off... me," I whimpered, struggling to articulate.

"Shit... sorry," he said, his voice shaky as he pulled me up, quickly letting go and grabbing his flashlight.

I gazed at my filthy shoelaces, my breathing calming, shame consuming me. Nicole's boyfriends, with their bragging and their touch, had conditioned me this way.

"Hey." His hand hovered. Our eyes met. "You alright?" Concern softened his voice.

"Yeah, sorry," I mumbled, embarrassed by my fluctuating emotions.

"Your house is close," he said. "You're exhausted, and it's dark. Let's walk and call Cooper or Tanner for a ride."

Fatigue hit hard as I tightened my ponytail. "Right. Took longer than I thought."

"No problem. Walk, or I carry you?" he teased, making me feel lighter.

I laughed; his ease provided comfort, just as baking had. We walked with the sounds of the forest wrapping around us.

I froze at the tree line west of my house, and Asher stopped, too. A man leaned against a battered old Toyota pickup parked askew in our gravel driveway, a haze of cigarette smoke curling around him. His clothes hung loosely as if they didn't quite belong to him anymore. His face was weathered and hard. He took a drag and exhaled slowly, eyeing us as though we'd interrupted something of which he wasn't proud.

"I don't know who that is," I said, pointing, my heart ticking like a wound clock. "Do you?"

The figure stepped forward, pushing off the truck, shining a flashlight that blinded us. "I know who you are," a low and sharp voice growled, like the rhyme's hiss in my nightmare: "And there he kept her very well."

21

Alexis

I instinctively stepped closer to Asher. The scent hit me before anything else, beer and sweat and something sour beneath it. My stomach turned.

"Ronny Moore," Asher muttered. His tone went flat.

"Nathan's dad?" I asked under my breath.

"Yeah," he said. "Luke's old partner."

Ronny moved closer, his steps wavering for a moment before he regained his balance. "You're Nicole's girl, aren't you?" he asked, eyes skating over me in a way that made my skin crawl. "Didn't know she had one still kicking around."

"Let's just head inside," Asher said tightly, guiding me toward the porch.

But Ronny wasn't finished. He nodded toward the backyard, where Ranger came bounding out. "Dog showed up in my garage. Thought I'd do Nathan a favor." He jerked his thumb toward the Toyota's scratched-up tailgate. "Not that he deserves one."

As if summoned, a familiar white F-250 barreled up the road. It was parked neatly at the edge of the drive, providing a sharp contrast to the rusting wreck Ronny had limped in. Nathan climbed out of the truck, his jaw already clenched.

"What are you doing here?" he snapped.

Ronny shrugged. "Doing you and Luke a favor returning her damn dog. He trashed my garage."

Nathan glanced over at Ranger, who was now circling my legs with his tail wagging.

"You left a full takeout bag on the floor again, didn't you?" Nathan asked monotonously.

Ronny's eyes narrowed. "Maybe if you actually came around once in a while, you wouldn't be such an ungrateful little shit."

Ronny grabbed Nathan's arm, but Nathan didn't respond and yanked it from his grasp. I noticed his fists clenching, and his jaw twitched as if he were holding back with every ounce of strength he had.

"Thanks for bringing Ranger," he said coolly, his voice devoid of any personal touch.

Ronny snorted, then turned his gaze back to me. "You're a quiet one," he said. "Just like your mom."

Asher stepped between us. "Get back in your truck, Ronny."

For a moment, I thought he might swing. But Ronny just laughed one of those slow, heavy laughs that curdled the air and stumbled toward his Toyota. He cranked the engine and backed out in a roar of gravel and rust.

Nathan let out a breath as if he'd been holding it for hours. "Sorry," he muttered. "He's..."

"You don't have to explain. Thanks for watching my dog," I said quickly as I lifted Ranger into my arms, his warmth calming my pounding heart.

Nathan nodded, rubbing the back of his neck.

"There's talk of a bonfire tonight by the Whispering Nook cave," Asher said, quickly looking at me, shifting gears like he needed a change in subject. "I was thinking we could get a bunch of people together. Something chill, music, sand, and fire. Just... a break from everything, y'know?"

I glanced at him. His voice was casual, but the intention behind it was clear: he wanted to help. To give us all a moment to breathe.

Asher caught my look and gave me a small, encouraging nod.

"We'll grab my brothers and Sadie," Asher said. "And meet you guys there."

Nathan's mouth pulled into something close to a smile. "I'll see you later, then."

Asher and I watched him drive away, the F-250 vanishing down the road in a hum of power and purpose. Once he was gone, we both stood in silence, the tension still clinging to the evening air like static.

Ronny Moore hadn't just brought back my dog.

He'd dragged something else up with him. Something angry, unresolved, and far too close to home.

I didn't say much after that. I just slipped inside, my skin buzzing from more than just the cold. The house felt too quiet, like it was holding its breath, so I moved on autopilot, shower, clothes, routine. I needed to shake off the feeling and scrub away the residue Ronny left behind.

I had just pulled on my shirt when something tugged at me, an unease I couldn't identify. I drifted to the window, drawn like a tightly pulled thread.

The backyard was dark, except for a faint glow from Kessler's yard. He was there again, shoveling under the moonlight, humming a tune I couldn't quite grasp. My pulse quickened. Was he mocking the rhymes or hiding something worse? Kessler's eyes met mine through the dark, cold, and unblinking before he turned away. I locked my door, the rhyme echoing in my mind, a warning I couldn't ignore.

22

Black Sheep

Piss. He was soaked to the bone, the stench sharp as his childhood shame. Like clockwork, he rose and stripped the sheets, grumbling at the mattress's brownish-yellow stains that had accumulated over the years. A man his age had no excuse for this childish flaw, but the rhymes in his head didn't care about excuses.

Since boyhood, he had never woken up to use the bathroom. Mornings brought his father's belt ten lashes across bare skin, followed by days locked in a musty closet, peeling faded blue wallpaper as punishment for being bad. The beatings didn't stop the bedwetting, so he developed a routine: setting his alarm early, swapping the sheets with a stash under the bed, and hiding the evidence before dawn.

Sleep eluded him today, except for a brief two-hour nap; his mind was flooded with Ladybug. Her face haunted his dreams, emerald eyes fading to murky seaweed, her sun-kissed glow dimming to ash. Not guilt, he relished the souls he had reaped, each hunt a pulse of ecstasy sharpening his edge. Nicole's blood had sparked the fire, but Ladybug's brokenness left him restless, an itch he couldn't scratch. She was no mere prey, he thought; her defiance fueled the chase, a riddle he must solve. That nagging unease, unnamed, coiled like the tattered nursery rhyme book he'd found in her closet, a taunt from her past, its pages whispering his own creed: "Ladybug, Ladybug, fly away home…"

Hatred for her burned, tied to Nicole's betrayal, but this other thing, desire, perhaps, gnawed at him. He had sent the ladybug photo, a taunt to keep her alert, but her depression dulled her, jeopardizing his prize. If she took her own life, he'd be cheated. He had to kill her to complete the rhyme and plant her in his garden.

He changed his plans, his mind racing as he burned the sheets in a rusted barrel behind the borrowed house, its for-sale sign creaking like the hull of his boat. With no car tonight, he walked like a ghost.

Ladybug needed to live a little longer; her fear fueled him, and her end was his rhyme.

23

Alexis

A bonfire. A party. My peers.

The Jeep ride hadn't eased it. Asher drove, Sadie's jokes filled the backseat, but my silence hung heavily. The pines blurred outside, a fleeting calm against my inner chaos. Asher's glances every few miles waited for words I couldn't find; his quiet concern was a lifeline I wasn't ready to grab.

I wished I could be the girl who belonged here, who laughed easily, who didn't carry a weight like a stone in her chest. I wanted to be normal, to be one of them. I longed to feel like I wasn't always watching, always waiting for the other shoe to drop. I wanted to forget and lose myself in something lighter.

I couldn't believe I was here, tucked inside the Whispering Nook, a sea cave illuminated by flickering flames and echoing laughter. The fire crackled, casting golden light across jagged walls etched with couples' names, their initials carved in hearts or scrawled in faded marker, a testament to stolen moments and whispered promises. The ocean hissed just beyond the mouth of the cave, its rhythm blending with the shadows dancing on the stone. Voices rose and fell, mingling with the scent of smoke, salt, and cheap beer that lingered in the damp air.

Sadie, vibrant in a frayed denim jacket, handed me a soda. Her grin was bright but strained, and her eyes darted to the shadows as if guarding a secret too heavy for the firelight.

"Come on, Alexis. Loosen up. It's just a party."

I tried. I really did. But my hands just wouldn't stop shaking.

Ronny's voice lingered sharp, commanding, barking at Nathan in a way that twisted my spine. It echoed Nicole's control, her calculated digs and venomous mood swings that bruised everything but skin. Ronny's grip on Nathan's arm, like a general commanding a soldier, mirrored her public smiles and private cruelty. I'd learned to read her wine glass like a storm warning, disappearing into plain sight. Now, that tightness clawed at my chest, fingers shaking as memories bled into the present.

Kaitlyn stood by the fire, arms crossed, staring into the flames as if they owed her something. When our eyes met, hers flicked away far too quickly. It was as if she hadn't meant to look. It was as if she didn't want to see me.

I walked over regardless. "Hey."

"Hey," she said flatly. No smile. No warmth. Then she turned toward a blond guy and muttered something under her breath.

I stood there for a second, stunned. We weren't best friends or anything, but she was the same Kaitlyn I knew, soft-spoken. Now, it felt like something had closed off behind her eyes, as if she didn't want me here.

"Don't take it personally," Sadie said from beside me. "Kaitlyn's hot and cold sometimes."

Guess others knew her better than I did.

The fire popped, sending sparks skittering into the dark. Asher appeared beside me, his hoodie unzipped and hair slightly windblown. "You okay?" he asked, voice low.

I nodded, but it was a lie. My skin felt too tight, and my body was too alert. I wrapped my arms around myself, wishing the sweatshirt I wore were thicker.

"You sure?" he pressed. "You look cold. Take this."

He pulled his hoodie off and held it out. I hesitated.

"I'm fine," I said, mustering a faint smile. "I'll warm up by the fire."

He gave me a soft smile so I conceded as I reached out and took the hoodie from him. I slipped it on and felt calmer. He just stood close enough to be a presence, not a pressure. His nearness wasn't unwelcome. Still, I was fraying at the edges, unraveling in too many directions.

Nathan jogged into the cave as though he'd just won a race, holding a Heineken bottle high like a trophy. The apple apparently didn't fall far from the tree. "I made it!" he announced, nearly slipping on a smooth rock. "Barely survived the tide."

"You okay?" I asked, raising an eyebrow.

"Totally. I only tripped like... twice." He wobbled slightly, beer sloshing. "Okay, maybe four times. But who's counting?"

"Asher probably is," Sadie whispered with a smile.

"Is it a competition now?" Asher said, smirking. "Because I'm pretty sure I could out-trip you."

Nathan laughed, pointing at him. "You? Mr. Brooding Lean Machine? Please. You probably do squats in your sleep."

"I do," Asher said with fake seriousness. "Dream squats. Very intense."

Even I had to laugh, the tension in my chest was easing just a little. For a moment, it almost felt normal.

Kaitlyn didn't laugh. She sat by the fire, staring at her phone screen as if it held all the answers. But I couldn't shake the feeling that something deeper was happening behind her silence.

A ladybug crawled across the top of my soda can, unnoticed by the others. Its tiny red shell glimmered like fresh paint in the firelight.

I shivered.

"Ladybug, ladybug…" The rhyme floated back again, intertwined with smoke and memory. The pumpkin. The blood. Nicole.

The laughter around me faded as the cave's walls closed in, containing more than just echoes. They contained the past. And perhaps something worse.

Something was still watching.

Sadie brushed past, whispering, "He's hot," and nodded at Nathan. I shot her a look as she joined him; their chatter flowed easily while they sipped beers.

Tanner sat by the fire with me, writing in a notebook as he watched Sadie laugh with Nathan, his eyes shadowed. "Sadie's tough, but her mom… Kate broke her in ways she hides. I'm scared she'll slip back into that darkness, or worse, this killer finds her. You get that fear, don't you?" He gripped his soda can, his knuckles white.

I touched his arm. "I do." He noticed me trying to see what he had written.

"It's poetry. Helps me keep Sadie close."

Emotions washed over me as I read. "It's beautiful, Tanner. You're… deep. Sadie's lucky. Why poetry?"

He shrugged as his eyes lingered on Sadie. "Words hold things together when I can't. Growing up adopted, I always felt… loose, y'know? Poetry is my anchor. But if I lose her…" His voice cracked, and he looked away.

I squeezed his arm. "You won't. We'll keep her safe. Write one for me sometime?"

Tanner smiled faintly. "Only if you don't tell Coop he'll call me Shakespeare for weeks."

"My lips are sealed," I laughed while sliding my fingers across my mouth.

He smiled, stood up, and walked over. I watched as he handed Sadie the poem, and she gave him a small kiss in return. There was hope for all of us.

I listened to the fragmented conversations as they reverberated off the walls. I loathed drunken men and their transformation from Jekyll to Hyde. Nathan's slurred words reminded me of Stephen Whitaker, Nicole's "gentle" guy, who was affectionate until alcohol changed him into a monster. When I was twelve, I woke up to find his arm around me, his hand over my mouth, the stench of whiskey as he groped me in bed. I stayed frozen, silent, until he fell asleep, and then I hid in my closet, tears streaming down my face, fear preventing me from dozing off. He disappeared afterward, but I've kept my door locked ever since, a knife always under my pillow.

"Hey, you okay?" Asher asked, his fingers brushing against my temple.

I blinked away at Stephen's ghost. "Yeah, fine." I wasn't. The memory was raw.

He didn't push it. He just stood close enough to be a presence, not a pressure. And yet… I felt that warmth anyway, not from the fire, but from him.

Asher wasn't like the boys my mom paraded through the living room; those men had sharp edges and smiles that twisted in the wrong direction. Asher didn't twist. He stayed. Quiet. Solid. He was leaving for college soon; I knew that. Maybe that's why I found myself stealing glances, memorizing the slope of his shoulder and the way his lashes caught the firelight.

Stupid. Selfish. But I couldn't help it.

The Trips began joking around with their silly banter, reminiscing about their time playing Little League football together and how terrible Asher was at the sport.

Cooper grinned and leaned back, saying, "Remember that one game when Asher tried to tackle the referee instead of the quarterback? Coach yelled so loudly that his whistle flew out of his mouth!"

Tanner laughed so hard that he almost spilled his soda while Asher groaned and threw a pebble at them.

"I was ten, and that referee was huge!" he protested, but their laughter echoed off the cave walls, drawing me into their warmth.

The tension in my chest eased a little. Even I laughed. Asher glanced down at me, his eyes flickering with something curiosity, perhaps. Or concern.

"You always laugh like it surprises you," he said.

I blinked. "What?"

"Like you're not used to hearing yourself happy."

The words hit harder than they should have because he was right.

I stared at the flames for a second, then back at him. "And you always say things like that when no one else is listening."

He looked away slightly but pressed his warm hand against my cold one. "Maybe I don't want anyone else to hear."

My heart stuttered.

We felt the walls between us. Yet, sometimes, something genuine slipped through the cracks.

He smiled, skeptical, his touch lingering. "Want a beer?"

I glanced at Nathan, gesturing wildly like a fool in the firelight. "No," I laughed hollowly. "Done with alcohol forever."

Asher chuckled. "You're right. Another soda?"

I nodded, eyeing the ice chest with Pepsi, Coke, and Sprite. "Sure." He pulled out a Coke, ice dripping like the chill of that text. Another ladybug skittered across the can, and I froze, heart pounding. Was this real?

As Asher sat down beside me, the soda burned my throat as I scanned the group. Four strangers by the fire remained silent, staring. Sadie and Tanner were making out on a log, which was no surprise. Cooper, Nathan, and two other guys chatted, beers in hand. Kaitlyn's friend, broad-shouldered with wavy blond hair, kept winking at me, though it seemed more like an eye twitch than a flirt.

"That's Zane Baker," Asher said, catching his gaze. "Big flirt."

I nodded, unease creeping in as I overheard Zane muttering to a guy standing next to him by the fire. "Nicole's secrets got her killed," Zane whispered, his voice low but clear.

"What's his deal?" I asked, nodding toward the guy whispering with Zane. His dark skin and slick, unwashed hair mirrored the storm brewing in his eyes.

"That's Trevor Thompson," Asher said, crushing his can. "William's son."

I choked on my soda. "Great. He probably hates me." William's alibi didn't diminish Trevor's glare, which was sharp as a blade.

Asher said, rubbing my arm, "No one could hate you."

Trevor's stare made me want to run away from this fire where ghosts danced. His family's pain and my suspicion clashed: Nicole's blood on my hands, the pumpkin's stare. Zane's mutterings replayed: Nicole's secrets? What did they know?

Sadie caught my eye, waving me over as she stood by Kaitlyn. I hesitated; Kaitlyn's gaze on Asher ignited a pang. Had they been involved? I pushed it away, concentrating on the crackling fire, then set my soda down and started walking toward them.

Zane swayed, blocking my path and slurring his words. "S-so, are they as s-soft as they look?"

"Excuse me!" I questioned, and my voice echoed.

"Your hair, s-skin, so s-soft," Zane said, reaching for me.

Cooper knocked his hand away. "Don't touch her," he growled. "Don't look at her. Nathan, get him home before I do something."

The Finns' protectiveness was it care or control? I grabbed Cooper's arm, shaky. "It's okay," I said, smiling to calm him. "I've heard worse."

He stared, his eyes softening. I nodded. "I'm fine." He nodded back.

"What's going on?" Asher asked, his hand on my back. I flinched not at him but at Stephen's echo. He pulled back, scanning the group. "Anyone?"

Cooper spoke, "Zane is an idiot. We're out." He tossed Asher the Jeep keys, muttering about Zane's disrespect.

I wanted the day gone, Ronny, Zane, the rhymes: "Peter, Peter…" My head throbbed, urging me to bed, to oblivion.

At 2 a.m., we piled into the Jeep, with Asher pushing for answers about Zane. No one spoke; a hush settled in. My phone rang with an unknown number, like the ladybug message.

24

Alexis

"Hello."

"Alexis, it's so good to hear your voice. I miss you, baby." A cold, faint laugh followed, like someone was playing a sick game with my head.

Air fled my lungs. "M-m-mom?" I stammered, my heart seizing. The fire's crackle from memory hissed, "Peter, Peter..." Was I hallucinating? Heavy breathing, then the silence line goes dead. The phone slipped to my lap, a sob tearing free as I froze, the voice echoing Mom's from years ago, reading rhymes.

"Alexis?" Asher's voice felt distant, a haze swallowing me. Nausea surged.

"Pull over," I choked, praying I wouldn't vomit in the Jeep.

"What's wrong?" he asked.

"Asher, pull over!" I yelled, my hand over my mouth.

He swerved to the side of the road. I stumbled out and vomited into the bushes, the world spinning like the pages of a nursery rhyme book. I heard footsteps crunching. Asher was there, gathering my hair. After five minutes of heaving, I slumped down, wiping tears and vomit with my jacket, my hair sticking to my face. I didn't care how I appeared.

The Trips and Sadie sat around me, their support fragile. "Hey, what happened?" Asher said, pulling me against his chest.

I sobbed, fear clawing deeper than the pumpkin's stare. "The person sounded just like my mom," I spat, my voice breaking. "Alexis, it's so good to hear your voice. I miss you, baby."

Gasps rippled among them, soft and astonished.

"There's got to be an explanation," Asher said, strained.

"Is there?" I glared. "Explain how someone sounds just like her."

Sadie hesitated. "Maybe she's still…"

I put my hand up, stopping her. "Don't." I sighed. "Sorry, guys. There's so much you don't know."

Asher pressed on, urging for the first time, as he grabbed my bag from the Jeep, noticing the nursery rhyme book. "Lex, you're carrying this alone. I don't think this book carries just memories. There's more."

I stood up, looking him in the eye. "I believe so, too."

He pulled me into a hug. "You don't think… she could be alive?"

Was she? Nobody, just blood, a finger, a rhyme. I had to know, even if it broke me. "I'm gonna find out," I said, my voice hard. I remembered Nicole's voice, soft and warm, reading rhymes before bed. Now, it was a weapon twisted against me.

Sleep never came. Not even the gentle hush of the waves outside the Finns' house could soothe me. I lay curled on the edge of the guest bed, still wearing Asher's hoodie, his scent lingering like safety I didn't deserve. The voice on the phone replayed over and over, crawling over my skin: "It's so good to hear your voice. I miss you, baby."

Nicole. Or someone pretending. But *who* would do that and *why*?

I slipped out of bed before sunrise, the sky outside just beginning to bruise with violet light. The house was silent. No footsteps. No pipes groaning. Just the occasional creak of the ocean-side structure settling in on itself.

Down the hall, I passed Sadie's open door, her soft snores confirming that she hadn't stirred. I tiptoed barefoot across the cold floor, holding my breath, pulse pounding like a warning drum.

Then I stopped in front of it: Dr. Finn's office. The door was closed.

The man kept secrets. He had to. He was a shrink. Confidentiality was part of the job. But he'd also been *my* mother's therapist.

My hand hovered above the doorknob. I shouldn't do this, but I had to. The knob turned with a soft click as I slipped inside, closing the door behind me until it latched with a muted click.

Dr. Finn's office carried the scent of cedar and ink. A framed diploma hung slightly askew over a massive oak desk. Books lined every wall, titles covering trauma, personality disorders, and attachment theory. There was no chaos, no sign of disorder, just perfect order as if nothing had ever unraveled here.

But I had. My mother had.

I crouched beside the locked filing cabinet behind the desk and tried the first drawer. Stuck. The second stuck. The third click.

My fingers fumbled through patient files, most labeled with numbers instead of names. But one folder caught my eye, the one that had been on Dr. Finn's desk.

I yanked it out and sat on the floor with my knees pulled tightly in.

Inside, there's a photo of my mom who looked to be around twenty years old. Beautiful. Polished. Her eyes are too bright. She seems like she could be smiling through a hurricane. Beneath the photo are pages of handwritten notes in Dr. Finn's scrawl. I scanned them, and each word made my stomach tighten.

The patient exhibits compulsive romantic entanglements characterized by excessive dependence on male validation. There is an obsession with maintaining the appearance of desirability. Reports indicate inconsistent maternal attachment. The father is absent and possibly abusive. Notable trauma occurred during formative years (see p. 3).

I flipped to page 3.

The patient was molested by their mother's boyfriend at age seven. She confided in their mother, who accused her of lying and punished her. This began a lifelong pattern of seeking approval from older male figures, particularly emotionally unavailable or controlling ones. Believes that 'being wanted' is the only way to matter.

I stared. The words blurred. My throat tightened around nothing. I didn't want to believe it, but I saw so many similarities.

Suddenly, everything about my mother made *sense*. The endless parade of men. The rage. The obsession with being desirable. The venom she directed at *me* if I ever looked too pretty, too bold, or too much.

It wasn't just narcissism. It was *wounded*. Wounds she never healed. Wounds she passed on like a curse.

The voice on the phone returned to me, now distorted. "I miss you, baby."

But the woman I missed had never truly been whole.

I shoved the file under my arm and stood, my legs shaky.

When I opened the door, Asher stood there barefoot, with his sleeves pushed to his elbows, his hair messy. His eyes landed on the file in my hand, then on my face. He didn't speak.

I pushed past him, but he followed, as quiet as the hallway itself. Back in the guest room, I sat on the edge of the bed with the file in my lap.

"I had to know," I whispered.

"I figured," he said. "You didn't sleep."

Silence stretched between us. I expected him to scold me or tell me that I shouldn't have looked. Instead, he sat beside me, close enough for warmth but far enough for respect.

"I don't know who she was anymore," I admitted. "She hated me."

"She was broken," Asher said. "And she didn't fix it."

I turned to him, surprised. He looked at me as if he saw more than just the girl unraveling, as if he wasn't afraid of what he saw.

"I'm trying not to become her," I whispered.

"I know," he said, voice soft. "That's why you won't."

He didn't rush in with more words; he just sat there beside me in the quiet. The file was still on my lap, heavy with truths I didn't want but needed. My shoulders trembled, but I kept still, holding everything inside like I always did.

Asher shifted slightly, turning to face me more directly. His voice was barely above a whisper. "Can I… can I hug you?"

The question affected me more profoundly than any lecture or apology ever could. He didn't assume. Didn't grab it. Just asked like it mattered.

I nodded, and the moment I did, he wrapped his arms around me, not too tight, not too light, just right. I pressed my face into his chest and let out a shaky exhale.

It wasn't about fixing anything; it was about not being alone while everything remained broken.

And at that moment, I believed him even if everything else was fractured.

25

Alexis

The bonfire's chaos still swirled in my head, smoke, Nicole's file, and Asher's hug, so warm I felt it linger, like a quiet promise I wanted to hold onto. Sadie had dragged me for coffee to "clear the haze," but I had slouched in her passenger seat, my temples throbbing. "Sadie, I'm done," I had said, my voice heavy. "Can we just go home?"

She threw me that stubborn grin, veering toward the coffeehouse. "Nope. A latte's calling your name, trust me."

I rolled my eyes, arms crossed. "Fine, but you're driving me home after." She winks, smug, and then parks.

We slipped into a dim corner booth, the rich scent of my latte cutting through my fog, soothing in a way I didn't expect. Sadie's usual fire faded as we sipped, her silver-ringed fingers twisting her dark hair.

"My mom's relentless about college," she muttered. "Says I'll be nothing if I don't get in."

I stirred my latte, mixing the cream like the memories of my mom and me. "Mine only cared when I messed up her plans," I said, my voice low.

Sadie twisted her hair, her eyes distant. "Mom wanted me to be nothing like her. I hid cash for months and snuck it from her purse to get here. When she found out, she…" She touched a faint scar on her wrist, her voice hardening. "I still left. You're stronger than you think, Alexis, you'll get through this." Her gaze flicked to the car outside, fear flashing.

"You okay?" I asked, unease prickling.

She flinched, dropping her hair. "Just tired," she lied, her smile brittle. The car peeled away, but her hands shook. As she drove me home, she gripped the wheel, silent, her eyes darting to the rearview mirror. I noticed that haunted look Nicole's men had worn it too, but I didn't push, letting the silence settle like ash, wondering what shadows clung to her.

At home, I found Dad in the backyard, tossing a tennis ball for Ranger, his throws sharp as he tried to teach him to fetch. I sank onto the tire swing, its chains creaking, while my thoughts tangled like the rhymes in my nightmares: "Can we talk about Mom's case? I want to go back to the house," I said, my toes dragging through the dirt, tracing an infinity loop that mirrored my endless questions.

"I don't believe that's wise," he remarked, pausing, his expression full of concern. He rose from the porch step, crossed the grass to me, and adjusted his watch, a compulsive tic, his fingers brushing the face twice to align it precisely while avoiding my gaze. "You've endured enough, Alexis," he said softly. "Revisiting what happened in that house won't be beneficial." His hand shook as he poured coffee, realigning the mug's handle three times before setting it down, his thumb tapping the rim in a rhythmic pattern.

His reluctance stings, stirring the same unease I felt in Sadie's troubled eyes. "Dad, I found her file," I blurted, voice low. "Dr. Finn's notes. About… what happened to her. The abuse, her mom betraying her, why she's… like she is…was."

Ranger whined at his feet. "Alexis, you shouldn't have." He stopped, his eyes flicking to his phone as a message lit up the screen. "Let's not talk about it," he said, but his voice cracked, betraying him.

I pressed on, the file's weight crushing me. "It said she was molested at seven. Her mom punished her for telling. That's why she's always chasing men, isn't it? Why did she hate me shining too bright?"

Dad's face tightens, and he looks away, tossing the ball halfheartedly. "Your mother's past... It's complicated. It doesn't excuse what she did, but..." He trailed off, lost.

After the weekend at the Finns', I came home and told him about the phone call. Her voice, "Alexis, it's so good to hear your voice. I miss you, baby," was a ghost on the line that shattered me. As expected, he took it hard, immediately calling the station to trace it. No surprise, the caller was too clever, no trace, a taunt.

"Dad, she's still out there," I whispered, the swing creaking beneath me. "And now I know why she's so broken. Don't I deserve to understand?"

"She's not, you know that." Finally, he locked eyes with me, his pain unmistakable. "You deserve peace, Alexis. Not her memories." Yet his trembling hands betrayed that he was just as haunted as I am.

"Then I need closure."

"You've said it yourself; you're still having nightmares, and with this last panic attack..." He trailed off, shaking his head.

I pressed my toe into the dirt harder, deepening the infinity symbol. This will continue forever if I don't end it... for my sanity. "Maybe this will clear up questions I've had," I said, meeting his eyes, holding his gaze to hide my real intent.

He stared back, then tugged my ponytail, a flicker of the Dad who'd hugged me in California, blood still fresh on my hands. He handed me Ranger's ball and said, "I'll ask Dr. Finn." Standing, he gave me a pointed look. "If he says no, don't ask again. Go to therapy and start healing. I know it's been tough, and not long since the… incident, but try to build a life here, with me."

"Daddy," I sighed, tears pricking my eyes, the word soft and rare. "I'm already trying."

He offered a tight smile and stepped inside, pulling out his phone. "Dr. Finn?" he asked, the door shutting behind him.

26

Alexis

Ranger bounced before me, springing like a rabbit instead of a German Shepherd. His eager barks pulled a smile from me despite the chill in my gut. I held up the ball. "This is what you want?" Jerking it in the air, I watched his eyes track it unwaveringly. He barked impatiently, and I threw it toward the trees.

He was lightning, catching the ball at the tree line's edge. It dropped from his slobbery jaws, and he growled, hackles rising, staring into the forest. My gaze snagged on a nearby oak, its bark etched with a ladybug carving smaller than the Finns' backyard one, its spots jagged, not smooth, a taunt like the rhymes in my nightmares. I jogged over, my heart racing, but Ranger growled before I could grab his collar, not at me, but at the shadows beyond. "Ranger?" His body jerked, bolting into the woods, bounding over bushes, weaving through trunks with eerie grace but he vanished, swallowed by the dense green.

"What's going on?" Dad yelled, sprinting across the yard, phone in hand, fingers tapping its case in a compulsive rhythm, a nervous tic to quell his unease.

I shrugged, anxiety coiling like the fog, the ladybug carving burning in my mind. "Ranger took off. Think he saw something out there." Or someone.

Dad ran a hand through his hair, adjusting his watch twice, another tic. "Probably a deer or some critter."

126

"Yeah, maybe." The cold in my stomach said otherwise, heavy like the gargoyle from Dr. Finn's office, the carving's jagged spots whispering, "Ladybug, ladybug, fly away home…"

"We'll give him half an hour. If he doesn't return, I'll call the Finn boys and Nathan for help."

I smiled at their names but shook off the distraction, feeling the carving's presence as a violation. Before I could reply, a gravelly rasp cut through the yard, making my pulse lurch.

"Luke! Alexis! Dog chasin' somethin'?" Ronny Moore stumbled out from the tree line, his flannel rumpled, eyes haunted, and boots scuffing the grass.

Dad's jaw clenched as he gripped the phone tightly, realigning it in his palm with his thumb. "Ronny, what the hell are you doing here?" His voice sliced through the quiet, edged with fury.

Ronny raised his hands, a lopsided grin on his face. "Heard the yellin', thought I'd check. Ranger okay? Need help?"

"He bolted into the woods," I said, my voice tight as I studied Ronny's gaze, flicking to me with unsettling focus. My stomach churned. Had he seen the carving lurking while we spoke of California earlier?

Dad moved closer, his voice a growl as he nervously adjusted his sleeve. "We've got it, Ronny. Go home."

Ronny's grin vanished, and his shoulders squared. "Luke, I heard you're headin' to California. I'm comin'. I know Ventura, know the players."

Dad's eyes narrowed, fury spiking, his fingers tapping the edge of the phone. "You were eavesdropping? You're not coming, Ronny."

"Why not?" Ronny snapped, fists balling. "I haven't touched a drop in five days. I'm clean. I can help Alexis."

The air thickened, and my skin crawled at Ronny's lurking presence, undermining our plans.

Dad's laugh was bitter. "Five days? That's nothing. You'd wreck everything, Ronny, sneaking around like that. We don't need you."

Ronny's face flushed, defiance flaring. "I'm tryin', Luke. I know things. I can help her end this."

A diesel growl cut the tension as Nathan rolled up, parking sharply at the edge of the driveway. He climbed out, jaw tight, eyes flicking from Ronny to me. "Everything okay here?" he asked, stepping closer, his stance protective but restrained.

I met his gaze, my heart calming. "Ronny was just leaving," I said, my voice firm, nerves buzzing from the carving's jagged warning.

Nathan nodded, his gaze fixed on Ronny. "You heard her. Go." His tone was calm yet sharp, reflecting his command of the situation.

My stomach twisted, Ronny's words heavy like the rhymes, his eavesdropping a betrayal gnawing deeper. Dad stepped between us, his voice a snarl as he realigned his watch. "Enough. Go home."

Ronny stared, his chest heaving, then muttered, "You'll need me," before turning, his boots crunching against the street as he faded into the fog. The tension clung, sour and spiked by the ladybug carving's silent taunt.

"What'd Dr. Finn say?" I asked, shaking off the violation, the carving urging me to move.

Dad sighed, his frustration etched deep as he adjusted the phone's position twice. "He thinks it's good for you." He paused, frowning. "Wants to come with us to help."

I rolled my eyes, twirling a finger by my ear. "Cuckoo bird here."

He frowned, stepping closer, his hand tapping the coffee mug's handle rhythmically. "No one believes that. You've endured hell more than anyone should." His tone steadied. "I'll organize California. A few days to sort out work. Is that all right? Or next week?"

"No," I shook my head, resolute, the carving's threat fueling me. "It's time. I want it over."

I wanted to end the rhymes before they ended me.

Forty-five minutes later, with flashlights in hand, we stepped outside to search for Ranger when he trotted into the yard, head held high, two mourning doves dangling from his mouth, a smug glint in his eyes. Relief washed over me, and laughter bubbled from Dad, Sadie, the Trips, and Nathan.

"Well!" Dad clapped his hands together, adjusting his watch once more. "Since you're here, let's have a barbecue. Call your parents, have them come over."

Quilts spread across the lawn, burgers sizzling, and chatter flowed, but Ronny's intrusion and the ladybug carving hung like smoke. There was a part of me that wanted someone to confirm what I was seeing was real, but I bit my tongue, hoping someone would mention the carvings to me.

Asher's eyes kept finding me, studying as if sensing my anxiety. I thought I masked it, but his gaze suggested otherwise, just like when he'd watched me with Mom's therapy files. Dad had set our California plans two days from now with Dr. Finn, which sent my nerves on a roller coaster, looping from anticipation to terror; Ronny's "You'll need me" was a discordant note.

I rolled my eyes as Asher stared again. "What?" I huffed. "Ketchup on my face?" I wiped dramatically, aware that I was clean.

He shook his head, his lips twitching. "No."

"Booger in my nose?" I crossed my eyes, flared my nostrils, and played the goof.

He chuckled. "No."

"Bat poop in my hair?" I glanced at the starlit sky, where bats swooped for bugs.

"Nope," he said, voice soft.

I threw my hands up. "Okay, I give up. Why the staring?"

He shifted his long, jeans-clad legs, lying on his side, eyes locking onto mine, serious. "You sure you're ready?"

I knew he meant California. My throat tightened as the carving's threat flashed before me. "Yes," I said, narrowing my eyes, willing him not to push.

He disregarded the signal. "Want me to go with you?"

I jumped to my feet, heart racing, drawing every eye. "Absolutely not!" I yelled, my voice slicing through the quiet, panic surging.

Asher looked taken aback, confusion creasing his face. "Why not?" he asked, standing, his voice steady yet tinged with hurt.

"Because," I said, my eyes darting to trees, quilts, the oak's carving, anywhere but him, California's weight too heavy to share.

His hand found mine warm, his thumb brushing my knuckles. I sighed, caught. "Babe, why not?" he pressed, Babe hitting soft but piercing.

I looked down, dodging his gaze, the carving's jagged spots burning in my mind. "I don't want you to see that part of my life," I whispered, glancing at the others watching, silent, Dad's frown deepening, his fingers tapping his phone again. "Any of you." I shrugged. "Dad has to come, and my... shrink," I smirked at Dr. Finn, earning laughs and easing the air. "But California's something I need to face to get better, to build a life here." A lie by omission—I'd hunt the Rhyme Reaper—but they wouldn't support that plan.

I pulled my hand free and walked to the house. At the door, I turned and met their eyes: Dad's worry, Asher's concern, Sadie's frown, her bells clinking as she twisted her ring, and Nathan's unreadable stare. "Thanks for caring," I said, voice steady. "I appreciate it, but I'm trying. Just give me time." I closed my eyes. "I'm tired. Thanks for coming."

As I stepped inside, the screen door creaked behind me. Asher's footsteps followed, soft yet deliberate. I froze in the dim hallway, my heart thudding, wishing I had locked the door. "Asher, please," I said, voice low, not turning. "I said I'm tired."

"I know," he said, moving closer, his voice rough. "But I need to know why you're shutting me out. I want to go to California. I can help."

I spun, my eyes burning, the carving's threat clawing at me. "I told you, I don't want you there!" My voice cracked, everything surging. "Why can't you let it go?"

He stepped forward, hands raised, calming a spooked animal, eyes searching mine. "Because I care about you, Alexis. More than I should." His jaw tightened, betraying a slip. "I've been trying to keep it together, but I can't watch you do this alone."

I pressed myself against the wall, the cool plaster grounding me as his rapid words overwhelmed me. "Care about me?" I retorted, my voice trembling. "What's really going on? Why are you pushing?"

He hesitated, his eyes dropping before returning to mine, raw. "It's not just you," he admitted, his voice low, revealing a secret. "I overheard Mom and Dad arguing. Mom said he's too focused on 'fixing' you, that it's not his place. Dad said we don't need to know why he's invested. Also mentioned your mom and nuns. It didn't sound right, Alexis. I need to go to California to figure out what he's hiding, what he wants with you."

Nuns? My breath caught as the hallway closed in, Ronny's spying and the ladybug carving now overshadowed by this betrayal. Dr. Finn's kind therapy and his offer felt tainted, a mask slipping away. "Fix me?" I whispered, hurt slicing through. "What does that mean?"

"I don't know," Asher said, stepping closer, his voice urgent. "That's why I have to come. To protect you, to find out. I can't let you face this alone."

"Stop!" I shouted, shoving his chest, his warmth lingering on my palms. "You're suffocating me, Asher! I can't handle this: your caring, your questions, your… whatever this is!" My voice broke, tears burning. "I need to do this alone. Leave me be!"

His face crumpled, and he hurt deeply, but I couldn't take it back. I stumbled toward my room, slammed the door, and locked it. The carving's jagged edges echoed, tangled with Dr. Finn's secrets, a storm I couldn't outrun.

27

Alexis

A day and a half later, we found ourselves in a private jet piloted by none other than Becca Shaw. Not only was she beautiful and seemed to hate me, but she had Dad wrapped around her finger and could fly a damn plane. Wonderful. Her arsenic-sweet voice grated on my nerves, and her frostiness chilled me. I stared out the window, arms crossed, ignoring Dad, which was easy since he was "spending time" with her in the cockpit, giggling like teenagers. Please don't crash, I thought, picturing the rumble of his LTD, much safer than this tin can.

"You okay, kiddo?" Dr. Finn asked, his voice calm, as it had been when he called my visions trauma, not madness.

I shrugged and glanced at him. "Yeah, wondering if we'll crash."

He chuckled. "Becca's flown for years. Don't worry, she'll focus." He cleared his throat. "I hope."

I laughed, twisting the hem of my AC/DC shirt, tension building. "Hope she can multitask."

"Yes, please," he grinned, nodding as he wiped his glasses with a handkerchief.

The thought of Dad kissing Becca or anyone grossed me out. I shuddered. "Ewe."

"Really, though," Dr. Finn said, eyeing me, "Becca and her ex, William, flew all the time till they divorced, and he moved away."

"Did Dad personally know him?" I inquired, observing Dr. Finn's jaw clench, much like Asher did when suppressing his anger.

Facing me, Dr. Finn answered, "Yes, and so did your mom." His brows furrowed, puzzled. "You don't know who William is to your dad?"

I raised an eyebrow. "No. Should I?" My stomach twisted; the caller's voice, Mom? Mixing with the closet book's rhymes.

His mouth opened, then snapped shut as if he had caught himself.

"Well, who?" I urged, gesturing for him to continue.

He rubbed his head, gripping his neck. "Ask your dad."

Giggles spilled from the cockpit as I gagged, tasting bile. "Really?" I said, glaring at the door.

"Yeah, guess not." Dr. Finn shed his suit jacket and tossed it beside me, pointless for a flight. Leaning forward with his elbows on his knees, he said, "William's your dad's cousin."

I froze, blood turning to ice. Livid. Why am I always the last to know? Dad knew he kept it from me. "What a coward!" I yelled, my voice echoing in the cabin, sharp as the knife I'd kept under my pillow after Stephen Whitaker.

I hated this rollercoaster life. Stomping toward the cockpit with Dr. Finn on my heels, I flung the door open recklessly. Two heads, Dad's and Becca's, snapped toward me, lips swollen from kissing. Dad's gaze held; Becca's flicked between me, him, and the controls, multitasking like a pro. I would have smiled if I weren't raging.

"So, you didn't think to tell me," I jabbed a finger at Becca, "Her ex, William, is your cousin, Trevor's dad?" My voice was unsteady.

Dad paled as he glanced at Becca and then behind me. "Luke, I'm sorry, I thought she knew," Dr. Finn said, his voice shaking.

Dad waved it off. "No, it's okay." He saw my fury. "I mean, I thought you knew who he was. William and I were close. You saw him a lot when you were younger. What does it matter? I wouldn't dump Becca just because you might disapprove."

The words stung another parent, who chose someone else. Tears welled in my eyes; my chest felt tight. "Dad, I don't care about your relationship," I said, shoulders slumping. "Just wanted to hear it from you, not someone else. Earlier."

He chuckled, and I stared incredulously. Laughing? "Well, at least she took it better than Trevor," he said, he and Becca laughing, sharing a joke I didn't get.

Crap. Trevor. "How'd he take it?" I asked, then paused. "Wait, that's why he was all broody, giving me death stares."

They exchanged wide-eyed glances, recalling the moment when Becca had dodged my questions at the café. "He didn't bother you, did he?" she asked, avoiding my eyes.

I pulled my soft jacket tighter over my shirt, shaking my head. "No, he didn't say a word. Avoided me." Just like I'd avoided Zane's drunken grab and Nathan's beer-soaked grin.

"Don't mind him," Becca said. "Trevor wasn't thrilled about the divorce. He'll come around."

"Not worried about being his friend," I said. "You and Dad aren't married, so I won't see him much." There's no need for stepbrother drama, not with the Rhyme Reaper lurking.

Dad rubbed his brow. "Sweetheart, I just asked Becca to marry me before you barged in."

My eyes flicked to her ring finger, a huge diamond glinting like a taunt. Well, shit. I walked into that one. The woman who despised me, her cold eyes at dinner, her voice like poisoned honey, was my future stepmother. Perfect. I turned, trudging to my seat, calling, "Don't expect me to call you Mom!" Dr. Finn chuckled; at least someone was amused. Mom? Never.

Back in my seat, I faced Dr. Finn, Asher's words from last night clawing at me. His dad was too focused on "fixing" me, secrets the Trips shouldn't know. "Dr. Finn, why are you really here?" I asked, my voice low and my eyes narrowing. "Asher said he heard you and Tami arguing about me, about you wanting to 'fix' me. What does that mean?"

Dr. Finn's face tightened, just like when he'd dodged my questions about Becca's ex. He leaned back and exhaled. "Asher shouldn't have eavesdropped," he said, voice careful. "I'm here to help you heal, Alexis. Your trauma, Nicole's death, the rhymes, it's heavy. I want you to find peace, that's all."

"That's all?" I pressed, unconvinced, Asher's concern for his feelings—his fear echoed. "Why do you care so much? What aren't you telling me?"

He rubbed his neck, eyes flickering with something unspoken. "You're important to our town, to… people I care about," he said, vague, like his therapy notes. "Let's just say I have my reasons for wanting you safe. Can we leave it at that for now?"

I stared, his evasion fueling my unease, and I didn't want to reveal that I had read Nicole's file. "For now," I said, my voice hard, but the rhymes swirled, warning me that secrets were piling up.

28

Alexis

Sun. The welcome in Ventura was almost warm, but home felt foreign—a lie. The salty air was thicker, heavier than Gold Beach's, no longer mine if it ever was. Pushing the thought aside, I rolled down the window of the rental car, a plain gray Toyota Camry, and stuck my head out, Golden Retriever-style, with no slobber, just a humid breeze thawing the cold tension from the plane. Confronting Dad about Becca, William Thompson's ex, had drained me, and I'd slept through the flight, even the refueling stop, which showed how little rest I'd gotten, chased by nightmares of insects, rhymes, "Ladybug, ladybug…" Strangely, I felt safer airborne than in my bed, where the call's voice, "I miss you, baby," waited.

We headed to The Resort at Marina Village, Ventura's fanciest hotel. When I'd asked why the splurge, Dr. Finn said, "You deserve the best," his tone odd. I figured it was really about the proximity to Nicole's house, the crime scene, taped off, waiting.

"Why not go now, get it over with?" I asked, anxiety spiking despite the cozy heat, my fingers twitching for answers to the nursery rhyme book's secrets.

Irritated, Dad snapped, "Sweetheart, you know why." The case was open, the house sealed with yellow tape, evidence untouched, needing a detective to enter, but they were swamped and unavailable until morning.

"We'll do something fun to keep your mind busy," Becca said, her voice grating, oblivious to my feelings.

Dr. Finn leaned in, whispering, "Relax, morning comes fast." He didn't know me either, fun wouldn't bury the pumpkin's eyes, the call's echo.

In the lobby, Dad grabbed our keys, saying he'd lucked out getting rooms during peak season. I had lived here for years, so I expected him to ask me because I knew Ventura's crowds from summers spent here. He handed Becca and me the cards. "You two're together."

I shook my head, shoving mine back. "Oh no, there's no way, Dad."

"Sorry, kiddo," Dr. Finn said, coughing. "I'm not sharing with you or Becca; it would be awkward and inappropriate."

He had a point, but rooming with my icy stepmom-to-be? Hell no. Grumbling, I stuffed the card into my jean shorts, remaining silent and feeling like a brat, but not caring that Becca's frost was colder than the Oregon fog.

In our room, Dad said to Becca, "See you in half an hour." I dropped my bags and flopped onto a queen bed, arm over my eyes, blocking her out.

"Your dad and I are hitting the station to clear things up, then we'll take you to dinner," she said, her voice trying for warmth.

I peeked, recalling our last dinner, her honeyed chill, my unease. "Great," I grumbled.

"Alexis," she scolded, motherly, jarring me to look. "Your dad's sweet. I love him. He's trying to make this easy for us." She sat beside me, patting my knee, her hand lingering cold despite her words. Was she trying to be motherly? I couldn't care less about

Dad and Becca. They could do all they want– I had a different focus.

I stared at her hand– slender, manicured, ageless. Unlike Nicole's, crooked from arthritis and worn, despite their similar ages. Unease twisted within me; was I ready for Nicole to be replaced? No, not after her neglect, her men's hands, and Stephen's breath on my neck. I stood firm, breaking her touch and feeling freer. "I'll try for Dad," I said, glancing at her as I headed to the bathroom. "Gonna shower."

Becca was gone when I emerged, relief washing over me—no more "bonding." I could accept her as Dad's wife, maybe, for his happiness, but a stepmom? No way. Her motherly act would spark wars if she pushed.

By the time I'd dried my hair and dressed decently in jeans, a tee, nothing fancy, she returned, swapping her gray suit for a red spaghetti-strap dress with a neckline plunging deeper than Nicole's club outfits. I froze, feeling small, my clothes plain compared to her glamour. She was outdoing Nicole, and I owned nothing like that, never had, never wanted to.

Inadequate, I stripped, yanked on my pajamas, and dove into bed with the sheets pulled up to my chin. Becca paused, earrings half-on. "What're you doing?"

I told her, "Stomach's off. Can't make dinner."

She rolled her eyes, seeing right through me. "Whatever, Alexis, thanks for trying. Feel better." The door slammed, and her words sliced the air. Her glare was cold, and she muttered something about her uncle under her breath, too low to hear clearly. Weird. Maybe I heard her wrong.

The rest of the night I spent watching reruns of *The Office*.

The next morning, after a hotel breakfast watched over by Dad and Dr. Finn, Becca's absence felt like a small blessing, however, that was short-lived as she picked us up in the Camry. Dad insisted on driving, so we headed to Nicole's house, its engine straining.

"Feeling better?" Dr. Finn asked.

"What? Oh, yeah, nerves," I said, truth slipping out, my stomach churning like when Ranger bolted into the woods.

"Kiddo, if it's too much, say so, and we'll leave," Dad said, his eyes on the road.

I swallowed hard, nodding. "Okay."

"Keep breathing steady," Dr. Finn started, but Dad cut him off.

"What the hell?" he yelled, slamming the brakes.

A few blocks from the house, traffic clogged the road, and black smoke curled up into the blue sky. "What's going on, Dad?"

No response.

"Dad?"

"I don't know," he snapped, flipping open his phone and mumbling to someone from the station, probably. "This damn traffic, give us five minutes." He tossed the phone into Becca's lap. "Keith, grab the light under Becca's seat."

Dr. Finn handed Dad a police light, which he fixed to the roof as he wove through traffic. The Camry wasn't an LTD, but it was nimble enough. "Damn it," he yelled, punching the wheel and veering right. The car jumped the sidewalk, lurching us forward.

Fear silenced me as confusion spiked. On our street, my stomach churned: police cars, fire trucks, smoke, flames. My house. Nicole's house. Screaming inside, I threw the door open, ignoring the shouts of Dad, Becca, and Dr. Finn rushing toward the blaze. A hollow sound swirled in my ears, like waves on a shore, as heat pulsed, flames licking but not touching. Tears burned like lava down my cheeks as possessions, Nicole's dresses, my track medals, and good and bad memories turned to ash, floating skyward like feathers that had vanished.

Gone.

Arms grabbed me, hoisting me bridal-style. I twisted, eyes locked on the house, not caring who held me, Dad, maybe, as the red front door's paint melted away, burning any evidence of Nicole's murder, the Rhyme Reaper's trail, the truth of that call.

Gone.

Hours later, we sat in the humid police station, hard plastic chairs digging into my back as we waited for the detectives. Stacks of file folders teetered on a gray desk, tempting my twitchy fingers to tidy them, a control I craved amid the chaos. Dr. Finn kept eyeing me, another bead of sweat rolling down my spine, soaked by my damp tee. Becca played the motherly role, braiding my hair away from my neck to cool me. I let her do it, numb; wasps could've swarmed my face, and I'd have sat still, the fire's ash heavier than her care.

My mouth felt like a desert, parched for water they hadn't offered, when two detectives approached. The burly one, lumbered forward, his broad shoulders straining against a sweat-soaked shirt that clung to his barrel chest. His close-cropped salt-and-pepper hair glistened under the fluorescent lights, and a faint scar jagged across his left cheek, giving his weathered face a rugged appearance. He somewhat resembled the guy from the airport, which I found odd.

The scrawny and wiry man moved with nervous energy, his thin frame overshadowed by his oversized shirt, damp patches spreading under his armpits. His sharp, angular face, framed by unruly dark curls, darted quick glances like a bird sizing up a threat. The burly man dropped a cardboard box on the desk with a heavy thud and extended a meaty hand. "I'm Detective Jacobs, and this," he nodded at the smaller man, "is Detective Fields. You're Miss Harper?"

"Alexis," I corrected, shaking his hand, voice flat.

"Nice to officially meet you," Jacobs said, his deep voice rumbling like gravel. "Last time, you were… incoherent." California, the pumpkin, my screams.

"Yeah, sorry," I mumbled.

"No need," he said, turning to Dad and Becca. "Detective Shaw, Detective Harper." He shook their hands with a firm grip before shaking Finn's hand as he introduced himself.

"Dr. Keith Finn, family friend," Finn said, not revealing that he was my shrink, though they probably knew that in small towns, gossip spread like wildfire.

"So, care to tell me what the hell happened?" Dad said, using his cop voice, no-nonsense, like when he'd grilled me about the swing vision. "Cut the bullshit."

"Arson, well-planned. Looks like it started in the attic. Accelerant traces gasoline, maybe. Someone wanted this gone," Fields said, his reedy voice cutting through the air as he lifted the box's lid and tilted it. A metal box with a wrinkled plastic cover glinted inside. "Thought it was electrical until the fire department found this. Dusted for prints, nothing. Bomb squad cleared it, no threats."

I froze, envisioning the pumpkin in my mind, Nicole's finger, "Peter, Peter…" and squeezed my eyes shut, dread coiling like a snake. "What's inside?" I asked, my voice barely mine.

Silence fell, all eyes on me. "Might be in your best interest…," Jacobs began, his bushy eyebrows knitting together.

I cut him off, my teeth clenched. "Don't tell me what's best. Tell me what's in the damn box."

Dad attempted, "Sweetheart ."

142

"No, Detective Harper," I snapped, glaring. "I want to know."

He sighed and nodded at Fields. "Go ahead."

Fields unlatched the box; my breath hitched as tears flowed freely, a sob tearing forth. My name, Alexis Jo Harper, scrawled in thick black ink, fire-damaged yet clear, stared back at me. Inside, folded neatly, lay Nicole's black cocktail dress, her last outfit, stained with the blood of my nightmares. Beside it, a crude drawing, inked on charred paper, depicted a ladybug with jagged spots, smaller than the Finns' backyard carving, its wings sharper than my oak's, a killer's mark reflecting my dreams. On top lay a page torn from the closet book, ladybugs bordering a rhyme, words twisted for me, crossed out or added in jagged ink:

"Ladybug! Ladybug! Fly away home. Your house is on fire. And your mother is dead. All except one escaped death, And that's little Jo, For she's scared To lose her head."

The station's hum faltered as a gravelly voice cut through, causing my pulse to spike. Ronny Moore shuffled in, with Nathan trailing behind, both looking out of place among the uniforms. Ronny's flannel was streaked with soot, his intense eyes fixed on me. Nathan's jaw was tight, his gaze darting between his dad and me, concern etched on his face, reminiscent of when he'd stepped in at the tree line.

"Luke, we came to help," Ronny said, ignoring a detective's raised hand. "Heard about the fire, know the area Nicole haunts. Let me in on this."

Dad's face hardened as he stood, his fingers tapping his phone in his pocket. "Ronny, I told you to stay away. Why the hell are you here?" he snapped, adjusting his watch twice.

Nathan grabbed Ronny's arm, his voice low and urgent. "Dad, I tried to stop you. You shouldn't be here." His eyes met mine, worry deepening. "Alexis, you okay? This is too much."

Detective Jacobs stepped forward, his eyes narrowing. "You were told not to interfere, Moore. Why show up now?"

Ronny's defiance flared, shaking off Nathan's grip. "I'm tryin' to help Alexis, damn it. In Nicole's case, Luke and I got notes from her before she died. Said Alexis might not be his, that she wasn't sure who the father was. We've been diggin' into it, and this fire's no coincidence."

What. The. Hell.

The room stilled, my breath caught, the rhyme's "little Jo" echoing with the drawing's jagged spots. Not Luke's daughter? My trust fractured, and it felt like a betrayal. The detectives' gazes snapped to Dad, then Ronny, suspicion sharpening. This explained Dad's distance, with his tics escalating.

Jacobs's voice was cold. "Notes? We cleared you, Harper. You two withheld evidence? That puts you both in the frame. Harper, Moore, you're detectives—you know better."

Dad's face paled, hands raised, his thumb adjusting the phone in his palm. "It's not like that. Nicole's notes were personally vague. We didn't think they were relevant until now," he said, his voice strained, fingers brushing the face of his watch, seeking order in chaos.

Fields scribbled furiously, eyes on Ronny. "You're too invested, Moore. What's your angle? And why drag your son into this?"

Nathan's voice cracked, pulling Ronny back. "Dad, stop. You're making it worse." He looked at me, pained. "I'm sorry, Alexis, I didn't want this."

144

I sat frozen; the box's contents, dress, drawing, rhyme and Ronny's words felt like a triple blow. "Not his?" I whispered, staring at Dad, the ground shifting beneath me. "You knew and didn't tell me." My voice hardened, distrust surging within me. "I need to speak to the detectives alone, and I don't want anyone else hearing what it's about. Not you, not Nathan, nobody."

Dad's eyes widened, hurt flashing across his face, but his fingers tapped the edge of the phone. "Alexis, sweetheart, we can..."

"No," I cut him off, standing with a resolve born from the ladybug carvings' threat. "It's private. I have to do this on my own."

Jacobs nodded, directing Fields. "Everyone out. Harper, Moore, you'll need to answer questions about those notes you received, so go with Fields. Nathan, Becca, Dr. Finn, wait outside." His tone was firm, his eyes studying me, sensing my urgency.

Dad hesitated, straightening his sleeve, then nodded, following Nathan and Ronny as Fields led them away. The station door clicked shut, leaving Jacobs and me in the humming silence, the box heavy in my lap.

Jacobs leaned forward, his gray eyes sharp yet steady, pen poised over his notepad. "Alright, Alexis, it's just us. What do you need to tell me?"

I swallowed, my fingers tracing the drawing's spots, the ladybug's sharp wings burning in my mind. "I've seen carvings," I said, voice low, steady despite my racing pulse. "Ladybugs, carved on trees. One in the Finns' backyard, big, smooth spots. Another on an oak at my house, smaller, jagged, like this drawing. They're not random. Someone's leaving them for me, watching me."

Jacobs's pen paused, his gaze narrowing, calculating. "Carvings? Where exactly, and when, did you notice them?"

"The Finns' was weeks ago, after... after Mom's case started," I said, the word *Mom* catching in my throat. The oak was a few days ago when Ranger ran off. This drawing is too close, too specific. The rhyme, the ladybugs, it's the killer, taunting me."

Jacobs scribbled, his voice calm yet probing. "You think these carvings are connected to the fire? To this box?"

"Yes," I said, gripping the box tighter. "The fire wasn't an accident. The killer knew I'd find this, knew it'd hurt me. I need you to check the trees and the carvings. They're clues, Detective. I'm sure of it. And the rhymes have deeper meanings and I believe they're tied to my mom."

He leaned back, studying me as the hum of the station filled the silence. "That's a bold claim, Alexis. We'll look into it. Send someone to the Finns', your place, and photograph the carvings. We'll check on the rhymes as well. But why keep this from your dad? From the others?"

I met his gaze, my resolve hardening. "Because I don't know who I can trust right now. Dad's hiding things, those notes, maybe more. I can't risk them knowing until I'm sure."

Jacobs's expression softened, but his eyes remained sharp. "You're carrying a lot, kid. We'll follow up, but you need to be careful. If someone's watching, you're in their sights. Stay sharp, and don't go poking around alone. Got it?"

I nodded, the weight of the drawing anchoring me. "I won't. Just... find out who did this. Before they come for me."

He stood, tucking his notepad away, then handed me his card. "We'll start with the carvings. I'll keep this between us for now. You did the right thing, telling me."

The station's heat closed in as he opened the door, my vision blurring, the rhyme's warning "lose her head" mixing with the drawing's jagged wings, Nicole's notes, and my fractured trust. I clutched the box, its contents a map to the killer's mind, my resolve to hunt the Rhyme Reaper burning brighter.

29

Alexis

All my breakfast ended up in the trash can, vomit splattering against the clear plastic liner until I was dry heaving, my body threatening to collapse like a crushed soda can. The contents of the box had confirmed it: my mother was never coming back. She was dead.

As Jacobs rejoined the others, he fixed his gaze on me, his tone calm yet urgent. "Can you tell us anything about the dress or this nursery rhyme?"

My stomach lurched. The Rhyme Reaper was out there, coming for me. "Dr. Finn, look at her," Becca cut in, her voice soft, concern etching her face. "She needs a break."

Dr. Finn squeezed my shoulder, his grip firm and his eyes searching mine. "Becca's right. Let's leave, come back later."

"No," I snapped, my sandpaper tongue scraping cracked lips, parched as the California heat. "Water, please." I glanced at Dad, his fingers tapping his phone, a reminder of the notes he'd hidden, secrets that fueled my distrust.

Every ounce of willpower kept my sanity intact, fraying like Nicole's dress in that box. My body felt heavy, stuck in tar, sinking with each flash. Stephen's breath, the pumpkin's seeds, "Peter, Peter…" circled in red, the call's impossible voice: "I miss you, baby." Was this real, or a nightmare, was the Rhyme Reaper waiting to end me? I wanted Nicole back, even her neglect, her men's hands, to escape this hell.

"Hey, kiddo," Dr. Finn said, shaking my shoulder and catching my bleary eyes. "Deep breaths. You're close to a panic attack. Work through it. I'd rather not sedate you."

I nodded, ragged breaths clawing in, the need to flee California burning hotter than the fire's heat. Gold Beach was home, not this. "My mother wore that dress the night she was murdered," I said, leaning forward, elbows on my knees, hands raking through damp hair. "The rhyme... It's from a book she read to me as a kid. I found it in the closet when I moved to Gold Beach." I glanced at Dr. Finn, his eyes widening in shock that I'd kept it secret.

"Any pages missing?" Jacobs asked, pen clicking, grating like the chaos of the station.

I frowned, confused. "No. Why?"

"He wants to know if you or one of us is the murderer or if he had access to the book," Becca said, glaring at the detectives, her cop voice sharp.

Air fled my lungs, a gut punch. "You think I killed her?" I choked, sobbing, tears mixing with sweat. "You think I could do that?" The pumpkin's red, the fire's ash, how could they see me in that horror?

"Hey, no one thinks you killed her, Sweetie," Becca said, reaching for my hand.

I yanked it away. "Don't." She no longer needed her hollow comfort, like the glint of her ring, a stepmom I'd never call Mom. "Listen, all of you." I squeezed my eyes shut, stealing myself. "Nicole wasn't perfect. She... let things happen to me." The memories of the abuse weighed heavily. "But she was my m-m-mom."

Jacobs asked, "We'd like to see this book. Could you send us pictures?"

"Um…I actually have it in my bag." I confessed, feeling questioning eyes on me. I reached down where my bag had been between my sandaled feet and pulled the book out. I handed it to Jacobs across the desk, and my grip tightened as he tried to take it.

Jacobs raised an eyebrow at me and cleared his throat. "It's okay, Alexis."

Fields came back after questioning Ronny and Nathan, asking for Dad to join him.

As Jacobs flipped through the book, the station's noise of ringing phones, clicking pens, and footsteps rubbed my nerves raw. Jacobs' pen was torture; I wanted to snatch it and hurl it; his calm infuriated me, as if he didn't grasp the box's weight, my name in ink, Alexis Jo Harper.

Jacobs nodded, satisfied yet annoyed, "Sorry, Alexis, this doesn't give us much since anyone could have this book. For now, the killer's trail remains cold, all loose ends."

Dad returned, his fingers straightening his sleeve, saying nothing about his questioning with Fields, Nathan, and Ronny already gone. I couldn't speak. Nicole was caged inside me, her perfume, crooked hands brushing my hair, sharp words, and blind eyes when men touched me. Memories crawled like spiders, unsettling as the fire's ash.

Jacobs cleared his throat, gaze shifting between Dad and me. "Couple more things before you go. Given the complications with the notes and your mother's case, we'll need a DNA sample from you, Alexis. And from you, Luke, for a paternity test. It's standard procedure when paternity is in question. We'll use a buccal swab quickly, just a cotton swab inside your cheek. No needles, no blood. We can do it here and send it to the lab. Results take about a week."

I froze, the words sinking like ice, the drawing's jagged wings flashing. A paternity test? My throat tightened, but Dad's hand found mine, squeezing, his thumb tapping the phone in his pocket. "It's just a formality, sweetheart. We'll get through it," he said, his voice steady, eyes betraying doubt, his hand brushing his watch's face, seeking order.

Fields stepped forward, holding two kits. "We need your consent, both of you. It's voluntary, but it'll help rule out discrepancies."

Dad nodded, jaw tight, his fingers realigning the phone. "Fine. Let's do it."

I swallowed hard, the station's hum pressing in. A swab, a week for answers I wasn't sure I wanted. But I nodded, voice a whisper, "Okay."

Fields handed us consent forms. We signed the pen heavy in my hand. A technician appeared, swabbing our cheeks, Dad first, then me. The cotton was soft, but the act felt invasive, peeling back a layer I wasn't ready to expose. They sealed the samples, labeled them, and the technician left with a curt nod.

Jacobs offered a tight smile. "We'll notify you once we have the results." He shifted in his chair, pulling a few sheets from a manila folder. "Also, it took the lab longer than expected to process the blood evidence. The amount of blood at the scene didn't match a single severed finger. After analysis, we found Nicole's blood mixed with feline blood. As someone staged it to mess with the cops," Jacobs muttered, his eyes narrowing as if he suspected more than he let on.

Dad stood up suddenly, leaning over the desk to look at the report. "You're saying this sicko staged the whole thing? Nicole could still be alive?"

Jacobs raised a hand, his tone measured. "Harper, we don't have definitive evidence to confirm whether she's alive or dead. The presence of animal blood complicates the scene, but it's not conclusive."

My head throbbed, struggling to process the implications. I'd been right all along. There was a chance Nicole was still out there.

"We're continuing the investigation," Jacobs said, his voice steady. "If anything new surfaces, we'll contact you immediately. For now, you're free to go." He began sliding the documents and evidence back into the case file, along with my dwindling hope that this case would ever be solved.

"You ready?" Dad asked, appearing before me, making me jump, his fingers tapping his watch's edge. I was desperate to flee California's hell.

30

Black Sheep

Not being able to keep closer tabs on his Ladybug had begun to jeopardize everything he'd planned, a gnawing itch that had festered since Nicole's blood first stained his hands. Previously, a single cat's death had sated him, its blood calming the rhymes in his head, a ritual born from Nicole's betrayal, her failure to be the mother Ladybug needed. But now, his need to kill surged thicker than the blood in his veins, a hunger only Ladybug's fear could quell. He'd tried to rein it in, to save his final verse for his Ladybug, whose emerald eyes mirrored Nicole's but burned with a defiance he craved to extinguish. Yet control slipped, and he scoured for cats, a frenzy reminiscent of the one on his boat months ago, watching Alexis from afar.

He'd lost it while hunting until the sixth cat was bludgeoned with his claw hammer in a girl's driveway, unaware of her eyes. Her screech pierced the air as she ran, but his was faster. One blow to her head made her crumble to the ground. In daylight, he risked everything, tossing her over his shoulder, her car keys glinting in the ignition as a gift. The trunk was packed with luggage for a planned trip, buying him time, her absence unnoticed; a reckless act born from losing sight of Ladybug, whose movements in Ventura had grown unpredictable since the police station.

As the boat rocked, the sun burning his back, he watched the portly girl, tied with zip ties on the deck, plotting her death. Cats

153

scurried around her; their blood coated his gloves, a ritual less sacred without Ladybug's fear to fuel it, a poor substitute for the terror he had once gotten from Nicole's pleading eyes. The girl's vomit choked, raw, and satisfied him, proof of his power, but she was nothing like Alexis: no emerald eyes, no glow to extinguish, and no trace of Nicole's charm that had first attracted him to her daughter.

"What else do you know about me?" he asked, tossing his knife between gloved hands, wondering if she'd call him Rhyme Reaper, the title from the news that he wore like a crown, earned with bells, shells, and ash, a legacy sparked by Nicole's blood.

She sobbed, mascara streaking her pudgy face. "N-n-n-nothing, I swear."

"What's your name?" He crouched, the knife grazing her cheek, leaving a red scratch with no blood. Her scream washed away with the waves, far from shore. He murmured under his breath, "All except one escaped death…" He twisted her blonde hair, roots tearing, growling, "Tell me!"

"M-m-megan….p-p-please," she cried, bloody snot dripping. "All I know… you… my cat, the cats."

Too much. She'd seen him, a mistake he couldn't afford, not with Ladybug so close yet so elusive, her defiance at the station, clutching that box, her mother's dress stoking his need to reclaim control. Steering toward the cave-lined shore, the boat rocked gently as the last of Megan's remains bound with the gutted cats slipped beneath the waves, swallowed by the sea's indifferent depths. The Rhyme Reaper wiped blood-slicked gloves on his jeans, the tang of bleach and salt stinging his nose. For a moment, the rhymes quieted, she choked sobs, and the cats' yowls faded into memory, a fleeting echo of Nicole's final pleas. But it wasn't enough. Ladybug's face, Alexis, with her emerald eyes flashed in

154

his mind, her fear the crescendo he craved, not this girl's pitiful whimpering. Megan had been a mistake, a messy detour, her death too loud, too close to shore, a reckless act born from losing Alexis's trail after Nicole's legacy pulled her deeper into Ventura's shadows. He needed control and precision. Ladybug's end would be his masterpiece, a requiem for Nicole's failure, not some driveway impulse.

As he steered the boat toward Crescent City's jagged coast, the sun dipped low, painting the water red like the blood he'd spilled—Nicole's, the nuns', and now Megan's. His thoughts churned, restless and plotting.

The Sutter Coast Hospital loomed in his plans, a stage for his next verse, a fiery taunt to lure Ladybug closer, to prove he still hunted despite her defiance. The infectious disease wing was locked, chained, and ready to burn. It would scream his name to the world, a distraction that kept the authorities scrambling while he closed in on Alexis, just as he once did with Nicole, her betrayal igniting his rhymes. He'd hacked their systems days ago, looping cameras and timing the chaos, a skill honed since Gold Beach, where he'd watched Alexis's every move, carving ladybugs to mirror Nicole's broken promises. The fire wasn't just destruction; it was a message, a call to Ladybug, her mother's daughter, to face him.

Docking beneath twilight's shadow, he removed his gloves and replaced them with latex ones while the navy coveralls rested in his bag. The boat's engine fell silent, but his pulse throbbed, rhymes surfacing like a chant birthed from Nicole's blood, now intended for Alexis. He stepped onto solid ground, the hospital's sterile silhouette beckoning him forward. Megan was gone, erased, yet Ladybug awaited. The fire would illuminate her path to him, a beacon to complete what Nicole's death had begun.

Bleach and stale mops filled the janitor's room; he glanced at the clock: 0200 hours, go-time. Two nurses, unconscious, zip-tied, and gagged, slumped against the shelves as he zipped up his navy coveralls. His surgical mask muffled his breaths, and his eyes glinted with purpose, the same fire that had burned when he stood over Nicole, her lies silenced.

He had hacked into the hospital's patient roster himself, targeting the infectious disease wing eight minutes before fire crews were set to arrive. Cameras looped through empty halls, his handiwork; chains secured the wing's entrance, preventing any staff from breaching it, a trap as meticulous as the one he'd set for Nicole. A bucket concealed of lighters, fluid, and matches, no weapons, just fire, the element that had consumed his message to Alexis, the box she'd clutched in Ventura.

Rhyme Reaper slipped out, grabbed his kit, and darted into the first room. Lighter fluid splashed on curtains, chairs, and fast-ignited targets. Still, he paused, eyeing the patient: an old man in his eighties with white hair, a steady heart monitor, skin paper-thin, pocked with oozing sores with green-yellow pus, like MRSA images he'd studied, mesmerizing up close. Infected, irrelevant, this burn was for Ladybug, proving he roamed. The urge to prod the sores tugged, a curiosity sparked by Nicole's own decay, her lies festering like wounds, but time pressed. He doused the sheets and lit a match, flames licking quickly. The man woke, screaming shrill, feminine, blood-curdling as fire melted the sores, and a heart monitor raced. He grinned, the mask hiding glee; the scent was not cat hair char but musky perfume, intoxicating, a faint echo of Nicole's scent. The man's arms flailed, useless, twitching, slumping, monitor slowed pain blackout, not death. The agony was worth watching, a prelude to Ladybug's fear.

Curtains burst into flames; he bolted, cries echoed, patients roasted—his symphony, a requiem for Nicole's failure. In the next room, an obese woman, awake and startled, lay in a bed overwhelmed by her bulk, eyes fixed on him. Grim Reaper incarnate, fitting. No curtains, no couch. He sprayed fluid on her face, blinded her, and a match flicked, igniting a whoosh as flames engulfed her. Her arms waved like white flags, no fight; a tea kettle scream pierced the air, weaker than Alexis's bonfire cry. He flinched as the smoke thickened, time seemed to freeze.

In the hall, he checked his watch for three minutes, tight. Alarms wailed, and sprinklers fought the flames, drenching him. He nodded in approval, sprinted to the alley exit, and coughed up smoke through his scorched lungs. Outside, fire truck sirens approached. He paused, carved a rhyme into a leather scrap with his knife, and pinned it to the janitor's door:

"Ring around the rotten flesh with sores forgotten, burn them, burn them, they all choke down!"

A taunt for Ladybug, her fear his fuel, a reflection of the rhyme he'd left with Nicole's body. He dropped a photo of Nicole at a Gold Beach bar, William Thompson's smile tight. Ditching coveralls in a bin, he disappeared, the rhyme echoing his hymn, Ladybug's hunt just beginning, her mother's legacy his to end.

31

Alexis

Almost a week after returning from California, I stood on the back porch, and the weight of Mom's absence carved a deeper wound. It was her birthday. The paternity test's looming results, which could come any day and threaten to reveal whether Luke was truly Dad, made this day even more difficult.

I whispered, "Happy Birthday, Mom," the words bitter and lost to the breeze. Was there anything happy about it? No, she wasn't here. Despite her neglect, those birthday moments—chick flicks, pajamas, Rocky Road ice cream, and her crooked hands—were gentle and sacred. I longed for that mom, stolen by the Rhyme Reaper's knife; her death left a void no research could fill.

I immersed myself in nursery rhyme histories, chasing the Reaper's twisted logic, but only heard echoes of that Ventura box's taunt: "Ladybug! Ladybug!" I was getting nowhere, and my frustration grew. I didn't know what I was thinking; I wasn't trained to be a detective.

The Ladybug rhyme had ties to nuns and fleeing fires to save oneself, more specifically, children. Did I escape the fire my mom had already stoked? Or was living with Luke somewhere I needed to flee?

I also searched our oak for new carvings, having high hopes of finding another one, but to no avail. Luke's tics, phone tapping, and watch adjusting had intensified since the station's questioning, and his silence about Mom's notes created a wall between us. Sadie still wasn't answering my phone calls, and I missed our friendship. I hadn't realized how close we had gotten, and now it was gone.

Dad's silence on her birthday hurt the most; no nod to our ritual, just a tight smile as his Ford drove away. I growled, stomping to the backyard, collapsing onto a blanket and stroking Ranger's sleeping warmth, a tether against the hole in my heart.

Clouds morphed above—dragon, ship, heart—beckoned escape from the shadows of Gold Beach. I'll never be safe. Rocking, I chanted, "Never be safe. Rhyme Reaper's out there. Never be "

"Yes, you will," Nathan said softly, startling me as he sat beside Ranger, petting him, dimples flickering. "Sorry, I didn't mean to scare you."

We hadn't talked about what happened in Ventura. Knowing my own issues with my mom, I understood Nathan's struggle in dealing with his dad. It's exhausting and something you'd rather get your mind off than keep rehashing things.

I shook my head, gnawing on my thumbnail. "It's okay. Glad you did." Another escort, but could I trust him? "Up for more boredom?"

He glanced at the forest, where Ranger once chased shadows. "Stay here, and I'll hit my squirrel-watching quota." Leaning closer, he whispered, "Or show you my secret talent… peeling bananas with my feet."

Laughter erupted, snorting and tears streaming as I fell back. His warm chuckle grounded me, a lifeline against the Reaper's taunts. Seconds stretched in his gaze until he offered his hand. "Come on, have fun."

I stood, feigning a pout. "I'm no baby, but yeah, I need fun." Anything to dull this ache. "What's the plan?"

"Town," he grinned. "No questions, let's go."

Drawn to his ease, I followed him to his Ford F-250, studying his flexing arms. Cute, but safe? No words passed between us as we drove, Metallica playing softly, our glances sparking flutters.

I couldn't get Stephen Whitaker off my mind. He had been cleared, but he was the only guy who stood out or whose name I could fully remember, who my mom dated. He was on my suspect list, and I'll investigate other men Mom knew, anyone who might be the Reaper. The thought took root, my resolve hardening.

In a residential area, he hopped out and opened my door. "Coming?"

"Where are we going?" I stepped down.

"Game," he said, hands in pockets. "Steal garden gnomes, one side each, don't get caught. Loser buys lunch."

"Gnome napping?" His nod doubled me over.

"Bored Gold Beach teens do this," he shrugged. "You in?"

"You bet." My track muscles itched.

He handed me a garbage bag. "Most gnomes, first to touch the truck, win. You're right, I'm left. Go!"

We bolted, legs burning. Five gnomes filled my sack at the first house. At the third, a tree displayed a fresh ladybug carving distorted, wings warped as if it were hurt, unlike the Finns' or my oak's. He's here, watching. My pulse pounding, I took a quick picture with my phone, then grabbed a gnome and sprinted, the carving's twisted form stabbing into my lungs, making it harder to breathe. House after house, adrenaline drowned the ashes, but the image lingered.

A driveway's red splatter paint made me flinch, and then Nathan's "You're gonna lose!" echoed with laughter. Sprinting, I slammed the hood of the F-250, with Nathan laughing from the bushes. "I win!" The victory was sweet, but the carving gnawed at me. I needed to send it to Jacobs.

His hands braced the hood, breath warm. "How many gnomes?"

"Twenty," I stuttered, his heat sparking, but the carving chilled me.

"Beaten by a girl," he chuckled, revealing an empty sack.

"Lost on purpose." I glared. "You made me run everywhere!"

"Wanted to buy you lunch," he smirked.

"Didn't need a game," I stepped closer.

"You needed more than moping," he said, eyes warm.

"You're right." But that carving.

"Let's return these." He jogged off, misplacing gnomes.

"Lunch is on you."

As we drove, I texted the picture of the carving to Jacobs. He quickly replied, "Thanks. I'll be there in a couple of days, and you can show me in person." I felt a small relief that he'd be in town; however, I wondered if there was more to his visit.

At Panther Den Pizza and Deli, Nathan asked, "Been here?"

I shook my head. "High school hangout?"

"Yep." Nathan grabbed my hand and pulled me to a booth.

The pool and video games buzzed, but Kaitlyn, the bonfire queen, glared–she was our waitress. Why was she so cold?

I met her stare. She huffed, "What can I get you?"

We ordered pizza and Cokes; she sashayed off. "What was that?" I asked Nathan, his gaze on her.

"She's my ex," he cleared his throat. "Dumped me for Zane a couple of months back."

"You still like her," I said, noticing his flicker.

"Yes and no. She was rough. Zane's my bro. He's liked her forever; they're a better match."

"She and I were friends," I frowned. "She's changed since the bonfire; she ghosted me."

"She cuts people off," Nathan said. "Don't take it personally."

Zane strode in, kissing Kaitlyn hungrily, causing her apron to wrinkle. I flushed and looked away. I've never been kissed. Am I kissable?

"You are," Nathan teased, his eyes fixed on my lips.

I chuckled, feeling embarrassed. "Said that out loud?"

"Cute," he grinned, easing my Kaitlyn knot.

"Alexis," Cooper called, walking in with Tanner and Asher. "Joinin' the livin'!" He punched my arm, stinging.

Asher's glance flicked to Nathan, who had a far-off look on his face. Could it be jealousy?

We spent time eating our pizza, chatting casually, and I felt Asher's gaze on my back from across the room while he played pool with his brothers.

Nathan must have noticed my awkwardness and asked, "Want me to take you home?"

"Yes," I answered.

Just as we were about to leave, Tanner yelled, "Bye Alexis! Don't be a stranger."

I gave them a small wave and smiled. "I won't." Asher was standing next to Tanner, gripping a pool ball so tightly that his knuckles turned white. I didn't say anything to him as I walked out.

Nathan drove me home, the truck rumbled through Gold Beach's dusk, the distorted carving gnawing at my thoughts. My phone buzzed with another text from Detective Jacobs: "Alexis, I wanted you to have this update. Fire at Sutter Coast Hospital,

Crescent City. Patients killed, rhyme left: 'Ring around the rotten, flesh with sores forgotten, burn them, burn them, they all choke down!' Photo of your mom with William Thompson found. I let Luke know. Be safe. See you in a couple of days." My stomach lurched. The Rhyme Reaper. He's in Crescent City, so close. Could he be here already? Gold Beach's carvings, now this northward, methodical, hunting me.

"You okay?" Nathan asked as he pulled into my driveway, the oak's shadow looming, its jagged carving echoing today's discovery.

"Yeah," I lied, forcing a smile, the weight of Whitaker's name and Mom's unknown men pressing harder. "Thanks for today." I slipped out, the truck's rumble fading as I climbed the porch steps, the house's stillness drawing me back to my hunt.

On my bed, I scoured the book, its rhymes "Peter, Peter…", "Mary, Mary…" and "Ladybug…" twisting like nightmares. Dad and Becca were chasing the killer, puzzled by my targeting, "Alexis Jo Harper," the "one that got away." I shouldn't be alive.

The distorted carving, its hurt wings, and Jacobs' message about the hospital fire prickled my spine, urging me to hunt Mom's men, Stephen Whitaker first, then William Thompson, and others she might've known. He's working his way up the coast: Ventura, Gold Beach, and Crescent City, his rhymes and fires a path to me.

I grabbed a notebook, my pen shaking, listing suspects: Whitaker, Thompson, and unknowns from Mom's past. Each one was a potential mask for the Reaper, burning lives, carving ladybugs, and closing in. The list was my map to unravel his game, to hunt him before he hunted me, for Mom, for the truth, no matter the cost.

163

32

Alexis

The buzz of Panther Den still lingered, but moving day pulled me back to reality: our house felt like a cage I couldn't escape. Not for me, though I wished it were anywhere but here, away from Becca's frost and Trevor's venom.

"Truck's here. Meet me out front," Dad said, passing me in the hall, eyes averted and fingers twitching toward his watch.

I saw his pain now: his work chasing Mom's killer through ashes and rhymes, honoring her despite her betrayal. Words that could mend us stuck in my throat.

Outside, sunlight stung as movers in blue jumpsuits unloaded boxes and furniture, piling them up in the driveway.

As I walked out to "help," Cooper caught me off guard. He set down a box, his usual smirk absent. "Lost a buddy in a middle school car accident, drunk driver. The guy walked free. Seeing you fight this killer, Lex… it's like giving him justice I never got. I'm not letting you face this alone." He busied himself with another box, avoiding my gaze.

His comment was completely out of the blue; however, his protectiveness warmed me as I grabbed a box. Having him around makes dealing with Trevor that much easier.

Trevor, Becca's son, grabbed one marked "Trevor's Shit Don't Open," his sour glare matching the bonfire's barbed wire tattoo on his bicep, his lanky frame tense with resentment.

He clipped my shoulder at the door, nearly toppling me. I grabbed the porch pillar to steady myself. "Hey, what's your problem?" I snapped, glaring.

"You are!" he spat, his voice raspy and aged beyond his seventeen years, as if a lifetime of smoke had settled within him.

I scoffed. "First time we've talked."

He shrugged, his eyes cold. "Maybe it's who you represent."

"Seriously?" Hands on my hips, I bristled. "Judging me for what Mom and your dad did?"

"Yep," he said, popping the *p*. "That, and him being accused of killing your slutty mom."

I surged onto my toes, poking his chest. "How dare you? Your dad slept with her, too. What's that make him?"

He grabbed my finger, bending it back, pain flaring through me. "You don't know my dad or your mom. Back off." His grip tightened, revealing a flash of something darker in his hazel eyes: anger or fear. "I don't wanna be here, sharing space with you." He shoved my hand away and stormed inside.

Cooper came out of the house, hearing the commotion. His form towered over Trevor. "Dude, what's your problem? You like hurting women."

Trevor's eyes widened as he stuttered, "N...n..no."

"All right, let's go." Cooper grabbed his neck and pushed him inside, muttering something about talking to the authorities...meaning my dad and Becca.

I slumped against the pillar and winced as my head grazed a brick corner. Trevor's venom wasn't just grief; it was personal, his hostility a wall I'd have to navigate in this house, and his presence a constant thorn.

Sunlight spilled across the window, catching a flicker of dark hair wild and familiar, like Mom's when we'd sit on the Ventura porch swing, her voice soft with nursery rhymes. Her face in the glass was a blur, but it brought me back to those evenings, her laughter warm before everything changed. The sounds of the movers faded; I could almost hear her reading "Jack and Jill," her hand brushing against mine. My chest tightened not with anger but with a longing ache, missing her. The reflection seemed to hum, "You remember." I wanted to stay there, drawn to her, to how she used to be.

Yes, I remember Mom. You once loved me. My heart ached, and tears spilled, darkening the concrete. When I blinked, she was gone.

Dad's boots crunched behind me. "Alexis, you okay?" His voice was tight, still stinging from our fight, his hand adjusting his watch compulsively.

I nodded, shaking the ghost away and wiped my eyes.

Before I could speak, Dad's phone rang, Ventura PD's number flashing. He frowned, answering. "Harper, is Alexis there with you?"

"Yes." Dad placed the phone on speaker. We both took a deep breath.

"Detective Harper, Miss Harper," Jacobs's gruff voice crackled. "Paternity test results are in." A pause, papers rustling. "Luke, you're not Alexis's biological father."

My heart stopped, shock crashing like a fist. "No," I whispered, disbelief choking me. "That's... wrong."

Luke wasn't my dad. The man who'd bandaged my scraped knees, who'd cheered at my track meets, wasn't mine by blood. Shock numbed my chest, like a wave crashing over me, stealing my breath. Hurt followed, sharp and jagged, slicing through memories of his smiles—were they lies? My whole life felt like a fraud, my identity unmoored, drifting in a sea of Nicole's secrets. Who was I, if not his daughter?

I clutched the pillar, nails scraping, tears stinging. "He's my dad," I said, voice cracking, staring at him. "I can't imagine you as anything else."

Luke's expression hardened, his gaze unfocused and jaw clenched, his thumb rhythmically tapping the edge of his phone—a subtle sign of his distress. For a brief moment, I noticed something shadowy in his eyes—anger or perhaps relief—but it vanished before I could discern it. "Understood," he replied, his voice devoid of emotion, as if he were swallowing glass. His hand twitched, yet he didn't reach out to me. "Thanks, Jacobs." He ended the call, leaving a heavy silence in its wake.

I stepped closer, trembling. "You're my dad, always." He nodded, barely, his gaze on the ground, pain etched deep. I'd hold him to it, biology be damned, and chase Mom's secrets, her men, and the Reaper's rhymes.

My phone buzzed with Asher's text: *Hey, I'm sorry for acting weird at the Panther Den. I was being stupid. I've been wanting to talk to you since you got back from California. I'm also sorry, I couldn't be there today. Overwhelmed with all this college paperwork. Are you good, Lex? Here for you.* His words and apology softened the blow of the news and warmed me, his belief a shield. Allies, not lovers, we'd face this chaos together.

Feeling anger creeping in, I stabbed out a message: *Just peachy. No worries about the den. I've been off since California. Guess who doesn't know who her real father is? Yep, me. Luke isn't my real dad. Oh and then there's this...I'll call you later.*

I sent the link about the hospital deaths. Not waiting for a reply, I pocketed the phone and spotted a ladybug on the pillar, its red shell glinting. A clue, a warning the Reaper was watching, and

Trevor's venom was a new variable in this house, but I'd be ready, my mental list growing, with Whitaker's name burning brightest.

33

Black Sheep

The echo of Nicole's birthday lingered in Alexis's whispered grief, her mother's absence a raw wound. The glow of the smoldering burn barrel in a Gold Beach forest sharpened Black Sheep's focus.

"How could you make such a huge mistake?" Spider demanded, his voice slicing through the dusk. He waved the Curry Coastal Pilot like a blade as he paced between a pine tree and the barrel's embers.

Spider, a code name from the nursery rhyme book, is fueling their plans, thrilling Black Sheep. His own moniker, Black Sheep, fit an outcast with blood-soaked hands, now the Rhyme Reaper, merging with a world he had shunned. Yet Spider's rage burned hotter than the barrel; his face aflame, veins bulging like Black Sheep's when he watched Ladybug from the woods, her emerald eyes haunting since the Ventura fire's ash.

"Are you listening to a damn word I'm saying?" Spider yelled, stepping closer, rolling the paper tighter, his eyes wild with the intensity Black Sheep felt when he carved that distorted ladybug days ago in Gold Beach, its warped, injured wings a taunt for Alexis, mirroring her growing fear.

"Yes," Black Sheep said, his voice low and steady, despite the newspaper's sting itching to provoke him, as his mind flickered to the men from Nicole's past, a long list of possibilities, wondering for a split second if the FBI's list included him.

169

"Well, explain why you screwed up our plan!" Spider's glare demanded the truth. "Don't lie, just tell me!"

Black Sheep stared at the barrel's glow, their pact against discussing set plans broken. Megan's scream, her body fed to the sharks, a reckless mistake deserving of Spider's wrath. Nothing could soothe him, not with Ladybug's pull lust, hate fraying his control.

He cleared his throat. "She saw me." The vague truth earned a newspaper swat to his head, sharp but deserved. Stronger, he could have dropped Spider, but guilt held him back. He glared, teeth gritted, "She saw me kill a cat."

Spider froze, then erupted, hammering him with the paper. "I told you to stop that shit! Ray's Food Place bulletin board's plastered with missing cat fliers, now a missing person!"

"Don't care," Black Sheep snapped, chest heaving. "The rest of the plan's solid. I needed a fix. Would you rather I kill Ladybug? She's driving me insane. Can't we take her now?"

The question disrupted the script, and patience was thin. Ladybug's defiance and her pursuit of the Reaper threatened his control, creating an ache.

"You can't. You'll expose us all. Remember, you came to me; you wanted this." Spider scrubbed his face, cooling off. "Don't screw this up again. Evidence gone?"

"Yes," Black Sheep said. "No prints, gloves on, clean kill." Like Nicole, the nuns, and the Crescent City fire.

"Your fix holds you?" Spider squinted, eyeing the barrel with skepticism.

Black Sheep nodded, savoring Megan's torn flesh, a cry that rivaled Ladybug's scream on the beach. She's mine, not Asher's, not Trevor's.

"Keep it together, no more deviations," Spider said. "Got a vigil to attend." He faded into the dusk, his restraint a mask that Black Sheep knew all too well.

Black Sheep circled his borrowed house, itching for his routine cats or Ladybug watch, but paused at the path to his Chevy Blazer, its rust blending into the shadows, unlike flashier rides in town. A tall, dark-haired man limped past, brushing shoulders with him, no words exchanged, a ghost-like shadow. One from Nicole's past? His list grew, the hunt sharpening, and Ladybug's end drew near.

34

Alexis

"Candlelight Vigil for Missing Local Gold Beach, Oregon Teen: The disappearance of 17-year-old Megan Lewis from Gold Beach, Oregon, on July 27 prompted a candlelight vigil at Gold Beach Park, which was attended by hundreds. Police released suspect George Giles, a homeless man, after confirming that he was in custody at the time. Search efforts continue with K9 units and volunteers from Curry, Coos, and Josephine counties. Megan's grandmother urges anyone with information to contact the Gold Beach Police at 541-247-6671 or the anonymous tip line at 541-247-5555."

I stood at the edge of Gold Beach Park, the vigil's candles casting flickering shadows across the crowd, their murmurs a dull hum against the ocean's distant crash. Megan Lewis's face stared from posters, her smile frozen. I shouldn't have come, but the pull of her absence dragged me here. I scanned the mourners, observing their pained faces, until a choked sob snapped my gaze to Megan's family.

Elaine, Megan's mother, her once-Broadway poise shattered, knelt by a candle wreath, clutching a crumpled paper she had pulled from beneath a flickering light. Her husband, Richard, leaned over, his lawyer's calm cracking as he read over her shoulder. Their faces drained, Elaine's hand trembling, and the paper slipped to reveal jagged black ink. I edged closer, heart pounding, catching the words before Richard snatched it back, his voice a raw whisper: "He's mocking the police. It's him."

The letter read:

"Little Miss Muffet sat on her tuffet,
Eating her curds and whey;
Along came a spider, who sat down beside her,
And frightened Miss Muffet away."
Sheriff's fools, you grope in the dark, but Megan's body was mine.
Her lies silenced, like the whore Nicole's, caught in my web. Your
nets are frail, while my threads bind tighter. Hunt me and fail.
                                                   -The Rhyme Reaper

A rusted spoon, taped to the page, gleamed with soot, its curve a grim nod to the rhyme's *"curds and whey."*

I knew that rhyme because it represented innocence and the fear of what challenges may come in life. It was another fitting one for this murder. However, did it connect to my mom?

Elaine's wail pierced the crowd as she collapsed into Richard's arms while he shouted, "Why taunt us?"

My blood ran cold, the *"spider"* echoing Mom's "Peter, Peter" carved in blood. Kessler's shovel loomed in my mind, his mutter of *"cleaning messes"* by the fence. The letter was a dare, aimed at Dad's police but slicing me, the Reaper's shadow creeping closer. I clutched my chest, breath ragged, watching Elaine's grief mirror mine, knowing Megan was gone and he was close.

The weight of the vigil urged me to act. My mind raced, forming a mental list: Who in Gold Beach could be the Rhyme Reaper? One man from Mom's past stood out, his menace in Ventura a clear mark, but other shadows from her life swirled in my thoughts, faces blurred, each a potential mask for the killer carving those symbols and burning lives in yesterday's fire. I'd trace their threads, starting with that man, then others Mom knew, to unweave the Reaper's veil. For a moment, I wondered if the FBI's list paralleled mine.

35

Black Sheep

The Rhyme Reaper crouched at the hill's crest, the distant roar of
the Rogue River a faint pulse beneath the whisper of the pines. The
bucket in his gloved hands, rusted and heavy with river stones,
gleamed in the dusk, its edge a silent vow. "Jack and Jill went up
the hill to fetch a pail of water." The rhyme slithered through his
mind, a venomous thread binding his rage to the night. Nicole's
face, her lies, her men flashed before him, her sins mirrored in the
couple climbing toward their doom. Mark and Laura Hensley,
lured by a forged note promising a picnic to mend their shattered
vows, laughed with brittle hope, unaware of the judgment
awaiting.

His hood cast a shadow over his face, a specter born of
betrayal. The nursery rhymes revealed the truth when his mother's
rope silenced her voice, each verse a blade to carve out justice.
Nicole's blood had nourished the first rhyme, her finger a trophy in
the pumpkin's shell. Mark and Laura would fall, their crowns
shattered for her sins, for the family they had torn apart with their
affair. The Rhyme Reaper's pulse thrummed, steady as the river,
his breath a hymn to the chaos he would unleash.

Mark's arm looped around Laura, his voice thick with wine,
promising love he'd never kept. "We'll make it right," he slurred,
echoing Nicole's hollow words to a boy who'd lost everything.
Laura's eyes flickered with doubt, her steps faltering; she knew

about Mark's nights with Nicole, the whispers that fractured their home. They reached the crest, the bucket glinting like a lure, its stones a weight they'd never lift.

The Rhyme Reaper stepped from the pines, a dark silhouette. "Evening," he purred, voice low, a predator's taunt. Mark flinched, Laura's gasp sharp as they clutched each other, rats sensing the trap. He moved swiftly, the bucket arcing through the air, stones slamming into Mark's skull with a wet crunch. Blood sprayed, a crimson mist, Mark's body collapsing like a felled tree. "Jack fell down and broke his crown." Laura's scream tore through the air, raw and fleeting, a sound the Rhyme Reaper drank like wine. He swung again, the bucket cracking her temple, bone splintering, her eyes dimming as she crumpled. "And Jill came tumbling after."

He pushed them, bodies rolling down the hill, limbs twisting in a grotesque dance, blood pooling in the dirt at the base. The picnic blanket lay crumpled, a mockery of their hope. Kneeling, he carved the rhyme into leather with his knife, the blade's edge singing: *Jack and Jill went up the hill to fetch a pail of water. Jack fell down and broke his crown, and Jill came tumbling after.*

He pinned it to Mark's chest, the words a verdict, a shadow of Nicole's carved shell. His fingers scattered clues, a shovel mark pressed deep, mimicking the old man's digging across the fence, Kessler's name a ghost to haunt the curious. A photo of Nicole and Mark in a Gold Beach bar, William's tight smile in the frame, dropped half-buried for the girl to find, his Ladybug, sniffing too close to his truth.

The Rhyme Reaper tossed the bucket into the brush, its clatter swallowed by the river's hum. He carved a smashed ladybug into the tree and then melted into the pines, heart calm, the rhyme's echo fading. They fell, like his mother fell, like Nicole fell. But the girl, his Ladybug, she'd climb this hill, her flashlight cutting through the dark, and he'd watch, her shadow, her reaper, until the final verse.

36

Alexis

The vigil had unraveled into a mess of tears and shouted accusations, the air thick with grief and suspicion. The letter, another twisted clue, turned the crowd feral. Dad's voice, low and tense, muttered something about the FBI stepping in, but I barely heard it over the whispers cutting through the chaos: "Megan's killer... Rhyme Reaper," one voice hissed, another replying, "just like Nicole's murder." My mom's name, Nicole, slapped me like a cold hand, linking her death to this nightmare. My chest tightened, the rumors clawing at me, too loud, too close. I couldn't breathe here, couldn't think. I had to get out.

The darkness helped me slip through the crowd, their frantic voices fading as I broke free, my sneakers crunching on the gravel path lit by my flashlight toward the picnic area. It wasn't just an escape. It was instinct, drawing me to a place that still held echoes of something good. The picnic area was where Mom and Dad used to take me, a quiet clearing by the Rogue River where we'd spread a blanket and eat sandwiches, their laughter bouncing off the pines. I could still see Dad tossing me into the air, Mom's voice calling out, "Careful, you two!" a slice of happiness before everything went dark. I needed that now, to feel them close again, even if it was just a memory.

The river's rush filled the air as I stepped into the clearing, the scent of pine and wet earth pulling me back. The picnic tables, weathered and chipped, looked smaller than they did in my childhood, but they still felt like ours. For a moment, I could hear Mom's soft nursery rhymes from our Ventura swing and see Dad grinning as he whittled a stick to make me giggle. My throat tightened, not with old bitterness, but with missing them, those simple days now so far gone.

At the vigil, I overheard a couple arguing, their voices sharp, mentioning a picnic "in the dark" at this very spot. I froze, my heart pounding. It was our place, where Mom and Dad took me for dusk picnics. Was the couple's fight a hint or just another echo of what I'd lost?

I jumped when I heard footsteps crunching on the path. Cooper ran towards me as my heart raced.

"Yo, Alexis. I saw you leaving the vigil. What are you doing out here alone?"

"My parents used to bring me here." I pulled the nursery rhyme book from my backpack, the pages worn from my grip.

My eyes scanned the hill ahead, pine trees stabbing at the sky, a rusted bucket glinting at the top. Something felt wrong, like the very air was holding its breath.

"What's wrong?" he asked, noticing my concern.

I began climbing, with Cooper silently following me. My flashlight beam sliced through the dusk, catching on crushed grass and then a smear of red in the dirt. My stomach lurched. Not again.

Cooper noticed, too, as he whispered, "What the hell?"

At the base of the hill, two bodies lay twisted in the shadows: Mark Hensley and his wife, Laura. I recognized Mark from my mom's old photos, his arm draped around her like a claim. Now his skull was caved in, blood pooling beneath him, while Laura's eyes stared wide beside him. The bucket lay dented nearby, streaked with red, a sick prop in the Reaper's game. A note was pinned to Mark's chest, the words carved into leather:

"Jack and Jill went up the hill to fetch a pail of water. Jack fell down and broke his crown, and Jill came tumbling after."

My hands shook, the rhyme searing into me, another cut from the killer's blade. Knowing the meaning of the rhyme, made me wonder if one of them had explored somewhere they shouldn't have.

I stumbled back, Cooper catching me as my flashlight trembled, revealing a fresh shovel mark in the dirt. Kessler's Pontiac GTO sat a hundred yards away, its hood still warm as we passed it. A photo peeked out from the soil, showing Mom and Mark at a bar, with William Thompson smirking in the background. My pulse hammered. Was William here? Or was this the Reaper's bait? Were they one and the same? Footsteps cracked behind us, and we spun, blinding Kessler with my light. He leaned on a shovel, his eyes glinting. "Always cleaning up," he said, voice like ice. We scrambled, the hill, bruising my legs as Cooper tried to help me, the rhyme pounding in my skull. The Rhyme Reaper was here, having made it up the coast to Gold Beach. Am I too late to figure out who this is?

My legs burned as we reached the road, and we both tried to catch our breath.

Cooper turned around in a circle as his hands pulled at his hair. "Was that…was that what I think it was? Oh, how sick? That was as creepy as a *Saw* flick, right?"

I had no words. I fumbled for my phone. I dialed Dad, my voice shaking as I spilled everything: Kessler, the bodies, the rhyme. "Alexis, stay put!" he barked, but I could hear the fear in his voice, sharp and raw. "You went off alone? Damn it, what were you thinking?"

"Cooper's here with me."

He seemed a bit relieved, but his words still stung, and I couldn't argue that he was right. I'd been reckless, chasing ghosts while the Reaper drew closer. He said he was on his way, but the line crackled with his anger and worry, a mix I hadn't heard since Mom died.

Minutes later, the FBI swarmed the scene, radios buzzing as agents fanned out across the hill. They'd been tracking the Rhyme Reaper up the coast, following a trail of bodies and twisted rhymes. My fear that the Reaper was coming for me was taken seriously. But it was too late. He'd struck again, here in Gold Beach, leaving Mark and Laura as his latest victims. Detective Fields stood by a nearby tree, his gloved hand tracing a small ladybug carving etched into the bark, its limbs jagged and torn from its body, the wood freshly cut. "Another signature," he muttered, photographing it as evidence. My stomach twisted. Mom loved ladybugs, always pointing them out in the garden. This taunt was meant for me.

They were hauling Kessler in for questioning, his shovel and warm car too convenient to ignore. His icy calm hadn't wavered, even as they cuffed him, but I couldn't shake the feeling he was merely a piece of the puzzle, not the whole picture.

As the agents continued to secure the scene, Jacobs pulled me aside, his notebook already open. "This ladybug carving," he said, voice low, "it's like the others we found in Monterey, Crescent City, all up the coast. The same ones you found, too, with the same knife work and mutilated limbs. Whoever's doing this, they're deliberate."

I swallowed hard, my mind racing. "Any leads?" I asked, dreading the answer.

He shook his head. "Not enough. The carvings are fresh, but the Reaper's always gone before we get close."

Detective Santos, the FBI's lead agent, interrupted with a sharp voice. "We need your statements, Alexis and Cooper. Stay nearby. Your dad's concerns are valid." I nodded, overwhelmed by the gravity of the situation.

"You doing okay?" I asked Cooper as I watched him take in the scene of all the authorities.

"Absolutely." He locked eyes with me. "This is intense. I don't know about you, but I'm ready to go full Donkey Kong on this Reaper!"

I snorted, trying to match his confidence, but I couldn't.

"I'm happy you were there with me."

"Me too." He placed his arm over my shoulders and gave me a gentle squeeze.

The Reaper was steps ahead of me, his rhymes and carvings tightening around me like a noose. A cold dread settled in my chest. I was running out of time to unmask him, and deep down, I feared I wouldn't discover who he was before he struck again. Somewhere out there, he was already planning his next move.

37

Alexis

A day after the vigil and the discovery of the Hensley's broken bodies, they found Megan's car torched at Frog Lake, ten miles southwest of my house, its charred skeleton confirming the Rhyme Reaper's letter. The town shuffled like zombies, faces gray, voices hushed, fear coiling tighter with each whispered rumor. Megan's family, her father, a retired New York lawyer, and her mother, a faded Broadway star, had the money to hunt for answers, but even their wealth couldn't coax help from Gold Beach's citizens. No one wanted to be the Reaper's next verse, leaving the FBI to chase shadows alone. They kicked into deep search, agents scouring every digital trace, cross-referencing nursery rhymes, ladybug carvings, and coastal crime scenes, piecing together the Reaper's path up the coast. But the deeper they dug, the more elusive he seemed.

Megan was dead; the Reaper's letter had crowed, but I had known before the words hit the paper. No one seemed to escape his clutches alive. Sleep was hard to grasp as the Hensley's bodies haunted me. I had told Dad, expecting Dr. Finn's trauma lecture, but he just stared, the lines deepening on his face. "Get rest, kiddo," he said, his voice heavy. The weight of their silence, along with Mom's secrets, pressed down harder.

My tired yet determined body sat with Jacobs at the FBI's makeshift command post. Asher was in the waiting room as he insisted on spending time with me, no matter what I was doing. I didn't protest welcoming his steady presence. With my hands shaking, I handed Jacobs the list of Mom's old boyfriends, the ones I could remember. Stephen Whitaker, Mark Hensley, and a few others, whose faces blurred in my memory. "This is all I've got," I admitted, my voice low. "She dated a lot of guys, and I was young. I don't… I can't remember everyone." Jacobs nodded, his face unreadable, but I felt the weight of my failure. What if the Reaper's name was one I'd forgotten? They'd let Kessler go that morning, his interrogation yielding nothing but incoherent ramblings about shovels and rhymes, no hard evidence to hold him. The FBI's search was churning, pulling threads from old cases, but the Reaper was a ghost, slipping through every net.

As we left the station, the weight of the nursery rhyme book tugged at my shoulders. The Reaper was steps ahead, his rhymes suffocating, but I wasn't just Mom's daughter anymore, haunted by her ghosts. I was Alexis, and I would run this race not just to survive but to win.

We stepped onto the darkening street towards Asher's Shelby, the air heavy with pine and salt, and I froze. I felt eyes on us.

I grabbed Asher's hand and squeezed hard, and he squeezed back, "He's here."

"What do you mean?" Asher glanced around quickly.

"He's watching us. I'm sure about it."

"Come on, Lex, we'll go back inside and get Jacobs." He tugged me toward the station; however, I didn't budge. "Lex?"

"He'll be gone by the time he comes out here." I was talking so low I wasn't sure he could hear me. "We're at the station. He'd be stupid to come and get me, but if he does, they could catch him."

Asher pulled me close to his chest. "What are you talking about? You're scaring me. You won't be bait, Lex!" His nose nuzzled the top of my head, breathing me in. "I can't let you. I don't want to lose you."

I no longer felt the pull of the eyes on me. "Let's go. I need to run."

Asher grabbed my shoulders and studied my drained face. "I'll go with you, but let's stick close to our houses."

I didn't argue.

School was just a week away, and the track coach had called, impressed by my California varsity stats. Running was my escape, the one place I could outpace the ghosts, but Dad's noose, fragile, handle with care, had tightened since California, since Megan, and now, after the Hensley's blood stained that hill. After heated negotiations, no running alone, ever, I hit my forest path. Ranger bounded leash-free at my side, and Asher on the other. Dad's orders were ironclad, a custodial hold born of fear, but Asher's steady presence made them more bearable.

Our breaths synced as we raced toward town, his long strides matching mine. Sweat dripped, and his scent of leather and flour, like bread baked into his car's seats, evoked warmth and a flicker of irritation. How could a sweaty guy smell so sweet? I huffed through my nose, annoyed. The pull to Asher, solid and constant, clashed with Nathan's dimpled grin and his playful ease. Both tangled my focus, pulling me from the Reaper's rhymes looping in my head: "Little Jo…" The nursery rhyme book burned in my mind, its pages heavy with Mom's handwritten notes, her secrets I couldn't yet crack. Had her choices, her men, and her lies unleashed this killer? Was I paying for her sins?

Asher nudged my shoulder, and I glanced over, catching his raised eyebrow. "You okay?" His eyes flicked to my lips, a habit

I'd noticed weeks ago, then back, his gaze igniting something I didn't want to name.

I forced a small smile. "Yeah, just need a break." We'd looped from his house to mine, but I'd coaxed him into another round, craving the burn to drown out the ghosts. Slowing to a walk, we sank onto a log, Ranger sniffing the underbrush nearby. Asher handed me his water bottle, the Princeton logo glinting like a countdown. His future, so certain, twisted my gut. I sipped, sadness pooling as I stared into the forest, swallowing a lump. Tears mixed with sweat streaked my face, and I prayed he wouldn't see.

No luck. His thumb and finger tilted my chin, forcing my gaze. His smile was soft, thrilled I'd stopped flinching at his touch warmed me, his face close, leather-vanilla breath fanning my cheeks. "You can talk to me," he said, tucking hair behind my ear, my shiver pulling his grin. "Anything, Lex. I won't judge. You're the strongest person I know, but you don't have to carry this alone. Not with me here."

I groaned, rolling my eyes, tears fading. "Glad doctor-patient confidentiality's ironclad at your house." Dr. Finn's sessions twice weekly, sneaking through Asher's home office, were a stalemate. My silence and nail-biting grated on him, just like when I'd clammed up about Stephen Whitaker, Mom's turned cheek, and her bruises I'd pretended not to see. "Your dad's not thrilled. I don't talk anymore, I don't want to. Mom told me to keep it for years. Secrets were safer, she said." Asher's eyebrow lifted, questioning, but he didn't push, steady as ever, unlike Nathan's playful prodding. "I'm afraid," I admitted, my voice cracking, tears spilling.

"It's okay to be afraid. Of what?" His voice was low, anchoring.

I stared skyward, failing to stem the flood. "The Reaper's coming for me. I felt it at the station, Asher. Those carvings, the rhymes, they're personal. That ladybug on the tree, its limbs torn off... Mom loved ladybugs. It's like he knows me, knows her." A sob broke free, raw. "I'm scared I'll never figure out who he is in time. He's always steps ahead, and I'm just... chasing ghosts."

Asher's arms wrapped around me, strong and safe, and I clung to him, the memory of being held so faint, Mom, maybe, on a birthday, before her men's hands, their cars, her lies. I cried harder, and his grip tightened. "You're not alone in this. Let the authorities do their job. Jacobs believed you about him being outside the station," he murmured, his breath warm against my hair. "Put some faith in others. I'm here, and I'm not going anywhere. Not yet." The 'yet' stung Princeton loomed, a ticking clock. I pulled back, searching his face, and saw a flicker of something new: fear, not just for me, but for himself.

"What about you?" I asked, wiping my eyes. "You're always here, steady, but... what's got you scared? You don't talk about it, cither."

He exhaled, running a hand through his hair, his smile fading. "Nothing gets past you, huh?" He glanced at the Princeton logo on the bottle, then away into the trees. "It's Dad. He's got this plan for me, the next Dr. Finn, fixing people like he does. But I don't know if that's me. Princeton's his dream, not mine. You're scared of losing yourself, Lex. I get it. Growing up, I didn't know where I came from, just that Mom and Dad chose me, Cooper, and Tanner. When I found out we were adopted, I kept thinking... what if I'm not enough for them? Now, with this killer, I'm terrified I'll lose you too." His voice cracked, eyes avoiding hers. He swallowed, jaw tight. "I want to be here for you, but I don't know how to stay and not let him down."

187

My chest clenched at the sight of him, vulnerable and struggling— the boy who'd always been my strength, now fragile beneath his own burden. "You're not messing anything up," I reassured him with a firmer tone. "You're the only reason I stay sane. But you can't stay for me, Asher. You need to figure out what you truly want, not what your dad expects." I hesitated, feeling the Reaper's shadow creep closer again. "And I won't give up. I'll find him, whoever he is. I have to—for Mom, all his victims, and myself."

I wanted him to go to school. Away from all this. To be safe.

He nodded, a spark of pride in his eyes, but worry lingered. "Just promise you won't go after him alone. I know you, Alexis, you're stubborn as hell. Let me help, at least until…" He trailed off, Princeton's shadow looming between us.

"Deal," I said, managing a half-smile. Ranger bounded back, nudging my hand, and I stood up, brushing off my shorts.

38

Black Sheep

"Shit, shit, shit," the Rhyme Reaper hissed, gloved fist slamming jagged bark, pain spiking through his knuckles but ignored. The pine's rough bite grounded him, a fleeting distraction from the fire in his chest.

For an hour, he'd followed Ladybug and Asher through the forest, keeping his distance to avoid Ranger's nose, his ragged breaths a humiliating reminder of his lesser stamina, no match for their track-honed pace. Alexis's legs flashed like they did in his dreams, on that beach where she'd smiled at him, unaware. His murderous glare fixed on their embrace, her tears staining Asher's shirt, twisting the rage that branded his heart—a scar carved deeper than the ladybugs he etched into trees.

He flexed his bruised fist, loosening it, jaw grinding, vein throbbing at his temple. How dare he touch what's mine? No one got this close, not Asher with his steady gaze, not Nathan with his Ford and gnome games, his dimpled grin that made her laugh. This wasn't the plan. Lust, love, hate for her, his chest ached, a tangled knot of need, Alexis Jo Harper. Mine. Always mine, since the day he'd watched her with Nicole, a child clutching ladybugs while he burned to be rid of her mother. Now Alexis was his, the final verse in his rhyme, and no one would steal her.

A growl rumbled low and primal as he fought the urge to charge, to snap Asher's neck, to claim her now in the dirt and pine.

His fingers twitched toward the knife at his belt—the same blade that had torn limbs from the ladybug carving on that hill, a taunt for Alexis and a nod to Nicole's garden obsession. But he stopped his breath from hitching. The FBI was everywhere, radios crackling, agents crawling Gold Beach like ants, their search tearing through archives, forums, and anything tied to rhymes or carvings. They'd found Megan's car at Frog Lake, his torch job, and still had nothing—no name, no face—just his rhymes mocking them. Pride swelled, sharp and hot. They'll never catch me. I'm the shadow they chase, the verse they can't solve. Kessler's release proved it—his incoherent ramblings about shovels and rhymes had wasted their time, just as Black Sheep intended. The old man was a pawn, a distraction, his warm car a planted clue to keep them spinning.

But pride conflicted with caution. The FBI's heavy presence, with vans parked at the station, and Jacobs sniffing every tree and carving from Ventura to Gold Beach, forced him to lay low—a cage he despised. His blood urged him to act—to carve the next rhyme into flesh—but one wrong move could unravel everything. Laying low ate at him; each day of inaction was a blade twisting in his gut. He wasn't made for patience; he was fire, not stone. Nicole had seen that once, before she dismissed him, her rejection a wound that festered into this symphony of death, with Ladybug as the crescendo. The nursery rhyme book, his copy from Nicole's time, was his guide—its coded pages a map to her fear, her end.

"And that's little Jo, for she's scared to lose her head," he muttered, lips curling. Time to clear obstacles and escalate—no more delays.

He shifted, crouching lower in the brush, eyes narrowing as Alexis and Asher stood, Ranger nudging her hand. She'd given the FBI a list of Nicole's men but not him. He'd made sure of that, staying a ghost in her childhood memories, a face she'd barely glimpsed. Her failure to name him was another victory, proof he was steps ahead, untouchable. But her tears, her fear, fed him too. He knew she felt him closing in. Good. Fear was his prelude, her surrender his prize.

As they walked away, he slipped through the trees, silent despite his bulk, his plan sharpening. He'd watched them leave the station. Asher was falling hard for her, and the Rhyme Reaper wondered if he had real love for her or if it was lust. Ladybug knew how to draw men in like her mother, and he bet his life on it that it was lust that only made him want to end her life more.

The FBI's search was blind to him, their leads dead ends, but he couldn't stay dormant long. Pride demanded action, and Alexis demanded completion.

He lingered in the shadows, his breath steady and his plan sharpening. As anger grew and became impossible to suppress upon seeing his Ladybug and Asher embracing, his stalking became a dance. Each step was carefully calculated to keep her on edge from afar, and each taunt a note in his growing symphony. He reached into his pocket and pulled out a small cloth bag, its contents faintly squirming. With a smirk, he dumped it on the ground, spilling writhing ladybug larvae right where she'd run. This grotesque, personal lure would draw her closer to his grasp, her fear his reward.

39

Alexis

Ranger's bark shattered the air, jolting me from Asher's arms and nearly toppling me off the log. His grip steadied me, sparing my pride, but his eyes darted to the woods, a shadow of doubt crossing his face. "What's up, boy?" I stood, inching toward Ranger, whose defensive stance was fierce at five months, not yet full-grown but acting like it, as when he'd chased doves or growled at shadows, ghosts, killers, and maybe the Rhyme Reaper himself.

Asher followed, his posture tense, eyes narrowing as he scanned the trees. "See something?" I asked, my heart racing and chills creeping up my spine.

He swallowed, searching my eyes, hesitant, as if he were weighing what to say. "Thought I did," he murmured, voice low, but there was an edge, something unspoken, as if he wasn't sure of me, either.

Ranger barked louder, and I frowned, irritation spiking. "Did you or not?" His guarded tone felt too much like Dad's evasions, Dr. Finn's probing, hiding truths I couldn't grasp.

"Lex, probably a deer, some critter," he said, squeezing my hand, soft yet unconvincing, his thumb lingering as if to reassure himself as much as me. But his eyes darted back to the woods, and I caught a flicker of suspicion as if he wondered whether I'd seen more than I was letting on.

My gut screamed, it wasn't a deer. "Doubt it," I snapped, yanking free. His hurt look was brief, but I noticed something else worry mixed with doubt, as if he was piecing together my recklessness, the nursery rhyme book, the Reaper's taunts. I bolted toward Ranger's gaze. "You know."

"Lex, what the hell?" Asher yelled, his footsteps pounding behind me, his voice cracking with frustration. He wasn't just worried now; he was scared. "Where are you going?"

My legs surged faster than California's tracks as I wove through trees losing Asher, my eyes sharp despite the dense green engulfing me. Do I know where I'm going? Probably, but instinct drove me beyond reason, past the ghostly voice and the ashes of the arson.

Movement to the right, I braced myself, rounded a tree, and froze. A four-point buck, grass hanging from its mouth, stood perfectly still, ears twitching as it chewed slowly, unbothered by my presence.

Asher was right—an animal. I sighed, bending down with my hands on my knees, smiling at the deer's calm demeanor. I stepped forward but then froze. "Ladybug," a whisper floated, kissing my ear, soft as fog.

I held my breath, doubting, but it came louder and closer. "Ladybug."

He's here. Gut deep, I had always known. "What do you want?" I called, no answer. "I know you want me." Silence. "Quit hiding, get me! No one else needs to die." My ponytail whipped as I spun, searching, arms out, reckless, stupid, offering myself like a perp in a lineup. "I'm here. Come on!"

"Ladybug," it hissed, inches away.

I screeched, bolting with legs pumping, lost but indifferent to anything but here. Footsteps echoed or seemed to behind me, but looking back revealed nothing. Facing forward, my forehead hit a tree, and I fell; my vision kaleidoscoped, and treetops spun. Darkness closed in, the rhyme's chant the last sound.

"Ladybug! Ladybug! Fly away home. Your house is on fire. And your mother is dead. All except one escaped death, And that's little Jo, For she's scared To lose her head."

My skin prickled, and my head pounded, waking me on damp ground with clothes soaked and chilling me like the Oregon fog after I found the Hensleys. I was afraid to open my eyes, terrified the Rhyme Reaper lingered, his "Ladybug…" echoing from the woods, a taunt like a nursery rhyme book's red ink. He'd had me unconscious, free to carve me like Mom. Forcing my eyelids open, a shot of pain shot through my brow, and I slammed them shut, the contusion throbbing—a reminder of the tree I'd crashed into while fleeing his voice.

My sight was useless, so I leaned on other senses. My body stiffened, and I stretched my legs, arms splayed, fingers curling into the dirt, grit lodging under my nails like ash. The prickling shifted, creepy-crawly, not my skin but something wriggling on me. Slowly, I opened my eyes; a speck hit my pupil, sparking a high-pitched scream as I bolted upright.

"Lex!" Asher's voice, urgent, cut through, his face pale as he reached me, eyes wide with fear but shadowed with something else, doubt maybe, or suspicion about what I'd brought on myself.

"Help me!" I yelled, brushing my face, now clear, but my body crawled with sticky, grotesque bugs with black, spiked, reddish-orange stripes, alligator-like, exactly the ladybug larvae from my nightmare. My heart hammered. "Help, get them off!" I screeched, swatting frantically.

"Lex, hold still. What are these?" Asher knelt, brushing at me with swift but careful hands, his voice gentle but strained, like he was piecing together a puzzle. His eyes flicked to the ground, then back to me, a question lingering about how I ended up covered in these, and why I wasn't surprised. "These aren't random, are they?" he murmured, almost to himself, his concern laced with unease.

I ignored where he touched, desperate to be free of them, their legs like needles, tied to the Reaper's taunts, the larvae he'd left to lure me, per my research after the arson box. "Little Jo…" Once gone, we sat, silent, watching them scuttle through the dirt, a grotesque retreat mirroring my panic's ebb.

Asher uncapped his water bottle, Princeton logo, a reminder of his leaving soon. "Here, drink," he said softly, handing it over, but his eyes didn't leave me, searching for answers I wasn't giving.

I guzzled, throat raw, and handed it back. "Thanks, I needed that."

He plucked a larva, shoving it into the bottle, its size resisting until he crushed it with his palm, leaving a streak on the plastic. I scrunched my nose, grossed out.

He saw, wincing. "Sorry," he said, but his voice was quieter now, his gaze lingering on the bug, then me, like he was wondering if I'd known about the larvae before or if I was hiding something dangerous.

I stared, silent, walls rising. Was it Asher? His voice could've morphed, whispering, "Ladybug…"

Where was Ranger? My eyes met his, his gaze questioning, but now I noticed suspicion there, too. Did he think I was reckless, or worse, involved somehow? Panic surged. Wouldn't Ranger have chased me, just like when he'd bolted after doves or shadows? If Asher was the Reaper, I couldn't reveal what I suspected, not after Megan's ghost. I stood, swaying, head pounding, pushing away his reach. Calmer, I realized I wasn't lost. My house was nearby, a path I knew despite the chase.

Breathing deeply, my voice steady, I asked, "Where's Ranger?"

I avoided his gaze, scanning the trees, but his silence drew my eyes. He crouched, shaking the bottle, squinting at the dead bug, his jaw tight. "He ran off when you did," he said finally, standing, his tone gentle but clipped like he was holding back. "We both tried finding you. Lost him." His eyes flicked to the woods, then back, and I caught it again, that flicker of doubt as if he wondered if I'd led Ranger into danger if my chase was more than fear.

His words grated, too much like Dad brushing off my ghost claims. Nonchalant, I shrugged. "Probably at the house," I said, starting back, my legs steady despite the cut stinging my forehead. But inside, Asher's demeanor was shifting. He'd always been my rock, but now I noticed cracks. He was scared for me, yes, but also of me, of what I might do next, and of what I wasn't saying. His Princeton future loomed, pulling him away, but so did his dad's expectations, the pressure to be the next Dr. Finn, to fix people like me. I'd seen him wrestle with it, but now he was wrestling with me too, my silence, my recklessness, the way I ran toward danger. Was he starting to think I was unstable, or worse, that I knew more about the Reaper than I let on? His kindness held, but suspicion was creeping in, a shadow I couldn't unsee.

Asher's voice broke my thoughts, soft but heavy with worry. "Lex, what's going on?" His eyes searched mine, warm but piercing, like he was trying to see through me. "One minute, you're terrified the Reaper's coming for you; the next, you're chasing him like you're not scared at all. That two-inch gash, the dried blood, those bugs, I don't think they were random, and you're brushing it off like it's nothing." He stepped closer, slow and gentle, hands open as if to catch me if I fell. "I said you could talk to me, and I meant it, but you're pulling away. Please... why are you putting yourself in harm's way?"

"Go home," I said harshly, the words cutting sharper than I intended. "I'll make it to the tree line, it's only two hundred feet. I don't need a babysitter." His hurt look twisted my gut, but I spun around, running without looking back. Asher's suspicion felt like a trap, and I couldn't shake the fear that he was hiding something. Either way, I'd let Jacobs know, and if he wasn't part of this, at least he'd be safe. Away from me, that was a magnet for bad things.

At the porch, Dad's stare petting a panting Ranger caught me off guard. He'd watched me approach, silent.

"Dad?"

He just stared, eyes unreadable."What happened to your head?" he asked, calm.

I rolled my eyes, wincing as pain flared. "Tree and I had a disagreement."

He nodded, still staring. No lecture?

Crap, he was mad. Ranger here, Asher gone, I alone, breaking his rules. "Don't be mad."

"I'm not." A grin spread, toothy, jarring.

"Okay," I drawled, wary.

"They got him."

I froze, knowing he meant the Reaper was arrested. But the woods... "Ladybug...", the bugs, Ranger's barks, screamed otherwise. "Are you sure?"

He scratched Ranger's head, nodding. "Positive. I can't spill details, but a lead panned out. The guy in Kansas, apartment plastered with clippings of our murders, handwritten rhymes on the walls. Trust me, he's in custody."

I sat on the couch, numb. "Think it could be one of the men Mom dated?" No relief, no joy. It felt wrong. What happened in the woods? "Dad," I said, spilling it: the voice, bugs, chase, rhyme.

He shrugged, waving it off. "Pssh, kid's prank, probably. Tell me if it happens again."

Brushed off. "Great," I snapped, bitter. "Now I can hit the party solo, no shadow."

"You can." He dug in his pocket, tossing keys. "Need these."

My eyes bulged. "You got me a car?"

"Not quite," he said. "I'm giving you my car," he added, tossing me the keys. Emotions churned his car, that sleek Ford LTD he'd polished like a treasure, now mine? He'd loved that car and swore it was his freedom.

My breaths heaved in shock. Who was he? Trying to break me?

"Whoa, before you flip, check it out," he said, rounding to the front. Reluctantly, I followed, bracing for his familiar black LTD, a mirror of his pride. Instead, forest green gleamed the same make and model, but reborn. "Dad?" He smiled.

"Knew you'd be shocked. I'm getting a new one with Becca, so this one's yours. Repainted, seats reupholstered, a fresh start." I stared at the car, its green paint gleaming like a lie. His casual shrug about moving on felt like he was playing a part. I didn't trust him. "You need some freedom, kiddo." His smile didn't quite reach his eyes.

I opened the door, sliding in, expecting his cologne, but it smelled new and clean. "Thanks, Dad," I said, a tear falling.

I sat in the car, checking it out as Dad went back into the house. I pulled my phone out from my track pants and dialed Jacobs, my hands trembling. "Jacobs, it's Alexis," I said when he picked up, my voice low to avoid Dad's ears. "Something happened in the woods today, a voice, ladybug larvae, a rhyme. Dad says the Reaper's caught, but it doesn't add up. I'm scared he's still out there."

Jacobs's calm "Tell me everything" soothed me, but I kept it brief and promised to meet tomorrow. After hanging up, I flinched as I pressed a rag I found on the seat to my forehead, not caring what it had on it. The nursery rhyme book's weight burned in my backpack, and a chill ran through me. Had I missed a clue, or was someone watching me right now?

40

Black Sheep

He'd spooked Ladybug intensely; her scream in the woods, "Come get me!" was intoxicating. Black Sheep craved her on edge. The ladybug larvae he'd plucked from a garden staged, deliberate, were tied to her nightmare bugs, her research he'd stalked, and the nursery rhyme book she clung to like a lifeline. Yo-yoing her close, then gone, kept her spinning, just as he wanted. But this wasn't just the plan. Her fear sparked something in him, a hunger he couldn't name, deeper than bloodlust.

Leaving the hardware store, paint cans clanking in his arms for Owl's next job, he bumped into a tall, thin woman batting lashes, her smile as fake as Sparrow's promises. Her beauty faded next to Ladybug's raw terror. He remained stone-faced, her perfume a cheap echo of Alexis's sweat-and-fear tang.

"We need to talk," she said, her voice clipped, the syrupy edge fraying.

He scanned the street—no pedestrians, no cars, neither his borrowed junker nor Nathan's F-250. "Why?"

"Can't avoid me forever," she whined, leaning in closer.

Curiosity narrowed his eyes. "Parked out back, fewer eyes." The alley resembled a ghost town, with no cars, making it perfect for secrets.

She glanced around, nodding. "Five minutes." Her sashay down the sidewalk was a performance he ignored, his mind on Ladybug's trembling voice.

Ten minutes later, leaning against his Blazer with arms folded, irritation churned. She was late, playing her games. Finally, she strutted up, hair flowing, supermodel-hot, fake boobs, faker charm. She was young, but venom aged her soul. He felt nothing, only a hollow ache for Alexis's fear.

"Boyfriend won't mind us alone?" he asked as she pressed a hand to his chest, her perfume choking, nothing like Ladybug's primal scent.

She leaned close to his ear. "Want him to catch us? Turn you on?"

He chuckled, masking the churn in his gut. "What do you think?" His mouth crashed into hers, hungry, hands frantic, hers, his until she pressed closer, and he shoved her back, scorched by truth. Wrong. He wanted Ladybug, not this. The realization hit like Mom's last ragged breath, a blade twisting. He wasn't Spider's pawn; he was the one running this murder spree. "You said talk."

Flustered, she exclaimed, "You're a damn light switch!"

"Sparrow, no games. What?" His patience was a fraying thread, and her presence served as a distraction from the scream echoing in his skull.

Inspecting her nails, she huffed. "How's Alexis? Ready to kill her?"

The air vanished, rage igniting. "You stupid…" He raised a fist, aiming for her nose, but froze. A girl propped the store's back door, black trash bag in hand, terror carving her face. Sadie. She'd heard. Not again.

Five strides, and he was on her. Sadie's eyes, wide as moons, locked onto his, trembling but unyielding. The door slammed shut, screeching, as he gripped her throat, lifting and slamming her against the brick. She went limp, gasping, but her gaze remained fearful, yes, but also a spark of defiance that reminded him of Alexis. Spider's warning screamed no more unplanned kills, but the silence was safer. "Sadie, if you wanna live, forget what you heard," he growled, breath hot, her eyes bloodshot. "One whisper, I hunt you, your family, your cousin's included. Clear?" His grip tightened, her face purpling. He eased it just enough for her to get air, watching that spark flicker. "Clear?"

"Yes," she rasped, her voice a thread, but her eyes didn't drop. Not like Megan's had.

He released her, stepping back and ignoring Sparrow's heat behind him. Sadie crumpled, clutching her throat and gulping air, but she didn't cry. Her fingers traced the bruising, black and blue, quickly spreading, and she looked at him not with surrender but with something calculating, as if she were memorizing his face. "Get inside, tell your boss you're sick, go home," he said, his voice flat as he noted the marks. "Scarves, turtlenecks, till it's gone. I'm watching."

Sadie yanked the door open and slipped inside, but her last glance wasn't fear. It was a promise, unspoken and dangerous. She wasn't Megan. She might not break.

"Entertaining," Sparrow said, smirking. "Think she'll keep quiet?"

He spun, nose to hers. "She's not Megan, yeah, she will. You do, too. No more solo meets, bring Owl. Sunday." Storming to his Blazer, tires screeching, rubber burning, leaving Sparrow in the dust. Ladybug's scream, "Come get me!" roared louder, but now Sadie's eyes haunted him, too.

41

Alexis

The back-to-school party loomed, a chance for normalcy with track tryouts, friends, and Dad's green LTD gleaming in the driveway. Normal. The word mocked me as I stood under the hot spray of the shower, water flowing over me like the damp chill of the woods, memories of bugs crawling in my mind. I shook my head, water dripping, grounding me.

Toweling off, I studied the mirror. The cut on my forehead, raw and throbbing, proved I wasn't dreaming. Normal or not, I'd fight for it, live like tomorrow could vanish—Reaper be damned. A knock snapped me out of it.

"Alexis?" Dad's voice muffled through the door.

"Yeah." I cracked it open, steam curling out. He held a garment bag, his smile soft but tired.

"Sadie dropped this for tonight."

I took it, brow furrowing. Sadie, who'd ghosted my texts despite reading them. "Okay." Suspicion prickled that her silence wasn't like her. Dad lingered, but I caught Trevor slinking past, his leer raking over me, cold as the breath in the woods. I squinted, hiding behind the door. Jerk. Dad didn't notice. "Gotta get ready."

"Have fun, don't drink too much," he said, pointing half-jokingly.

"I won't be drinking," I shot back, rolling my eyes. He knew me, didn't he?

In my room, I tossed the bag on the bed. A note fluttered out: *Heard you didn't have a costume. I thought of you. Wear it. Love, S.*. Had Asher talked to Sadie? My pulse spiked, warmth flooding me with his leather-and-flour scent, his steady hands, safety. Then dread crashed in. The woods. Bugs. His voice, soft, teasing, now twisted. Safe? Or a cruel jab?

I unzipped the bag, breath catching a red, form-fitting dress, black spots, spaghetti straps, glittery wings, and antenna headband. A ladybug. Bile surged. I flung it down, sinking to the floor. How could she? A sick joke, me the punchline.

The Kansas perp Dad mentioned felt too tidy and too remote. This costume screamed Reaper or a cruel prank. Trust fractured, sharp as Mom's betrayal

Was Sadie aiding the Rhyme Reaper?

Reaper or not, I'd play dumb and dig for answers and be the bait to draw him to me. I grabbed the costume, my resolve firm. Tonight, I'd be bold, unravel Asher's game, and live like there's no tomorrow.

In the kitchen, whispers drifted to Dad and Becca, heads bent over the Curry Coastal Pilot, murmured about Megan's case, the Hensley's, the Rhyme Reaper, and the Kansas suspect. Coffee steamed as their hands brushed, smiles too intimate. I froze, unseen, watching their love young, real, unlike Mom's string of men. It stung to see Becca slip into Mom's place so easily. I lingered for a moment before sliding onto a barstool.

Dad looked up, glancing at my robe. "Thought you were getting ready."

I faced Becca, throat tight, forcing vulnerability. "I… need help. Mom didn't do girlfriend stuff, sleepovers, or makeup. I act like I've got it together, but…" I trailed off, gauging her. Was she here for Dad or something else?

Becca's hand shot up, her grin too eager. "I'd love to do your hair and makeup." She glanced at Dad, whose smile glowed too brightly. "Mind?"

"Not at all. Thank you," he murmured, leaning to kiss her ear. She giggled softly, beaming with joy.

It wasn't gross, but it twisted something within me. Their ease, her place in his heart, left me feeling like an outsider. Still, I needed her help. "Come on, my bathroom's bigger," Becca said.

I followed, clutching the costume. Inside, she eyed it. "Wow."

"Different from plain Alexis," I said, nerves tingling. "Hot, but…"

"Sexy," she said, reading me too well.

"Yeah, not slutty. Just…"

"Classy."

I laughed, but it felt empty. "Can you make me… not me?"

Her hazel eyes glinted, too, knowing. "One condition. No peeking till I'm done."

For an hour, she tugged and curled my hair, brushes sweeping across my face. We talked about school, her small wedding, and colors. It was sisterly, not motherly, yet I kept her at arm's length. Was she too perfect, too eager to bond? I painted my nails red to match the costume while she styled waves, stepping back with a smirk. "Done."

I turned, my heart pounding. The mirror showed smoky eyes, lashes brushing my brows, bold red lips matching my nails, and hair falling in luscious waves—a stranger, confident and powerful. The cut on my forehead was swollen, but she had skillfully hidden the bruising. "Thank you," I said, hugging her, the warmth caught me off guard.

"Got black heels?" I asked, grinning.

"Sweetie, you have no idea about my shoe stash," she chuckled, but her relaxed demeanor made me feel uneasy. It seemed too reminiscent of Dad, too slick. Was she concealing something, or was I merely paranoid, spotting Reapers in every shadow?

42

Alexis

The LTD vibrated, the Finns' house pulsing with music, while cars, pickups, sedans, no Shelby or F-250, sprawled across the driveway and yard. My heart, a caged bird, fluttered as I pulled down the mirror. "You can do this," I told my smoky eyes, reapplying Becca's lipstick and smacking my lips. Stepping out, my heels bit into the gravel, protesting as I grabbed the door to steady myself. Breathe. Fanning my armpits, I walked, each step defying the old me. "You can do this."

Inside, music drowned out the drum of my heart, providing relief. Without it, the thump would have betrayed my nerves. The front room transformed into a nightclub with rainbow strobes, a disco ball, and bodies grinding against each other. I scanned for Sadie and the Trips but had no luck; faces blurred like spectral warnings haunting my dreams. I pushed through the crowd, my bedroom dance moves being my only practice, praying I wouldn't flop. In a clear spot, I closed my eyes, letting the bass guide me, my head rolling, hands gliding upward, suspended, with music flowing through my limbs. For the first time, I felt free, a new Alexis, untethered from "Ladybug."

A spark trailed from my wrist to my neck, familiar Asher. "Lex? Never thought I'd see you here, wearing that," his breath wrapped around my ear, melodic, laced with surprise. "Stunning. Dancing like no one's watching, alone. But oh, everyone's watching." Asher carried an effortless charm; his Jack Sparrow costume amplified his roguish allure.

What? My eyes snapped open, every gaze locked on me, staring. I grimaced. Great, hi, classmates. I stilled, facing Asher, his smile perfect, eyes hungry, better than Depp. His hands, soft and firm on my bare shoulders, burned hot and cold, but trust faltered. The costume, the note, someone was pulling strings, and Asher's presence felt too convenient.

"Did you send it?" I demanded, voice sharp, stepping back. "The costume, what's your game?"

His brow furrowed, confusion etching his face as his usual composure cracked. "Lex, I didn't send you anything. I'm here for the party, same as you." His voice carried a hint of hurt, as if my accusation stung more than he expected. Asher wasn't used to being questioned; people gravitated toward him and trusted him. My distrust continued to shake him, and if he was innocent, my treatment of him was unfair.

His denial struck like a slap. I wanted to believe him, those earnest eyes, that cracked voice, but my mother's warning echoed louder. Fear clawed at my desire. The old Alexis would've crumbled and apologized, but I was done being that girl. "I can't trust you or anyone," I whispered, shoving his chest.

He stumbled, calling, "Lex!" as I bolted, music swallowing his voice, the Reaper's rhymes haunting my steps. I was no longer running from fear but toward truth, no matter how much it hurt.

The backyard glowed with fairy lights, magical, yet nothing felt right tonight. Groups laughed, carefree before the grind of homework, while I sat shivering on the porch step, sweat chilling me, arms wrapped tight. Sadie was my best friend, my anchor. I needed to talk to her to get answers about the costume and the note. She'd been my confidante, but with the Reaper's rhymes in my dreams and the arrival of the costume, could she be involved? Was she working with Asher? The thought twisted my gut, but I had to know.

Determined, I slipped upstairs, dodging partygoers, and found her room with the door ajar. The space was cluttered with posters, clothes, and a desk piled with papers. My phone's flashlight revealed printed sheets. Nursery rhymes, with one standing out: "Ladybug, Ladybug, Fly Away." My twisted nickname. My breath caught in my throat. Sadie's room, her papers betrayal loomed. Heart pounding, I snapped pictures with my phone, my hands steady, leaving the papers untouched. I'd confront her and demand the truth, but not tonight. I needed more.

Descending the stairs, I nearly collided with Asher, his pirate costume towering over me. "Lex, please, talk to me," he urged, his eyes pleading; he was no longer the untouchable charmer but a boy desperate to be believed. "Whatever's going on, I told you I wanted to help." His insistence felt genuine, yet it unnerved him as well. Asher, who thrived on helping, was losing it. My rejection forced him to confront his own vulnerability and to question why someone he cared about viewed him as a threat.

"I can't trust anyone," I retorted, stepping around him with a hardened determination. I was set on uncovering the truth, beginning with Sadie. If she and Asher were plotting something, I would bring it to light. The Alexis who once avoided conflict was no more; I was reshaping myself in this trial of uncertainty.

Trevor appeared, his sharp features twisted in a scowl, blocking my path. "Where are you running?" he growled, stepping closer and more aggressively. Trevor was a volatile presence at home, and his hostility felt personal, as if my presence threatened some unspoken plan.

Asher stepped in, grabbing Trevor's shoulder. "Back off, Trevor!" he snapped, his voice firm, his protective streak surfacing. This wasn't just about keeping the peace; Asher was staking a claim, demonstrating that he wasn't the enemy. Trevor glared but eased back, shaking off Asher's hand, his retreat a reluctant acknowledgment of Asher's influence.

I seized the moment, darting past them to my car, gravel stinging my torn nylons. Sliding into the driver's seat, my hands shaking, I turned the key. Through my windshield, as I backed away, Trevor's silhouette loomed in the moonlight, his cold stare piercing the glass, with Asher beside him, watching with concern. My tires screeched as I peeled away, their figures shrinking in my rearview mirror.

I had to rely on myself now. The costume, the nursery rhymes, Sadie's possible betrayal, Trevor's aggression, every clue was a thread in a tangled web. I would confront Sadie, unravel her ties to Asher, and keep digging alone until the truth was revealed. And if she didn't provide me with any information, I would have to pass the pictures to Detective Jacobs for him to investigate.

43

Alexis

A large, calloused hand covered my mouth, silencing my screams. The fuel oil smell on the man's hands made my stomach wrench, and black spots invaded my vision. There were men all around me, gripping and slicing their fingernails into the flesh of my legs and arms while I thrashed and kicked at them, while they dragged me along. One whispered, "Ladybug, ladybug, fly away home..." his voice was a chilling echo of the text, tying their cruelty to Mom's sins. The smiling crescent moon and the billion radiant stars reflected off the ocean's surface but cast the men's faces into shadows. Who were they?

Everything around me was eerily silent. I couldn't hear the water lapping at the shore. Even my breaths were soundless.

Disoriented, I couldn't remember how I'd gotten there.

Before I knew what was happening, my feet were plunged into the icy water, causing me to suck in a breath of air, but no oxygen came. Only then could I taste the oil from the man's hand, and I gagged as bile burned its way up my throat.

The strength of all the men pushed me deeper, inch by inch. The water exploded against my hot skin like tiny icicles. Twisting and turning under their vise grip was useless because the harder I fought, the tighter they contracted.

The rough hand shifted to my forehead, almost as if he were checking my temperature. His face remained shrouded in shadow, but I saw the gleam of his teeth when he smiled before pushing my head under the water. I had no time to suck in a breath as the water engulfed me, stinging my nostrils and filling my lungs. My body was exhausted, and I knew it was a lost cause, yet I still battled against the ocean water, which pulled at my legs as it dragged me deeper and deeper. The murky water washed away the men's shadows and gave me clarity. Six heinous men, my mother's boyfriends who'd abused me, stood side by side while their trench coats floated on the ocean's surface, watching me sink into the depths of the sea. Like a ladybug's shell, a faint red mark burned on my wrist where one had gripped me, a riddle from the Rhyme Reaper's game.

I jerked awake, gasping for air in short, spastic breaths. I ran my hands over my bed, praying my sheets weren't soaked. I sighed; they were dry, just a nightmare. Fully awake and entangled in my sheets, I still felt as if I was drowning, but I didn't want to free myself from their embrace. My wrist itched, and I froze, spotting a faint red mark, like the one in the dream, whispering of eyes watching me. The mark pulsed a taunt that I'd end up like Mom, broken into pieces if I didn't solve the killer's riddle. Did I do that to myself?

First day of school. Great!

Everything was so messed up, including my puffy eyes from crying on and off since Saturday night. Awesome, lucky me. I looked great at the party and made a good first impression, but then I had to go and ruin it with all the drama surrounding Asher and Trevor. And what else? I had to top it off by looking all swollen and blotchy on my first day. Stupid me. The nightmares were constant and still a mystery. I couldn't figure out if they held hidden meanings or if I just had them due to all the stress I'd been under. Deep down, I knew they signified something, but I just couldn't find the courage or strength to decipher them. The whispered rhyme gnawed at me, riddles I had to solve or join Mom in pieces.

Why was I struggling to see things clearly?

Because it was all just too damn confusing, that's why Asher made me feel things I'd never felt before. Could I genuinely believe that he would hurt me after giving me something so soft and wanting? That he was the killer, despite having so many opportunities to take my life, yet choosing not to? I covered my face with my pillow and screamed. The scream didn't erase the rhyme or the fear that I was wrong about him, about everyone. No matter how many times I yelled and how much I screamed into that stupid pillow, it never changed anything.

So, I did the only thing I could to distract myself from my drama and prepare for school.

Showing up to school in baggy jeans and an 'If You're Single So Am I' t-shirt was the opposite of sexy; it was more like: "Boo-Yah, I'm not going to let any of you get the best of me." However, I hoped they had better things to focus on and would worry about their own lives. But when I walked into the building, hope was left outside. With every turned head and widened eye, their whispers of disgust assaulted me. Yep, they had no lives of their own. I adjusted my backpack on my shoulders, feeling even more awkward when I finally reached my locker. They had started to gather around me, which I found rather odd.

Their stares on my back made me shudder as they crawled up my spine. What was up with these people? Had they never seen a new student? After struggling with the combination on the lock, I finally got it open and placed my unwanted folders inside but kept the one thing that linked me to the serial killer – my tattered nursery rhyme book. I ran my fingertips across the various characters on the cover and stared at it before shoving it back into my bag. A ladybug sticker, peeling at the edges, clung to the cover, its red shell glinting, a taunt from the killer's riddle. The sticker's edges curled like the note from the bonfire, whispering secrets I couldn't yet read.

Taking a deep breath, I faced the whispering crowd and their judging looks. None of them were familiar to me, yet their eyes held unspoken secrets.

Impatience and annoyance coursed through my veins like anxiety, but just as I was about to speak, someone interrupted me. "Considering what happened this weekend, you don't look shaken up." It was Trevor, with Zane right by his side. I wanted to smack the smug looks off their faces.

How dare they? And seriously, were they blind? I looked like shit.

With narrowed, hateful eyes, I stared down at Trevor, hoping he would spontaneously combust. "Whatever happened between me and Asher is my business, not yours. So why don't you all get a life!" Yeah, I wasn't going for popularity.

The whirlwind of gasps drew me in, and I focused on them completely as I was engulfed in a flurry of loud murmurs. "Asher was dating her?" "She doesn't know?" "Who doesn't watch the news?" and lastly, the one that left me frozen and expelled the air from my lungs was: "You'd think since her dad's a detective, he would've told her that her mom's murderer is still out there."

Those words felt like an invisible force. My back hit the locker, supporting me as the only thing preventing me from crumpling to the floor and curling up into a ball. I was sure my face had turned ghastly white, along with my knuckles, which hung tightly at my sides. Beads of sweat formed at the edge of my forehead. I wanted to wipe them away, but doing so would give the onlookers a sense of satisfaction. They would win, and I was sick and tired of losing.

With the tennis ball-sized knot in my stomach and perspiration streaming down me like I'm a roasting pig, I lifted my chin to the crowd. I would fall apart at home, but not in front of my so-called peers. Fighting back tears and hoping they wouldn't see my lip tremble, I lied, "Of course, I know everything that happened." With that, I clung to my backpack as I elbowed and pushed my way through the crowd.

My throat burned as I passed the scattering, blurry crowd. I had to hold it together. No one was supposed to see that I was dying a slow, torturous death. I would never escape my nightmares because my life was one. Was there anyone – the police, the FBI, my dad – ever going to stop this killer and end my agony? With a shaky hand, I pushed open the double doors. I wanted to escape or wake up, but before I could cross the threshold, someone yanked on my bag and pulled me back inside.

"Where do you think you're going, huh?" Zane hissed into my ear when he wrapped his arms around me and held me against him by my hips. He rubbed, then dug his strong fingers into my jeans so hard there'd be bruises tomorrow. "Asher's gone, so it's time you see who you really want. You should wear that costume again." His voice dropped, a venomous edge like the men in my nightmare. He rubbed his nose down my jaw and then licked the pulse of my neck. His hot, minty breath sent chills down my wet skin, making me shudder and curse myself for wearing that red atrocity. "Like that, don't you? I can make you shake in ways he never could." He bit my ear lobe and pushed his hips into my backside, making me whimper.

I closed my eyes and pictured how the Trips would save me. Asher's face was etched in my mind. I remembered how his ocean-blue eyes lit up with happiness and compassion as he told me about the scar across the bridge of his nose, which he got playing pee-wee football. I wished my green eyes could convey how much I needed him, but he was merely a figment of my imagination. Please help me! No, I needed to help myself now. I couldn't rely on others. Just when I was about to go postal on his ass, someone intervened.

"Zane, what the hell are you doing?"

I never imagined it would be the stunning Kaitlyn to rescue me, but I felt relieved nonetheless as Zane quickly released my hips and stepped back.

I turned around and pressed my back against the door. As my chest heaved, I hoped to leave unnoticed when Kaitlyn pointed her hot pink fingernail at me. "You, don't go anywhere." She turned and got right in Zane's face.

However, I tuned out everything she was saying to him as I glanced over Kaitlyn's shoulder and saw Sadie, dressed in skinny jeans and a snug black tee, walking toward me. Relief eased my throbbing head, but then she narrowed her eyes and walked past me, flicking her black hair over her shoulder.

I shouldn't have been surprised to think she'd still be my friend after how I treated Asher, but I was. At least, I expected her to ask for my side of the story. One way or another, I was going to get the answers I needed from Sadie.

Kaitlyn and Zane's conversation escalated violently when I redirected my attention to them. Zane's face remained a picture of calm as Kaitlyn pounded her tiny fist repeatedly into his broad chest. The only indication that he wasn't a statue was the swing of his surfer blond hair as his body absorbed her blows like a punching bag.

Grateful for Kaitlyn's dramatics, I slipped outside and let the door close with a soft click. The salty air calmed me as I took a few deep, shuddering breaths and walked toward my car. With each step, I could still feel Zane's grip on my aching hips. It was another experience I would carry with me for the rest of my life and a reminder that I couldn't trust anyone, including myself.

I gripped the handle of my car and rested my forehead against the damp, cold window as my tears pooled at my feet. So much has happened. Can a person endure only so much before losing their mind?

I wasn't sure how much longer I could keep fighting. I needed answers, but despair had started to feel like part of my DNA, and I couldn't shake the sense that my life would end abruptly soon. Without a doubt, he was coming for me, part of me wanted him to end it, end me.

My hands began to shake as the nightmares I had about my mother resurfaced in my memory. Her chalky, once full of life, eyes bore into me. That would be me, dead, because I couldn't figure out this damn riddle. Riddle? Wait a minute. I stood up and gazed at my reflection in the window. Nursery rhymes were like riddles, right? What if my nightmares or the things I saw were the riddles? The answers were there, and I was sure of them. If I could figure things out, I might not have to face death.

Not today. I smiled and slipped my bag off my shoulders, determined to revisit the book, compelling me to unravel the killer's game before he claimed me. The book's weight in my bag felt like a lifeline; its rhymes offered my only shield against the encroaching shadows.

"I wouldn't let them get to you," a voice said.

"Shit!" I jumped and dropped my backpack into the puddle; brown water splashed onto my jeans. I groaned and rolled my eyes when I saw Nathan sticking his head out of his truck window. I hadn't realized he was parked several spaces away from me. His strong, slender fingers brought a cigarette to his mouth, and I watched his lips wrap around the end. Smoke streamed from his nose and mouth, never diverting his glazed, brown eyes from me. I narrowed my eyes at his cigarette again. Of course, I recognized the sweet, woodsy smell on him, but I didn't want to believe he would do something like this. His eyes held a flicker of something: Guilt or hunger? That echoed the nightmare's shadows. "Nathan, what are you doing?"

He looked away and took another drag from his joint. Smoke billowed around him, and I noticed a large bruise on the underside of his jaw.

I stepped in his direction, the smell of marijuana growing stronger as I approached. "What happened?" I reached up and lightly touched his bruise with my fingertips. He flinched so hard that he hit the top of his head on the truck door. I staggered back when his face contorted in pain.

"Dammit!" His eyes were wide and vicious while he rubbed his head. "Don't. Touch. Me. Again."

Not wanting to gaze into his cold eyes, I concentrated on how frequently his jaw ticked and clenched.

What was his problem? Something had happened to him, and by the size of the bruise, I knew it wasn't good. Plus, seeing Nathan smoke weed was quite unusual for me. No doubt, his anger was fueled by the high. The school bell rang, and with one last scrutinizing look at Nathan, I spun on my heel and headed back to the school. His truck screeched and peeled out of the parking lot as I reached the stairs.

44

Alexis

The grass felt cool against my legs as they lay in a wide 'V' on the football field. After the day I endured, it felt great to stretch.

My run-in with Nathan left me all out of sorts. I wished that the invisible bubble I was in would make me disappear. Half of what the teachers lectured on breached my guarded area. I tuned out everyone's voices, lived in my head, and, every chance I got, I flipped through the nursery rhyme book. Judging eyes followed me, and I could tell they were laughing at me only by how their bodies shook with their tight eyes and their flapping jaws.

Asher sent me a series of text messages. I saw the first one, *"Please, we need to talk,"* but I left the rest unread. Despite my longing for him, I lacked the courage to reach out, believing it was better to keep things unchanged. He left for college yesterday, which gave me some relief, knowing he wouldn't come searching for me. Yet, his messages felt like a lifeline, suggesting he might hold the key to the mystery I was struggling to understand.

The field had become busier, and many students were here preparing for tomorrow's tryouts. I stood with my legs shoulder-width apart, bending down to stretch.

45

Black Sheep

The overgrown trees cloaked him in shadow, creating a cocoon of bark and breath as he stared at her, his Ladybug. His siren. Every movement she made was stitched into his memory: the graceful lines of her legs, the soft glint of sweat on her collarbone, and the way her dark ponytail swung like a metronome to his escalating pulse.

She stood at the edge of the track, her breath visible in the crisp afternoon air. To him, she was art, flawed, feral, unknowable. A creature shaped by pain and tempered by survival.

His gloved hand twitched against his thigh, aching to reach through the veil of branches and touch the warmth she carried unknowingly. But he didn't move. Not yet. Watching was enough for now.

A bead of sweat traced down her neck, disappearing beneath her collar. He imagined its path, feeling it in phantom trails across his own skin. The fear pulsing beneath her calm, the instinct telling her she was being watched, was what intoxicated him the most.

Fear was the purest truth.

She turned slightly toward the trees, her shoulders tightening. She knew. Not who. But that. She felt him. That awareness spurred his breath and made the world shrink to the space between her heartbeat and his.

Silently, he reached into his coat pocket and withdrew the small, worn blade. Its edge kissed the bark with familiarity as he carved a small ladybug, simple, crude, sacred, into the base of the tree that concealed him. Each mark represented a moment she had unknowingly bled into his story.

"Soon," he promised. Soon, she would understand why the rhyme had chosen her, why it whispered her name between its lines. "Ladybug, Ladybug, fly away home…"

He didn't blink as she turned back to the field, unaware of how close she was to her fate. How close he was to hers.

But this wasn't the moment. The verse wasn't finished. The story had rules, and so did he.

For now, he would remain the shadow. The chill behind her neck. The breath she swore she imagined.

The final stanza would arrive. And when it did, she would finally understand what it meant to be the last sheep in the rhyme.

46

Alexis

Fear tightened its hideous grip around my heart. The hairs on the back of my neck stood up straight. I spun around, searching for the eyes I knew were watching me. Everyone in my line of sight was chatting with one another or chugging down water. Go figure, I'd been glared at all day, but not when I could be in imminent danger. The chances of being grabbed and taken into the trees without anyone noticing were alarmingly high.

Trees.

With my heart pounding in my throat, I took a few steps closer to the wooded area, only to stop when my head began to spin. The trees blurred in and out of focus. Branches reached toward me like a thousand fingers beckoning me to enter. I staggered back, blinking hard, when I saw my mother standing among the trees. She was a beautiful, dark-haired angel in a red dress, nothing like her corpse. Another hallucination brought on by the fear within me. I stepped toward her, but she raised her hand in a silent warning and smiled softly. This was real, well, at least to me.

My trembling hand covered my mouth as I sobbed. "Mom, I miss you," I confessed, words I never thought I'd speak, but they were true, nonetheless.

Her smile was sad, one I had never seen when she was alive. How could it be possible for her to be on God's side and not

Satan's, given what she allowed to happen to me? Could angels really be wicked?

Why couldn't she have been the mother I needed—a mother who would protect her child from the evils of the world? The weight of the gargoyle pressed heavier against my chest. I always needed my mother's love, and I always had.

"Please, just tell me what I should do," I cried. "Is he coming for me? Am I going to die?" I fell to my knees and clutched my chest. "Please, Mom." I needed her to answer, but I know I sounded crazy.

She turned and ascended into the light as if it were a doorway to another dimension. The luminous glow contracted until it was the size of a golf ball. It fluttered and spiraled toward the heavens like a firefly, then exploded into a million tiny teardrops against the blue sky.

This was unhealthy. I wasn't healthy.

Overwhelmed and nauseous, I collapsed onto my hands and knees on the grass by the track and vomited until only bile remained. Exhaustion enveloped me; every muscle felt as if it had been ripped from my bones. If I could, I'd curl up into a ball right here and never move, but I was too close to the trees, which brought me more fear. He was out there. The forest held the killer's eyes and watched me.

This was all in my mind, my own manifestations coming to the forefront.

"Alexis?" Coach Chloe Adams asked, touching my shoulder. "Are you all right?"

I nodded and wiped my mouth with the back of my hand. "I'm okay." I cleared my throat. "I think I just pushed myself too hard." Then, I stood and faced Coach Adams. It was time to think clearly and decide whom to trust.

After showering and convincing Coach Adams I was okay, I sat in my locked car as it idled. I told myself I would feel safer in the school parking lot than at home, where there would be no one around. The idea of being alone made me uneasy. I needed to be somewhere public.

Not far from school, I sat in a nook at Gold Beach Books and Biscuit Coffeehouse, trying to soothe the pain in my stomach and the rancid taste of vomit with a 'triple chocolate coronary' muffin and a tall glass of ice-cold milk. There weren't many people here, but I felt safe enough.

With help from the lovely old lady who owned the store, I found a copy of *The Secret Meanings Behind Nursery Rhymes*. Two hours passed, and the meanings of the rhymes began to make sense when a shadow fell across my book. I turned in my seat and held my breath. Sadie stood like a statue, her hands on her hips and her lips twisted into a pissed-off snarl. I raised my eyebrows. Our gazes locked for so long that I almost looked at my wrist for an imaginary watch while waiting for her to explain. She huffed, rolled her eyes, dropped her books onto the table, and sat down.

Her icy blue eyes studied me for a moment before she spoke, "Alexis, what's wrong with you? Asher's a mess, calling me nonstop to get you to talk. You're breaking his heart." Her voice was louder than it should have been in a bookstore.

I sighed and prayed that I wasn't making a mistake by trusting her, and then I told her everything that had happened with Asher. A small part of me hoped she would be able to shed some light. Her eyes widened, a flicker of fear or guilt crossing her face before she looked away.

"You really think Asher and I are helping the Rhyme Reaper? That's insane, Alexis!" She raised her voice loud enough for people to stare.

I cringed and shielded my eyes from onlookers. "Sadie, keep it down! We're in public," I hissed through clenched teeth.

"I don't care! You're being so damn stubborn!" she lowered her tone, then slumped into her chair.

I leaned forward, my voice barely above a whisper. "Sadie, why did you give me the ladybug costume? And what about the papers in your room? The ones about the nursery rhymes." My heart pounded as I watched her closely.

Sadie's face paled as she fidgeted with her sleeve. "I… I just wanted to help, okay? I knew giving you the costume wasn't a good idea. And I saw some stuff and thought I could figure it out, but I couldn't." She grabbed the crumpled ladybug papers from her school bag. "Look at this, Alexis, it's got to mean something." Her hands shook slightly as she handed me the papers, her eyes darting to the door like she expected someone to barge in. She couldn't meet my eyes. I knew she was lying, and it twisted my stomach.

I threw my hands up in the air. "These don't explain anything. Please explain to me why you gave the costume to me, Sadie. Tell me!"

"Asher didn't know. It was all me," she said matter-of-factly, folding her arms and looking more like a five-year-old than a senior in high school.

Ugh! I believed her, but she only made me more confused. "I don't know who to trust anymore."

"You're blind, Alexis. Open your eyes before it's too late!" she yelled again, grabbed her bag, and stomped out of the coffeehouse.

No doubt about it. She knew something.

I had no intention of following her, but as darkness began to settle, I gathered my resolve and drove home, accepting that I would be by myself.

47

Alexis

The tune *"This is the song that never ends"* became *"This is the day that never ends"* when I pulled into my driveway and saw Nathan dangling his legs from the tailgate of his truck. I closed my eyes, pounded my head against the headrest, and took a deep breath. No matter how much time I gave myself to work up enough courage to face Nathan, it wouldn't be enough, so I yanked the keys out of the ignition and slammed the car door shut. I had no plans to cower before him. He needed to understand that his outburst freaked the shit out of me and was uncalled for.

He jumped off the tailgate when I approached him and walked toward me. I decided I couldn't wait any longer. "You know I've had the worst first day ever. It's like the universe declared a holiday for my misery. Mail carriers will thank me for the day off. So, whatever you're gonna say, save it." I didn't finish my rant when Nathan stepped closer, his face tense, hands shoved deep in his pockets.

"Alexis, I need to talk to you," Nathan said, his voice low and rough, cutting me off. His eyes darted around as if he were afraid someone might overhear. "It's about my dad. He's been acting... weird for weeks. I had a huge fight with him tonight, and I just needed to tell someone."

I frowned, my frustration shifting to unease. Come to think of it, I hadn't seen or heard anything about Ronny since my house fire. My eyes looked at the dark bruise on Nathan's cheek, half-hidden in the dim light. "Is that how you got that bruise? Did Ronny hit you?" My voice was sharp, my mind scrambling to connect the dots.

Nathan's gaze fell, his hand brushing the bruise as he nodded slowly. "Yeah… he did. We were screaming at each other, and he just lost it. Decked me across the face." His voice cracked, heavy with shame and anger, and he kicked at the gravel, his hands clenched. "He's been off, Alexis, secretive, locking himself in his office, taking calls at all hours. Tonight, he tore into me, called me a failure, and said I'm wasting my life. I've never seen him this bad. I don't know what's wrong with him, and he won't tell me anything."

"I'm so sorry, Nathan." I stepped forward and took his hand. He tensed at first, then relaxed.

He hesitated, his jaw tense, then pulled a crumpled piece of paper from his pocket. "That's why I'm here. I found this in his office. It's a note… from your mom, Alexis. To my dad." His voice was smooth, unsure, as he handed it to me, his fingers trembling slightly, his eyes searching my face.

I unfolded the paper, my pulse racing. The handwriting was unmistakably my mom's, with its careful loops, Nicole's. I read it out loud, "Ronny, you're my safe place in this chaos. I don't know what I'd do without you. Yours, always N." A love note. My stomach churned as a mix of betrayal and dread hit me like a punch. "What the hell is this?" I whispered, my voice barely audible.

"I don't know," Nathan said, his tone urgent. "But it's not just this note. Dad's been hiding stuff, files, other notes, things he never used to care about. He's even kept things from the FBI, Alexis. I saw him shredding papers one night when he thought I wasn't home. I think he knows something, maybe about your mom or whatever. I'm not saying he's in on it, but he's not acting right." He swallowed hard, his eyes stormy with suspicion. "If he's digging into something, he's not telling me."

I gripped the note, my mind spiraling. "Why not take this to Jacobs? If Ronny's hiding stuff from the FBI, they need to know." My voice shook, the note's weight making my hands tremble. "This could be big, Nathan."

He flinched, his face tightening. "I can't do that, Alexis. Things are rough with my dad, but Ronny's still my dad. He's the only one I've got left in my life." His voice broke, raw and heavy, and he looked away, his hands clenching. "I'm not ready to turn him over to the FBI without knowing what's going on. Not yet."

I stepped back, my thoughts a tangled mess. "So you're just handing this to me? Nathan, I'm already dealing with a lot. Now this?" I shook my head, the weight of it all crushing me. "I have to tell Jacobs about this note. You're putting me in a bad spot."

"I know, and I'm sorry," he said, his voice raw. "But I found that note yesterday, and I've been freaking out. I didn't want to believe my dad was hiding something, but after tonight's fight, I couldn't ignore it. He's not himself. I'm scared he's in over his head." He ran a hand through his hair, looking lost. "I'm telling you because I trust you. I don't know who else to go to. I thought you'd want to know."

I exhaled, my breath shaky. "I do. But this… this changes everything, Nathan. If Ronny's keeping secrets from the FBI, and my mom was involved with him, I can't just sit on this." I folded the note and shoved it into my pocket, my mind racing with questions about my mom, Ronny, and Sadie's papers. "We need to figure out what he's hiding, but you can't hold back stuff like this again. If you find anything else, you tell me, okay?"

He nodded, his expression heavy. "I won't. I promise." He hesitated, then stepped back toward his truck. "I gotta go. I just… I needed you to know." The slam of his door startled me; then he peeled out of the driveway, his tires screeching, leaving marks like he did in the school parking lot.

I stood there, frozen against my car, the note burning a hole in my pocket. What was that? My mom and Ronny? Ronny, Dad's old partner, hiding notes from the FBI? Could Ronny be my dad? And now Sadie's nursery rhyme papers, too? I had to tell Jacobs, but the thought made my chest tight.

I blinked and took a deep breath, trying to calm my staccato heartbeat, and then I started to chant, "I will not turn into my mother; I will not turn into my mother!" Those words felt like a knife twisting in my gut, promising I'd end up like her if I didn't solve it.

48

Alexis

The fluorescent lights in Jacobs's makeshift office buzz like a hornet's nest, drilling into my skull. I slouched in a creaky chair, twisting my backpack strap until my knuckles whitened. The love note from Mom to Ronny is a hot coal in my pocket. Sadie's nursery rhyme papers claw at my brain, her lies from that coffeehouse fight replaying like a bad song. She's been ghosting my texts, and I'm done waiting for her to crack. Jacobs is the only one I trust, the only one who doesn't look at me like I'm some broken kid chasing shadows. I needed him to see what I saw, to make sense of this Rhyme Reaper mess before it swallowed me whole.

Jacobs leaned back, his face marked by hard lines and keen detective eyes, scanning a file as if it held the answers. "Spill it, Alexis. What's so urgent?"

My phone buzzed, probably Asher again. I've got a dozen of his texts sitting unread in my inbox, and I'm not bothering to check them. Sadie's silence hurt worse than my messages going unanswered. I swallowed hard, my throat raw. "It's Sadie. She's got these… printouts in her room. Nursery rhymes, like the ones the Rhyme Reaper's obsessed with." My voice cracked, and I hated how weak it sounded. "She lied to my face, said she was helping, but she couldn't even look at me. Now she's ignoring my texts, giving me death glares at school. I'm freaking out she's in deep with something bad."

Jacobs's eyes narrowed as he scribbled on a notepad, the pen scratching like nails on a chalkboard. "Nursery rhymes? Are you sure? Did she give you an explanation on why she's got them?"

"Nope." I shook my head, my gut twisting. "She flipped out at the coffeehouse and stormed off. That was a couple of days ago. Now it's just… silence. She's dodging me, and I know she's hiding something." Sadie's panicked face flashed in my mind, and her shaky voice served as a warning I should've heeded.

He nodded, still writing. "We'll look into it. If she's got something on this case, we need to know. What else you got?"

My fingers grazed the note, and my heart stuttered. This part's going to gut me, even with Jacobs. "Yeah. There's more. Nathan Ronny's kid gave me this." I pulled out the crumpled paper, its edges worn from my obsessive folding, and slid it across the desk. "It's from my mom to Ronny. A love note. Nathan found it in Ronny's office. Said Ronny's been weird, hiding stuff, shredding papers. He's keeping secrets from you, from the FBI."

Jacobs unfolded the note, his jaw tightening as he read Mom's loopy scrawl: *Ronny, you're my safe place in this chaos. I don't know what I'd do without you. Yours, always N.* He set it down, his eyes hard. "This is big, Alexis. Ronny was Luke's partner. If he's holding out on us…again." He rubbed his temple, looking older than he should. "Nathan thinks his dad's mixed up in this?"

"Not exactly. He's just… spooked. Ronny punched him in a fight and called him a failure. Nathan's a mess, but he won't rat him out. Ronny's all he has. I didn't know who else to tell." My chest ached as if I were betraying Nathan, but Jacobs was my only lifeline.

He leaned forward, his voice low. "You did right coming to me. We'll check on Ronny, keep it quiet. Sadie's papers, too. We are looking into those rhymes; they are connecting them to your mom, but I can't go into detail right now. But Alexis, you gotta stop playing the lone wolf. The Rhyme Reaper's no joke, and you're not bulletproof."

"I'm not playing," I snapped, my blood hot. I caught myself lowering my voice. "I'm trying to figure out what happened to Mom, what Sadie's hiding, what Ronny's up to. No one else gives a damn." Not Luke, not Becca, and sure as hell not Trevor, who'd love to see me fall apart. Jacobs is the only one who doesn't make me feel like I'm losing it.

He held my gaze, his eyes softened just slightly. "I hear you. But you bring this to me, no one else. Promise."

I nodded, my throat tight. "Yeah. But you'll tell me if you get anything on Sadie, right?"

"I'll try," he said, which felt like a cop-out, but it was all I was getting. He stood, and I was dismissed. "Go to school, Alexis. Stay out of trouble."

I got home, and Ranger was at the door, his shaggy black fur a warm blur as he shoved his wet nose into my hand. "Hey, boy," I muttered, scratching his ears. His tail thumped like a heartbeat, the only thing that kept me from unraveling. I tossed my backpack by the couch, where Dad was sprawled with a beer in hand, staring at a TV blaring some robbery story. He wasn't watching, just... existing, bearing the weight of raising me even though I wasn't his kid.

"Late again," he grumbled, not looking up. His voice is rough, like gravel, worn down by years of being a detective.

"Was at the station," I said, keeping it short. I wasn't in the mood for a fight, especially with Trevor's smug ass somewhere in this house. "Talked to Jacobs."

Dad's eyes locked onto me, fierce. "About what? Alexis, I told you to drop this Rhyme Reaper shit. You're going to get hurt."

I stiffened, and Ranger nudged my leg, sensing my anger. "You're not doing anything. Someone's got to find out what happened to Mom." The words slice through the air, and his expression darkens.

"Watch your mouth," he snapped, slamming the beer down. "You don't know what you're stirring up. Ronny's already losing it, and you're digging into his life?"

My pulse spikes. "You talked to Ronny?" The love note burned in my mind. Secrets.

Dad rubbed his face, exhausted. "Yeah, last week. He called, sounding paranoid as hell. Wouldn't say why. Just… back off, Alexis." His eyes met mine, filled with fear, the kind that's been eating me alive since the fire.

Becca walked in from the kitchen, dish towel in hand, her blonde hair messily tied back. She attempted a smile, but it wobbled as if she were walking on eggshells. "Dinner's almost done, Alexis. You okay? You look… rough."

"I'm fine." I crouched down to pet Ranger, avoiding her gaze. Becca has been pushing to become family since her and Dad's engagement, but I wasn't ready to let her in, not when Mom's past was bleeding into mine.

Trevor slinked in, hoodie half-zipped, earbuds swinging. He glared at me, all venom and sharp edges. "What'd you do now, Alexis? Piss off the cops again?" His sneer made my skin crawl as if I were some screw-up he had to deal with.

"Shove off, Trevor." My hands formed fists. Ranger growled, low and steady, and I stroked his fur to keep us both calm.

"Enough!" Dad yelled, his voice cutting through the tension. "Trevor, help Becca. Alexis, please go to your room," he added.

I didn't fight it; I grabbed my backpack as Ranger's paws thumped behind me. In my room, I slammed the door and collapsed on the bed, with Ranger curled up next to me, his warmth the only thing keeping me from falling apart. I pulled out my phone, scrolling past Asher's texts and Sadie's infuriating silence. No replies, just quiet. Mom's note, Sadie's lies, Ronny's secrets, I was suffocating.

Three weeks later, Ventura High's halls felt like a pressure cooker, each whisper and stare like a blade. I had spent three weeks avoiding Sadie, who glared at me in the cafeteria but wouldn't answer my texts. Trevor made it worse; his jabs at home sliced deeper every day. Yesterday, he leaned over the breakfast table, smirking, "Sadie's probably done with your crazy, you know." I almost smashed my mug, but Ranger's head in my lap kept me grounded, his soft nudge pulling me back.

I ignored Nathan's texts as well; his warnings about Ronny replayed in my mind. Jacobs hasn't called, and the Rhyme Reaper is out there, his shadow creeping closer. My nursery rhyme papers were stashed under my mattress, too dangerous for me to look at, knowing the possibility of spiraling was clear. I had to stop digging.

I was late for chemistry. My sneakers squeaked on the linoleum as voices drifted from the teachers' lounge. The door was cracked, and Mrs. Hargrove's voice reached me, low and heavy. "You remember Nicole Roberts? Alexis's mom? God, it's been forever, but seeing Alexis… It's like her ghost is here."

I froze as my backpack slipped off. I moved closer, holding my breath.

"She was a mess," Mr. Delaney said, his voice thick with pity. "Chasing boys, starting fights, breaking hearts left and right. I felt bad for her, but she burned every bridge. No friends by graduation."

Mrs. Hargrove sighed. "No wonder Alexis is so alone. That fire, her mom's death… now this thing with Sadie. It's like history is on repeat."

My throat felt like it was on fire, and I backed away before they spotted me. Nicole was a walking disaster, with no one to call her own. Was she running from something or someone herself? My backpack felt like lead; Sadie's secrets and Mom's past weighed me down. I'm not her, but every step felt like I was slipping into her skin.

49

Black Sheep

The Rhyme Reaper crouched in the frost-laced pines, his white suit a specter against the brittle darkness of November night, the air sharp with salt and the threat of snow. His goggles glinted, cold and predatory, as he watched Sadie trudge up the icy gravel path to her house, her black hair tucked under a knit cap, breath clouding in the chill. Her shoulders slumped, burdened by months of silence since that bookstore spat with Alexis had carved a wound the Reaper savored. His lips curled beneath the mask, a silent snarl of triumph. "Little Bo Peep has lost her sheep…" The rhyme coiled in his mind, a venomous thread binding his rage to the girl who'd tethered his Ladybug.

Ladybug had been poking around, asking too many questions; her relentless probing threatened his carefully woven web. She thought Sadie was dodging her, nursing a grudge over that coffeehouse fight, but Sadie would soon crack under the weight of her secrets, and he couldn't risk her talking. The Rhyme Reaper's gloved fingers tightened around the syringe in his pocket, its needle-sharp as the truth. Sadie's absence wasn't betrayal; it was his design, a meticulous strike to unravel his muse's fragile world. Ladybug's guilt, her frantic texts and unanswered calls fed his hunger; each pang of her heart was a note in his twisted symphony. Sadie was his now, a lost sheep to be snared, and tonight, he'd claim her.

The ocean's roar was a pulse muffled by the frost that crusted the pines. The Rhyme Reaper's breath was slow, deliberate, his pulse steady as the tide, savoring the hunt's edge.

Sadie fumbled with her keys at the front door, her porch light casting a feeble glow that flickered against the ice-slicked steps. She was alone. Tami and Dr. Finn at the hospital, her cousins scattered, no one to hear her bleat.

His boots pressed into the frozen earth, silent and honed from nights spent stalking Ladybug, her emerald eyes dimming under his gaze. This wasn't the bloody hill or the hospital's burning flesh, but the thrill was the same, the rhyme's cadence guiding his steps: *And can't tell where to find them...*

He moved a blur of white against the dark, closing the gap in seconds. Sadie's key turned in the lock, and the door creaked open, but his gloved hand clamped over her mouth before she could cross the threshold, stifling her gasp. His arm snaked around her waist, yanking her back into the shadows, her body rigid with shock. The syringe flashed, the needle piercing her neck with surgical precision as the sedative flooded her veins, just as it had to Ladybug in California. Her muffled cry faded, her limbs slackening as she crumpled against him, a lamb caught in his snare. Leave them alone, and they'll come home. The Rhyme Reaper's chest thrummed with dark glee, the rhyme's promise fulfilled, another knot in his web.

He affixed the forged note to the Finns' front door and then dragged her through the pines, her weight negligible, like a feather compared to the bodies he'd hauled. Pausing by a gnarled pine, he reached out, his gloved hand tracing the ladybug he'd carved into the bark weeks ago, its delicate lines a silent ode to his muse. The woods opened into a clearing where his beat-up Chevy Blazer waited, its tailgate open like a hungry jaw. He tossed Sadie inside the vehicle, her body crumpling onto the cold metal, her hardware store apron tangled with her scarf, and her knit cap askew. The tailgate slammed shut, the sound sharp and final.

His senses pricked at a rustle disturbing the frost-heavy dark. Ladybug wasn't here, not tonight, but her presence haunted him, a ghost in his mind. The Rhyme Reaper's lips curved into a predator's smile. She'd blamed Sadie's silence on their fight, on her own paranoia, never suspecting the spider weaving her despair. Her LTD wasn't parked nearby, but he felt her all the same; her guilt was a beacon he'd ignited with every unanswered call. Not yet, Ladybug. Sadie was the bait, and Ladybug, his masterpiece, would fall when he chose.

He slid into the Blazer, the engine roaring to life, a guttural growl that enveloped the forest's icy hush. Headlights sliced through the pines as tires crunched on frost when he pulled away, Sadie's limp form a silent trophy in the back. His fingers tapped the wheel, humming softly, "Little Bo Peep has lost her sheep…" The rhyme was his hymn, a vow to his Ladybug, her fear his fuel. Ladybug thought Sadie hated her, but the truth was colder: Sadie was his, a cat, and a piece of the puzzle she'd never solve until he broke her.

The rearview mirror caught the house's fading porch light. The Rhyme Reaper's smile widened, goggles glinting as he pressed the gas, the Blazer vanishing into the November night. The tide was rising, his web tightening. Nicole had been his first lamb, Sadie the latest, and Alexis would be the final verse—she screams the crescendo of his rhyme.

50

Alexis

Numbness clung like a stubborn fog. I didn't know how to feel; nothing felt finished. My breath fogged the sliding glass door; a fragile veil against the ache of Sadie's absence, vanished into November's jaws.

Leads on the killer had grown stagnant, as cold as the mid-November air seeping into Gold Beach. Detective Jacobs told me he was heading to talk to the Finns, but he admitted they couldn't pin down Ronny either, his words laced with frustration, the trail as elusive as the snow burying the town.

The town's chill matched my own, my heart heavy with despair, echoing the ashes of the hospital fire and the weight of the nursery rhyme book. School buzzed with parents imposing tighter curfews, kids plotting secret parties, sneaking past rules. But I had no energy for rebellion, my world gray as winter's blacks, with no reds or oranges left from fall's fleeting warmth.

Grief engulfed me. Asher's calls ten daily at Princeton, now once a week, faded. Moving on was painful. School overlooked me after the Asher drama and the Reaper news blackout, leaving me feeling isolated. Track practice was half-hearted, schoolwork was routine, sleep was endless yet exhausting, and my eyes resembled black pits. All happy memories were slipping away, my attempts to reach them failed, and their backs were turned.

I avoided Dr. Finn's appointments; his voicemails triggered Asher's memories, but the Finns' home, once welcoming, was now overwhelming. Guilt consumed me; I'd wrongfully blamed Asher, not the Reaper. Despair intensified.

Dad and Becca's wedding plans soared, love radiant, but my misery of wearing sweats to school, making no effort, dragged me down.

Brushing dull, brittle hair, Becca's crimson dress–her choice– hung loose. My frame had thinned, lips cracked and ashen, blending with sallow skin and desperate for color. Becca's lipstick tube taunted me, red as Mom's, her beauty a mask, club dresses and makeup hiding the real Nicole, while ratty pajamas revealed cruelty and Stephen Whitaker's hands unstopped. I couldn't wear it, not with her ghost.

"You really should put that on."

Trevor's voice jolted me, and the lipstick clattered into the sink, reminiscent of his venom at school.

"What're you doing here?" I glared, leaning weakly against the sink. His tuxedo bow tie was loose and looked sharp, but hate burned inside me.

He glanced at the sink, then at me. "Seriously, put some color on, that red dress makes you paler."

"Shut up," I growled, adjusting the fallen spaghetti straps, feeling like a saloon girl, not myself. Great!

"What's wrong anyway? You look like a skeleton." His eyebrows were raised, teeth flashing, smug.

"None of your business. Leave," I whispered, shoving him out and stomping to the closet for shoes, the heels mocking me.

He raised his hands. "Delivering a message, Luke wants two space heaters from the attic."

I whined, "I'm dressed, why don't you? Why heaters?"

"Mom's bitching too cold for guests and wants them cozy. Your dad's got me scrounging neighbors for spares," he said, pointing. "You get the attic." Shrugging, he left.

This is why you shouldn't plan an outdoor wedding in November in Oregon.

"Awesome," I grumbled as my zipper got stuck, so I threw on my lavender robe, glaring at the heels while my socked feet stood defiant. I yanked the rope of the attic ladder in the garage, and the steps unfolded like the pages of a nursery rhyme book. The shadowy opening exhaled a bitter draft as dust parted, pushing me upward, urgency prickling like bugs in the forest. Each step quickened; the garage light faded, and the air felt musky and claustrophobic. A chill crawled up my spine, hairs rising, half screaming to run, half whispering to look.

"Stop being a baby," I muttered, fumbling for the string and clicking on the light. It flickered, my eyes adjusting, and then I screamed as my head smacked against a beam. "Ouch!" Rubbing the spot, I stared at a photo on an easel. It was my four-year-old smile, Mom's hand on my left shoulder, and Dad's on my right, our last family shot, a summer fireplace staple of Dad's. A sense of wrongness washed over me as I noticed the words scratched onto Mom's purple dress: *I loved you, Whore!* Tears pooled, and a sob choked, "Dad…" I crumpled, my knees hitting the wood. Her infidelity? Discolored papers peeked out from behind.

Ten minutes later, I had uncovered three letters, their words heavy with dust and secrets. One signed K dripped soap-opera sap, making me laugh through tears as attic cobwebs tickled my nose. Another, B's graphic scrawl, churned my stomach. I shoved it back, bile rising. The third, R's loopy poem, stunned me—its love for Nicole embraced her flaws. R was probably Ronny, his devotion chilling now, knowing he was out there, untouchable.

Why hadn't she found happiness with K, B, or R, breaking Dad's heart? What void drove her to ruin us all? I pocketed the letters, no secrets left, and grabbed the heaters, leaving the light on and the stairs open. Dad owed me answers about Kansas, about the killer still out there.

As I stepped into the backyard, the wedding ceremony was just moments away from starting, but a chill hung heavier than the dark clouds overhead. Icy gusts whipped through the tent, barely tempered by ten sputtering heaters. Yet the guests chatted, their laughter oblivious to the brewing storm. The wind's howl echoed the "Ladybug, ladybug" whisper from my nightmare, a riddle I couldn't shake.

Suddenly, Becca's mother thrust an ugly bouquet into my hands, tore off my robe, and pushed me in front of the bride. My bare feet sank into the cold grass, unnoticed by the crowd, while Trevor's leer burned into me.

A sign, not a mere omen but a celestial verdict that this marriage was cursed to fail, shattered the fragile moment. The sky split open, a raw, festering wound in the heavens, spewing winds that screamed with the primal rage of a hurricane. They tore through the wedding tent, a merciless force that spat on the brittle vows being sworn. Women's painstakingly sculpted hairstyles disintegrated into frantic, knotted snarls. Hair pins flew like shards of a shattered illusion. Men staggered, clawing at their partners' skirts to shield them from the gusts' savage assault, their efforts crumbling against the storm's unrelenting hunger. The tent's canvas thrashed like a dying creature, its poles creaking and ropes fraying as if the very structure revolted against the farce of this union.

Dad snapped into detective mode, his voice a razor slicing through the bedlam. "Secure the area!" he bellowed, the command ringing with the iron of his detective's badge. He moved with precision, rallying guests to brace the buckling poles and snatching scattered chairs from the wind's grasp. His gray-streaked auburn hair whipped in the gale, but his focus remained on the crowd, not me, leaving me stranded in the chaos. I stood rooted, the wind's shriek coiling around me like a strangling vine, my heart hammering as if I were back in Ventura, staring at Mom's blood-drenched bed, the pumpkin's carved rhyme "Peter, Peter, Pumpkin Eater" searing my mind. Or in Gold Beach, choking on whispers that the Rhyme Reaper still hunted.

Becca's mascara-smeared glare stabbed through the tumult, not pleading but venomous, a hatred that burned colder than Mom's icy stare in life. Her face was a grotesque mask, with black rivulets of mascara oozing down her cheeks like tar, pooling in the creases of her snarling mouth. Her eyes glinted with malice that echoed the attic's scrawled "I loved you, Whore!" a condemnation I couldn't outrun. Her sodden dress clung to her frame, the fabric stained with mud and something darker, dripping in viscous streaks that reeked of decay as if the storm had dredged up the rot of her secrets.

No one saw the tent pole quivering behind her, its rope unraveling like a hangman's noose, but I did, wind-torn, splintered, ready to strike. A vision seared into my mind: the pole impaling her, her scream drowned by the gale, blood gushing to soak her dress like Mom's gore-soaked bed, the rhyme twisting, "Ladybug, your mother is dead…" No, Dad loved her and had lost Mom to the Reaper's blade; he couldn't lose Becca, too.

I lunged forward, my dress ripping at the seams with a sickening tear, and slammed my shoulder into Becca, sending her sprawling into the mud as the pole tore free, its rope lashing like a flayed tendon. I grabbed the splintered wood, my hands shredding

243

against its jagged grain, but my feet slipped in the churning sludge, the pole wrenching from my grip. I slid past the tent, a tangled wreck dress, panties bared, caked in rancid mud that smelled of rotting flesh. My head cracked against a tree, stars exploding in my vision, and I tumbled down a rain-slicked hill into a festering sludge pit, its stench a putrid assault. The muck engulfed me, warm and viscous, seeping into my mouth, a vile slurry of bile, decay, and something alive writhing, crawling. Maggots squirmed in the red-slimed ooze, their pale, bloated bodies pulsing against my tongue, clogging my throat. A wriggling mass burrowed into my ear, its slimy churn deafening as I screamed, spitting, thrashing, the slime coating my teeth, drowning me in a nightmare's rancid ocean.

"Alexis!" Dad's voice knifed through the darkness, flashlight beams stabbing through the twisted trees, illuminating the maggots swarming my face, their glistening trails weaving through the muck in my hair. Hyperventilating, I retched, vomit mingling with the pit's fetid stew, my chest heaving as the rhyme's final line clawed at my mind— "And that's little Jo…" I sank deeper, the sludge sucking me under, my vision blackening, the storm's *sign* sealing my fall into the Reaper's shadow.

51

Black Sheep

The Rhyme Reaper, masked and drenched, watched Ladybug slip into the mud, guilt twisting within him. His pit dug for cats lay gutted as he spied her silhouette behind the curtains, his mind filled with porch thoughts. He had carved those memories while imagining her, but her choking on maggots and muck wasn't his plan, not like Nicole's pumpkin. Indirect, revolting, not her end, not yet.

Leaping from his perch, hidden by trees, he knelt, plunging his arms to his shoulders, quickly finding her.

He had no time; Detective Harper's beams drew closer. He yanked her free, wiping mud from her face; her pulse was weak, and she wasn't breathing. Prying her mouth open, he removed maggots and mud before starting CPR.

52

Alexis

Warm air filled my lungs as I pushed the masked figure away, rolling over and coughing up muddy maggots that clung to me like the insects from my nightmares in the woods. My head throbbed, sharp pain radiating from where I'd struck it against a jagged rock during my desperate scramble, the scene blurring in and out like a flickering film. Shielded by the dense, gnarled trees, their branches clawing at the sky, I was hidden from the world, the storm's howling wind and thrashing rain drowning out the sounds of my struggle. My heart pounded, a frantic drumbeat, as I turned and met his hunched stare, his eyes glinting with malice through the slits of his mask, though they flickered in my hazy vision. "Ladybug," he rasped, his grubby hand reaching toward me. The Rhyme Reaper. This was it. This is where I met my end.

His fingers grazed my cheek, rough and cold, and a memory slammed into me the night Mom died. I was passed out on the couch, the TV's static humming, when a shadow loomed over me. A hand, the same rough touch, brushed my face, the air thick with the stench of sour breath and blood. I stirred, catching a glimpse of a figure slipping into Mom's room, the *"Peter, Peter"* note later found in the pumpkin, her severed finger glinting with her wedding ring. The Rhyme Reaper had been there, his touch and breath marking the moment he stole her life. Now, that same foul breath hit me, rancid and sharp, curling into my nostrils, confirming it was him, even as the world tilted and blurred, the storm's roar muffling our deadly dance among the trees.

I screamed, scrambling back against a tree, its bark biting my spine, tears streaming as the woods echoed his chilling "Ladybug…" from the text, the costume, though the storm devoured the sound. My vision swam, his masked face fading in and out, but I felt him lunge, the knife's cold edge pressing against my throat, a thin sting blooming where it bit. His kills flashed before me, each a shard of terror in my fractured sight. I nodded, wincing as the blade pressed deeper, his face inches from mine, fingers tracing my trembling lip to the bloody cut on my head, the pain flaring with each touch.

Sucking on each bloodied finger, he hummed with a perverse delight; his murky eyes gleamed with intent though they flickered in my unsteady gaze.

"What did you do to my mother?" I choked, the pumpkin's rhyme haunting me, its words scrawled in blood. He laughed a remorseless cackle, shaking his head, the sound swallowed by the storm's fury. "Please, I won't tell," I begged, my voice cracking, my head pulsing as the world blurred once more.

Twigs snapped. "Alexis!" Dad shouted, his voice barely piercing the storm's howl. Ranger's bark cut through, sharp and frantic. The Reaper vanished into the shadows, swallowed by the trees, leaving behind mud, maggots, and a whispered, "Not today…" that the wind tore away as my vision faded while I slumped against the tree.

53

Alexis

After a thorough scrubbing and sixteen stitches later, I lay completely still in the rock-hard hospital bed. It was the last place I wanted to be. I tried to talk my way out of coming in, but lost that battle because when someone's skin is tinted red, covered in maggots, and has a large gash at the base of their skull, they don't have much of a case. The sterile air stung my nose, sharp with antiseptic, masking the pit's rancid tang, maggots writhing, "Ladybug…" echoing like a warped engine hum. My stitched scalp throbbed under fluorescent glare, each pulse a reminder of the Reaper's knife, its cold edge drawing blood, more vivid than the needle's prick, tied to Mom's carved pumpkin.

On the way here, I rambled on and on about the serial killer, but Dad just sat calmly listening to me, then patted me on the leg and said, "Alexis, I think you hit your head too hard." With my head pounding, I stared, slack-jawed, as he returned to driving. What the hell was wrong with him? My jaw dropped, pain spiking like a misfired piston. His new car hum mocked, with dashboard lights flickering like a weak pulse against my racing thoughts. No one believed me when I said the Rhyme Reaper was there and saved me. Why?

I slammed my head into the pillow and winced. Here I was, trying my hardest to catch this killer, but no matter which way I turned, there was a brick wall in the way. Dad should have tried his best, but he didn't. Jacobs didn't even seem to be doing anything! I'm sick and tired of feeling like nothing is being done. The pillow's starch dug into my neck, pain flaring like a hot nail in my skull. Dad should've been scouring the streets, not sitting placidly, blind to the pit's truth. Exhausted by his calm, I burned. The monitor's beep taunted me, syncing with my pulse, each tick a countdown answer, now.

"Have you rested at all?" Dad startled me, making me jump. "Sorry." He held a hand up and then pulled a chair closer to the bed. His voice sliced through the room's hum, causing my pulse to spike. "Sorry." He raised a hand, dragging the chair closer; its screech was like metal on asphalt, grated against the worn spine of the nursery rhyme book.

I gave him no response but narrowed my eyes and studied his face. Something was off; besides the paleness of his complexion, it was devoid of any emotion whatsoever. I locked eyes, silent, his face a ghost pale, blank, hiding something, like the attic's dust-choked letters, "I loved you, Whore!". What's he burying? The room's cold bit into my knuckles, my fingers curling tight, ready to pry the truth from his silence.

I crossed my arms over my chest and huffed. "What's going on, Dad?"

He sighed and started to ramble, "We've been so blind. He's been here all along…." He continued to talk, but all that echoed in my mind was that he'd been here all along. His words blurred, but 'blind' stuck, cold as the warped hum in my head, not a lullaby but a blade, Megan's unfound shadow. Was he finally listening to me? The IV drip echoed a slow tick like rain on a windshield.

"Dad, stop!" I sat up, feeling a slight head rush, and grabbed his hand. "You're not making sense. What are you talking about?" I shot upright, my head swimming, holding his hand, pulse racing like tires on wet pavement, my grip tight as I searched his eyes for cracks, for the truth, now.

Dad's eyes locked on mine, unblinking, as if he were bracing for a crash. "Ronny Moore," he said, voice flat as the hospital's hum. "The FBI arrested him tonight."

My heart lurched. Ronny Moore? I slumped back against the stiff hospital pillow, my breath snagging in my throat, a strange half-gasp that burned. It was him, the guy in the pit; it had to be Ronny. The dots connected: the loopy "R" in that attic letter, his absence when Jacobs couldn't find him. It made sense, the pieces clicking into place like a lock. My scowl deepened, eyes narrowing at Dad. "You're serious? Him?"

I couldn't outrun the nightmare. The Rhyme Reaper's trail was a bloody map. The FBI had mobilized every small-town cop they could find, all of them sifting through evidence scraps, blood, rhymes, and lies, hoping to stop him before he sliced through my world next. But Ronny, the guy who wrote love notes to Mom, the monster whose blade tasted my blood? It all made sense.

Dad leaned forward, hand heavy on mine, anchoring like a tow hook, his touch warm but weighted, like he was holding back a tidal wave. "Look, Alexis, there's stuff about your mom you don't know. She wasn't exactly…"

"Faithful," I cut in, my voice sharp, slicing through the room's antiseptic buzz. "I know, Dad, the paternity test," I said as if he'd forgotten. I was ready to let Dad in on the letters I found. My mind spun, replaying the knife, that voice, "Ladybug."

"I found the letters."

Dad's eyes widened, then shut tight, a quick flinch as if I'd punched him. "You found those?" His voice cracked, raw, and he cleared his throat, his hand tightening around mine. "Yeah. Ronny was one of them. And it makes sense he's the Reaper. I saw his temper flare while we were working together. The guy could snap like a frayed rope. He bottled it up, but when it blew…" He shook his head, eyes distant, as though he was seeing Ronny's rage replay.

I leaned forward, my brow furrowing as the monitor's beep quickened. "Yeah, it makes sense?" Ronny was scribbling odes to Mom, the monster Mom pushed away. "How does a guy go from love poems to carving up Mom? Everyone else?"

Dad shifted in the hard plastic chair, uneasy, as if he were sitting on broken glass. "Love like his… it twists into something dark. Obsession, rage, he had it in him. I saw it." His words landed heavily, but they didn't fit, like a wrench in the wrong socket.

My neck had fingers kneading tense cords. I gasped as thoughts skidded like tires on ice. "Obsessed, that's for sure." I held back; I needed to talk to Ronny and get some answers.

"I'll never get over your mother," he said, his voice low, his eyes staring through the hospital walls at some ghost of her. There was more; I could feel it, but he was clamming up.

"You okay? Are you looking rough? Need the nurse?" He stood halfway to the door, worry creasing his face, but it felt like a dodge, sidestepping the real fight.

I shook my head, my voice steady despite the churn in my gut. "No, I'm fine. Just wanna go home." The "fine" was a lie. The puzzle was fitting together, with some pieces still scattered like pages from a nursery rhyme book.

The door creaked open before Dad could respond, and Tami Finn stepped inside, her face pale and eyes red as if she'd been crying for days. Dr. Finn followed closely behind, his usual calm unraveling, his tie loose as though he'd tugged it one too many times. My stomach twisted. Tami's hugs were warm, but her arrival felt like a warning shot.

"Alexis, honey," Tami said, her voice soft but shaky as she crossed to my bed. She squeezed my hand, her fingers cold and trembling. "We heard about the wedding, what happened... Are you okay?" Her eyes searched mine as if she were looking for cracks she could patch.

Dr. Finn cleared his throat, standing stiffly by the door. "You're tough, kid. If you need anything, you tell us." His voice was steady, but his knuckles were white, gripping his coat as if it were a lifeline.

I forced a nod, throat tight. "I'm... yeah, I'm okay. Thanks." Lies piled up, but their worry was heavy. Tami's hand lingered, and I caught a glance between her and Dad, something unspoken, heavy.

"Alexis," Tami began, her voice dropping, "we're worried about Sadie, too. She's... she hasn't been home. Left a note, said she was going to stay with her mom, Kate, for a while." She swallowed hard, her eyes glistening. "She's been off, so we thought she just needed space, but she seemed scared like she was hiding something. It's been days, and Kate hasn't heard from her either."

Dr. Finn stepped closer, his jaw tight. "Jacobs is coming over later; however, we were wondering if you knew anything?"

My heart slammed, a cold spike in my chest. A note? Sadie, with Kate? That didn't make sense. Sadie's mom was a mess, rarely around. My mind flashed to the knife, the voice "Ladybug." I gripped the hospital sheet, knuckles white. Sadie wasn't with Kate. She was gone, and I'd missed it, too caught up in my own paranoia to see the truth.

"I... I don't know," I choked out, voice barely steady. "She hasn't talked to me since the fight. I thought she was pissed at me." Guilt clawed my gut. Tami's face crumpled, and Dr. Finn's hand rested on her shoulder, both looking at me like I was their last hope.

Dad's hand found mine again, but it felt empty, his eyes avoiding mine. The room's hum pressed in, the puzzle pieces sharper now, cutting deeper. Ronny in cuffs, Sadie missing, and the Rhyme Reaper's shadow stretching longer than I'd feared.

"Maybe Jacobs should ask Ronny about Sadie." Had he done something to her? Was she part of his sick nursery rhyme obsession? I couldn't shake this awful feeling.

54

Black Sheep

They came like lambs.

Asher led first, shoulders squared and righteous. Tanner followed behind, bold in his words but unsteady in his hands. Cooper, sharp-eyed yet hesitant, trailed close enough to second-guess but not enough to stay away.

They followed the Reaper's trail willingly. Believing every word.

He'd said he saw Sadie, injured and limping near the Whispering Nook where they'd once gathered, laughing, shouting, and drinking. The memory of warmth and fire still lingered in their minds.

That familiarity was the leash.

The Reaper walked behind them, unseen but close enough to hear every breath. The forest grew quieter as they moved, like it, too, was waiting.

When they arrived at the clearing, the cave gaped before them like a yawning mouth. Cold air drifted out from within.

That's when they noticed it. Before them, its edges were jagged. Snagged on one of the rough stones was a scrap of Sadie's flannel shirt, the familiar red and black plaid now torn and damp, fluttering faintly in the cold draft from within.

Tanner frowned. "This doesn't feel right."

Cooper's jaw clenched. "It's a setup."

Asher moved anyway. "If she's hurt, we don't wait."

That was all it took. One crack in their unity, one flash of doubt buried under loyalty, and they were in.

Inside, the cave had changed.

A small fire flickered at the center, casting grotesque shadows across the damp walls. The air was filled with the scents of moss and old blood.

They were not alone.

Three masked figures emerged into the firelight.

Each wore crude, expressionless masks crafted from bone-white plaster. No mouths. No eyes. Just pointy ears and black holes staring back. Like mice.

Sparrow stood slender and poised, her long yellow braid cascading over one shoulder. In her hands, a crowbar twirled.

Beetle loomed at her side, short and stocky, brass knuckles already glinting on his fists.

Owl was the largest: broad-shouldered, unmoving, with a long hunting knife gripped loosely in one gloved hand.

"What the?" Tanner started

Beetle struck first, delivering a brutal jab to Tanner's ribs that sent him crumpling.

Cooper turned, but Owl was behind him, wrapping one massive arm around his throat and pulling him backward in silence.

Asher lunged toward the firelight, reaching for something, anything, but Sparrow moved quickly. The crowbar whistled through the air and struck his back, sending him crashing to the dirt stoned floor.

The Reaper watched from the cave mouth, unmoving, unflinching.

It was beautiful.

The three boys writhed, bleeding and stunned. But they were alive for now.

"Bind them," he ordered quietly.

The zip ties were pulled tight. Ankles first. Then wrists. Gags are tied off with deliberate care.

Asher groaned. Cooper fought the restraints. Tanner's eyes were wide and dazed.

The Reaper crouched beside them. Slowly and carefully, he dipped his finger into a can of red paint and began to write in looping script across the cave floor:

"See how they run."

He stood, brushing his gloves clean.

"They'll wake up soon," Sparrow murmured from behind her blank white mask.

"And when they do," the Reaper said, smiling faintly beneath his own, "they'll realize the rhyme was about them all along."

He turned toward the shadows at the back of the cave and gave a slight nod.

From behind a jagged rock formation, Beetle and Owl emerged, dragging something heavy.

Sadie.

She was gagged and bloodied, her flannel shirt torn, and dried blood caked along her hairline. Her eyes fluttered open as they dropped her onto the cave floor beside the fire. Rope bit into her wrists. One ankle was swollen. Her breathing was shallow but steady.

Asher let out a muffled yell through the gag. Tanner attempted to roll toward her. Cooper growled through clenched teeth.

The Reaper crouched beside Sadie and brushed a strand of blood-streaked hair from her cheek with gloved fingers. "You've been very useful, Sadie."

Her eyes flared with helpless rage.

He stood and faced the masked trio.

"Take her," he said, voice low and measured. "Bring me Ladybug."

Sparrow nodded once, already reaching for the rope to pull Sadie to her feet.

"She'll come," the Reaper added, watching the flames reflect off his painted mask. "She won't let Sadie burn."

His smile returned, slight, serene, hollow.

"Pain is a powerful invitation."

55

Alexis

My home was a sanctuary from Gold Beach's turmoil, where the town simmered over Ronny's trial in Portland's maximum-security prison, his haunted eyes etched in my memory. Luke urged Nathan to confront his father in jail for answers, while Jacobs pressed Ronny about Sadie's fate. The townsfolk cursed Nathan's name, and pity stirred within me; his father's sins weren't his. Yet my guilt ran deeper, connected to my failure to protect Sadie. The town's whispers had poisoned me, and my harsh words shattered our friendship. I misjudged Asher as well, ensnared in regret. Old taunts about my mother stung, but they paled beside Nathan carrying his father's crimes.

Numbness clung like a heavy shadow. My breath fogged the sliding glass door, a fragile barrier against Sadie's absence, swallowed by November's chill. The Finns and police searched for her, their voices muffled by snow, while my head injury kept me on the sidelines. I stirred cocoa, its bitter steam rising, and opened Asher's unread texts, pleas for help finding Sadie sent days ago. His voicemails, raw with worry, burned with every word. I had been in the hospital during Dad and Becca's wedding vows since their wedding had been a disaster, their joy clashing with the search for Sadie. With the serial killer caught, Dad claimed a honeymoon, leaving Trevor and me behind.

Snow blanketed Gold Beach, sinking cold into my bones. Ranger pressed against my leg, a fleeting comfort. I pressed my palm to the glass, condensation weeping as I watched snowflakes dance, each unique yet joined, unlike my hollow days without Sadie, Nathan, or Asher.

Stepping onto the porch, the snow bit through my thin boots and jeans. Ranger's crunching footsteps trailed behind me. Once I reached the center of the yard, I closed my eyes and gazed up at the sky. The soft, cold flakes pricked my skin before melting away. Sticking out my tongue, I wanted to taste the purity of the snow, hoping it would wash away the guilt that had been gnawing at me ever since that fateful night in May. The wind's howl carried a faint hum.

Ranger's bark shattered my trance, nearly toppling me as the spell of snow broke. He stood rigid, snarling at the post light, his fur bristling and eyes locked on the forest's darkness I couldn't pierce. The glare was blinding, like the intensity of a headlight. What's out there? My pulse quickened, my breath clouded, my hands flexed and poised to act. Reaper?

"What, boy?" I shouted, my voice lost in his growl as I tugged his collar. "Inside!" My shoes and socks were now soaked, cold seeping through. I pulled, but he anchored, snarling at shadows with his hackles raised. Squinting, I caught sight of it—a hooded figure, white-clad, bursting from the snow, charging, shoulders broad—not Ronny. Ranger's roar shook the air; teeth bared, and my heart slammed like a blown tire.

Fear locked my joints, not frost, and my eyes flicked between Ranger and the figure. Time dragged, my pulse hammered, and the snow's crunch became a dull roar. Protect. My mind raced, calculating distance, angle, and action.

Ranger was my only shield, so I screamed, "Sick 'em!" His ears flattened as he charged the hooded shadow, a snarling blur against the ghostly veil of snow. The figure, with cruel intent, drew a pickaxe from its sleeve, the blade gleaming savagely. Dread tore at my chest, my vision blurring with panic. As Ranger leaped, the axe arced upward mercilessly, ripping through his chin, flesh splitting with a wet, splintering crunch that pierced from neck to skull. Blood sprayed, hissing in the snow, steaming red, entrails spilling, Ranger's eyes blank. A guttural choke faded into deafening silence as the figure hoisted the axe, Ranger's mangled form dangling, fur matted, the snow glowing crimson. My heart shattered, screams choking on blood's metallic stench, the Reaper's hymn sealing my failure.

Time stood still as blood dripped from my beloved Ranger, seeping into the snow and staining its purity crimson. My knees sank into the snow, the cold penetrating through, yet it didn't register. Ranger lay broken, his fur soaked in blood, his eyes once alive with trust now vacant. A sob tore from me, jagged and wild, as I reached for him with trembling hands. He was my rock. He had stood by me through every loss and scream in the dark, his warmth a lifeline. But now he was gone, stolen by the Rhyme Reaper's blade. Tears froze on my cheeks, but I didn't wipe them away. *I failed you, boy.* Rage flared beneath the sorrow, igniting a fire. This wasn't the end. I stood, my legs unsteady yet firm, wiping my face. The Reaper wouldn't break me, not yet.

A choking sob tore from my throat as I turned my eyes away from his lifeless form. Gazing at his murderer, I met his dark, merciless eyes behind goggles, his broad shoulders indicating he was male, a shadowed predator tracking my anguish. "How could you?" I screamed, tears scalding my cheeks. Before I could blink, he hurled Ranger down, yanking the axe free with a sickening crunch, the stench of blood rising and sealing my dread.

I was his next victim. Determined not to let that be the outcome, I turned on my icy heels and ran up the porch steps, almost slipping. I went in through the open back door and locked it behind me. My chest heaved, and blood pounded like after a sprint, safe for now.

The ghostly man surged forward, axe raised, shattering the glass wall. Shards erupted outward like a broken headlight as he plunged through. I ducked, shielding my head; with glass raining down and my heart pounding, nowhere felt safe. He stumbled but quickly recovered, looming four feet away, predator close. My eyes darted around for a weapon or an exit, my mind raced, refusing to be prey.

Heart pounding, I lunged for the hourglass lamp, yanking its cord free with a snap. I hurled it at his head; my legs braced for a fight. His arm shot up, deflecting it, causing the lamp to shatter down. His eyes, black and furious behind goggles, bored into me like steel from a pit. I steadied my breath, calculating my next move now.

Looking from the shattered lamp to the figure before me, I encountered dark, furious eyes peering through ski goggles, glistening with savage intent. Before I could flee, he lunged, grabbing my arms and dragging me close. I thrashed with all my strength, my body twisting against his towering, unyielding bulk, air getting squeezed out. My defiance ignited; I kicked his shins with icy feet, screaming, "Let me go!" My raw cry echoed. A gunshot pierced the living room ceiling, plaster dusting down like snow, silence crashing in. My mind raced two, not one, a team's trap. I had tried to put it together, however there were too many missing pieces from this puzzle.

A sharp, familiar voice cut through the wreckage of the shattered doorway. "Ladybug, stop, or your friend will die." My captor spun around, and my eyes locked onto Sadie, her face obscured by a green blindfold, tape sealing her mouth, dried blood crusted on her nose, and a jagged slash across her forehead. Her arms were tightly bound, a gun pressed firmly against her temple. Next to her stood another figure, masked and dressed in a white suit, a silent partner to the first. Words escaped me as I took in the scene: two men, moving like a pack, holding us captive. My mind raced, questions cutting through the chaos. Sadie, why was she here? Was she tangled in this, or just another pawn? This wasn't the work of a lone hand; the pieces screamed coordination.

I was utterly lost, my mind reeling as I tried to comprehend the chaos erupting around me. Words escaped me as I watched the two men overpower Sadie and me with swift, ruthless force. The gunman's voice cut through the air, sharp and restless. "Beetle, blindfold her and gag her. The neighbors might hear," he snapped, a nervous edge betraying his urgency. "Black Sheep'll lose it if the plan falls apart."

Black Sheep? The name echoed in my mind, a mystery I couldn't solve. Before I could think further, Beetle acted. A blindfold tightened over my eyes, plunging me into darkness. A rough cloth was shoved into my mouth, sealed with duct tape. Zip ties cut into my wrists, the pain flaring like raw exhaust, stealing my breath. Desperate to hold onto something, I counted the steps. I heard two, maybe three, clinging to the sound amid the haze.

In that suffocating moment, the signs I'd ignored crystallized: the serial killer's ruthless efficiency stemmed from a team, not from one madman. The truth struck: Ronny was a fragment, not the whole, entangled with others, many hands weaving a merciless web. My mind spun, pulse pounding, ears straining for clues amid echoing boots, the cave air thick with dread. Who was Black Sheep? The plan faltered, but why? What sinister shift happened? Could Ronny really be involved in this? My heart raced, questioning his role in this relentless buildup nightmare.

Sadie and I were thrust into the backseat of a car, our shoulders brushing in a fleeting moment of solace amid the shared dread. It reminded me of those grueling, sweat-soaked track stretches when we pushed each other to keep going. Not today, I thought, drawing strength from her warmth beside me. She was alive, right here, and I was determined to keep it that way. My breath came in muffled gasps as I flexed my fingers against the tight zip ties binding my wrists. My mind focused on one urgent goal—escape.

I realized that the farther we moved from my house, the fewer our chances of being found. Time wasn't on our side, and I had to act quickly. Sadie hadn't left; she had been taken, just like I was. We were caught in this nightmare by forces beyond our control. And now, with each tick of the clock, the distance between us and safety grew wider. I had to come up with a plan to escape together and survive.

Sadie's muffled cry pierced through me as I shifted away from her, careful not to attract attention. I turned my back to the door, pretending to rest my head against the seat. With my hands bound, I fumbled awkwardly, searching for the handle. My fingertips brushed against the cold metal, and I whispered a silent plea before testing it. A soft click sounded. It was unlocked.

Adrenaline shot through me as I yanked the handle, and the door swung open. A cold blast of wind hit me hard. I planted my feet on the ground and threw myself out of the car. The world spun as the abductors' angry shouts and the screech of tires filled the air. I crashed onto the asphalt, rolling repeatedly before finally stopping. Pain shot through my body. My limbs felt numb, and my skin was scraped raw from road rash. It was a reckless move, but I was still alive, and bruises would heal.

I had to keep moving if I wanted to save Sadie. Gritting my teeth, I rolled onto my side, but a sharp, excruciating pain shot through my right shoulder, making the world spin. The blindfold had slipped down to my neck, and I squinted, trying to make sense of the deserted highway stretching out around me. If a car passed by, I could flag it down and get us both out of this nightmare. But through the haze, I saw them—the two men—closing in. I staggered to my feet and ran, my legs weak and unsteady. For one fleeting moment, I thought I might make it, then a brutal yank on my hair pulled me back. I stumbled into one of the men's arms. With my hands still bound, I kicked wildly at the other, fighting with every ounce of strength I had left. This was for Sadie. I couldn't give up.

Something pressed against my temple, and a click sounded nearby—probably a gun. I froze, fear gripping my muscles. They didn't want me dead, not yet, but the warning was clear. I had to be smart to protect Sadie's life and my own, but there was no time to think. Before I could react, something solid struck the side of my head. Bright, blinding pain flared, and then everything went black.

56

Black Sheep

A commotion at the cave's entrance, a jarring clatter of boots and
ragged gasps snatched Black Sheep's attention away from the
flickering fire. He stumbled, the heat of the flames searing his skin
as he stalked toward the disturbance, his pulse pounding with
irritation and anticipation. Beetle and Owl staggered in, dragging
two petite figures over their shoulders. The firelight danced across
their battered forms, casting jagged shadows. Black Sheep's gut
twisted. More targets? No. It was Sadie and his Ladybug.

In the corner, Asher, Cooper, and Tanner jerked upright, their
chains rattling against the stone, biting at their zip-tied hands.
Their blindfolds had slipped, revealing bloodshot eyes widened in
terror at Sadie's battered body, her face bruised, lip split, clothes
torn and Ladybug's worn frame, her skin pale and scraped, hair a
tangled mess. Asher, the youngest, his face gaunt, inhaled a
trembling breath, a faint whimper escaping as if Sadie and
Ladybug's arrival tightened the noose of their own captivity.
Cooper's hands twitched in their shackles, his gaze fixed on
Ladybug with helpless dread, while Tanner, his knuckles bruised
from futile struggles, shrank back, chains straining, eyes wide with
panic, fearing they might share the girls' fate. Victims of his
cruelty, their presence served as a grim reminder of his control,
each new captive heightening their terror.

Black Sheep ignored their pathetic stares, his world narrowing to Ladybug. He lunged, snatching her worn body from Beetle's grip and cradling her against his chest, her faint warmth seeping through his shirt. Her head lolled, boneless, and her matted hair swayed like a broken doll. A sharp, unwelcome worry stabbed him. "What's wrong? What'd you do?" he growled, his voice low and edged with rage.

Beetle raised his hands, shaking his head. "She's a damn wildcat. Threw herself from the car and busted herself up. Had to knock her out to get her back in."

Black Sheep's jaw tightened, breath catching as he carried her to the back of the cave, where a tattered blanket lay on the cold stone. He eased her down, the fire's glow revealing her worn state: torn jeans exposing scraped skin, her face hidden by hair, sticky wet with grime. His fingers brushed the strands from her blindfold, exposing duct tape over her mouth. A swollen lump throbbed on her temple, and he traced it gently, his touch lingering, torn between care and obsession. Cuts and smudges marred her cheeks, and he peeled the tape from her lips with slow precision, her faint breath grazing his fingers. Her fragility stirred his desire, warring with a pang of guilt.

His gaze drifted to her shirt, which had slipped off her right shoulder, revealing skin gleaming in the firelight. He licked his lips, imagining its softness, but froze at the angry red mark and bulge beneath her collarbone, a dislocated shoulder, its pain all too familiar. "Get over here," he called, voice tight with urgency. Beetle and Owl dropped Sadie, her battered body hitting the sandy floor with a groan as Tanner scrambled over to her body. "Her shoulder's out. Leave the zip ties. She'll scream when I pop it back."

Owl clamped her bound ankles, knuckles white, as Black Sheep slid behind her, easing her upright with her back pressed to his chest. Her worn frame felt fragile, and her shallow breaths created a faint rhythm against him. Beetle pinned her arms while Black Sheep gripped her shoulder, his fingers sinking into the swollen flesh. He paused, the damp air of the cave heavy in his lungs, the crackling fire a distant pulse. Then, with a swift, brutal crunch, he yanked the shoulder back into place. The sound echoed, sharp and sickening.

Ladybug's scream shattered the cave, a raw, anguished wail ricocheting off the walls. Asher flinched, chains clinking, while Cooper muttered, "Shit…" under his breath, and Tanner looked away, their faces pale. She thrashed, her bound limbs straining against their grip, her blindfolded face twisted in pain. Black Sheep held her tighter, her screams vibrating through him, a twisted satisfaction coiling in his gut. He stroked her hair, his lips brushing her ear, shushing her, but each gentle sound fueled her defiance, making her cries grow fiercer.

"You son of a bitch! Let me go, you sick bastard!" she rasped, her voice raw, head jerking as if to bite him. Owl and Beetle laughed, but Black Sheep's expression darkened, humor gone. Her rebellion ignited a fire, threatening to break his fraying control.

She was unravelling him. His hand clamped over her mouth, fingers pressing hard, and he yanked her head aside, breath hot against her ear. "I could snap your neck like a chicken bone if you don't shut up and settle down," he hissed, voice venomous. The cave stilled, her sharp breaths puffing against his palm, the only sound save for Asher's faint whimper, eyes locked on her trembling form.

"I'm taking my hand off," he said, each word measured. "Don't make me regret it. One more word, and I'll tape that pretty mouth shut. Got it?" She nodded jerkily, and he released her, standing abruptly, boots grinding sand into stone.

He paced, kicking at the ground, frustration gnawing at his chest. Everything was out of order. Sparrow was late, and his plans were falling apart. Time slipped through his fingers like sand. He yanked the pistol from his waistband, the safety's click piercing the silence. Tanner gasped, "No, please..." his voice barely audible, the Mice's fear a low hum against Black Sheep's rage. Ladybug had upended his world, her defiance tugging at his heart. He was done, ready to end it all to escape this hellhole town, the U.S., and never look back.

With narrowed eyes, he stalked toward Ladybug, pressing the cold barrel of the pistol against her forehead. Her head trembled, and a faint whimper escaped her lips. His heart thundered, drowning out Cooper's panicked plea, "Don't!" and Beetle's shout, "Easy, man!" Her worn beauty tempted him to be better, but he couldn't let her rule him. He squeezed his eyes shut, a coward's choice, picturing her blood painting the cave wall. His finger pulsed on the trigger, the moment stretching, heavy with her life in his hands.

"You son of a bitch!" Beetle roared, charging and slamming Black Sheep against the cave wall with a bone-rattling thud. Pain exploded in his skull, vision blurring as Beetle's fists pounded his face, eyes, mouth, and nose, crunching. Black Sheep swung back, fists meeting flesh, but Beetle's rage overpowered him. Owl lunged, grabbing Black Sheep's arms and pinning him upright against the rough stone, his grip like iron. Blood trickled from Black Sheep's nose, the metallic taste sharp on his lips.

A sharp click sliced through the chaos. Sparrow stood at the entrance of the cave, her pistol pressed against Black Sheep's head, her eyes blazing with fury. "Put him down, Beetle," she ordered, her voice low and deadly. Beetle stepped back, his chest heaving, as Owl released Black Sheep, who slumped slightly but stayed on his feet. Sparrow's gaze never wavered, the gun steady. "I'm done with your threats against me, my family, all of us. You treat us like scum, but you need us. Do you want our help? Start acting like it, or I walk, and you're done."

Asher, Cooper, and Tanner froze, their chains clinking softly, bloodshot eyes darting between Sparrow's pistol and Ladybug's trembling, worn form. Terror carved deep shadows into their faces as if the shifting power of the cave threatened to crush them. Asher's breath hitched, his gaunt frame shaking, a faint whimper escaping him as he saw Sadie's battered body, her face bruised, lip split, clothes torn and Ladybug's pale, scraped skin and tangled hair. Cooper's hands twitched in their shackles, his gaze locked on Ladybug with helpless dread, while Tanner, knuckles bruised from futile struggles, cradled Sadie tight against him, eyes wide with panic, fearing they might share the girls' fate. Victims of Black Sheep's cruelty, their presence served as a grim reminder of his control, each new captive deepening their terror.

Black Sheep's jaw clenched, and rage burned in his chest, the metallic taste of blood lingering. He would not be humiliated. This was his vengeance, but it was their game. Sparrow's words sank in, her gun's cold barrel a stark reminder he needed to regain full control.

He exhaled sharply, the cave's damp air chilling his lungs, and raised his hands slowly, palms open in surrender to act in their game, but he made the rules—he was in charge. "Alright, Sparrow," he growled, voice low, he reluctantly pretended. "I can't handle all this, Asher, Cooper, Tanner, Sadie, all of 'em. It's too much. I need to focus on Ladybug, she's the one that matters." His eyes flicked to Ladybug, her worn body trembling, scraped skin glowing faintly in the firelight. Obsession flared, softening his gaze, but the weight of his crumbling plans hardened it again. "We're still waiting on Spider," he added, tone clipped. "He's out there now, rigging explosives on the bridge. Once he's back, we move. But I need all of you if this is gonna work. To kill all of them, we need the bridge to go down to block the authorities." His eyebrows arched as he eyed his team. "Unless you're interested in getting arrested?"

Sparrow's eyes narrowed, her pistol steady, yet she nodded slightly, acknowledging his warning without lowering her guard. The cave held its breath, with only the fire's crackle and the Mice's chains breaking the silence. Asher's faint sob shattered the stillness, his head bowing in defeat, while Cooper and Tanner's ragged breaths echoed their fear. Black Sheep's chest tightened, his control as fragile as the bridge Spider was wiring to blow.

57

Alexis

I recognized the Rhyme Reaper's identity the moment he held me tightly in his arms, the damp chill of the Whispering Nook seeping into my bones, its jagged, name-painted walls shimmering with firelight like the bonfire I had danced around months ago. The memory of that night's laughter, with sparks rising into the starry sky, clashed with the acrid smoke and coppery taste of blood now filling the air, the stalactites dripping above like silent witnesses. Why hadn't I seen it sooner? Deep down, I had sensed but ignored the red flags pointing to him: his comforting embrace followed by sudden coldness, veiled anger, his cunning words, and problems with his dad. The clues were countless, etched into the cave's shadows like the "Peter, Peter" note scribbled in Mom's blood-soaked room.

But why? I knew he would kill me, but why the hesitation? I would play his game to uncover the secrets surrounding Mom's murder, even if it meant dying. Asher was here, chained to the cave's slick rock, and I wouldn't let him die for me, not after what I had put him through. I didn't want anyone to die because of me.

"Black Sheep," I said, voice steady, testing, drawing him out.

He yanked me up, and I winced as the sharp cave wall dug into my back, its rough edges scraping my worn skin. Nathan's deepened voice growled, "I told you to keep that mouth shut," his words echoing off the cavern's jagged ceiling.

The smell of smoke emanated from his body, and the heat of his breath against my skin reconfirmed my suspicions. He'd tried to mask his voice, but I knew. "I know you're going to kill me," I snapped, my voice trembling but defiant. "What do you want? Why are you doing this? What about your dad? Is he helping you?"

"Don't tempt me. You'll die like your whore mother deserved," he spat, hatred for Mom dripping venom. He laughed, a cold, jagged sound, and confessed to Alexis, "You know that letter your mom sent my dad? I made sure it surfaced. It was one of the ways I framed him and kept the FBI chasing him while I continued my plan to finish you." He let out another maniacal laugh, loud enough that it bounced around in the cave. "And you believed me."

My eyes widened. He was good, too good. Brilliant, even. I didn't recognize this man as a wolf in sheep's clothing—Black Sheep fit him. I was tired of this lunatic controlling my life. The cave's oppressive weight and its damp air, thick with mold and blood, pressed in, but I needed to keep his focus on me. "I know who you are... all of you. You think you're so clever. Well, think again, Nathan!" I said, defiance crumbling into desperation. "You don't have to do this. You're not a monster. I'm not my mother. Let us all go. We can end this."

My blindfold was torn off, my vision hazy from exhaustion and scrapes, yet I glared at the cruel face of Mom's killer, his deranged eyes gleaming in the flickering firelight across the cave's jagged ceiling. Nathan's jaw tightened, conflict flickering within him. "You're wrong. I am a monster. You're mom created me. And you know what….I'm happy she did. This is me, and I am like your mother, but you're nothing like her," he muttered, voice cracking. "That's why it's so damn hard to kill you." He stepped closer, gun trembling. "But you're hers. Her blood, her shadow. She destroyed me with her lies, her men. You need to die! But other's need to die first." He unlinked the Finn's chains, and with hands bound, they propped themselves against the wall.

I seized the moment to get his full attention, voice low, as tears fell. "Nathan, you loved her once, didn't you? I see it. Killing me won't undo her mistakes. Let me live for you, not her."

His eyes darkened, a storm brewing. "Loved her?" he snarled, his voice breaking as he approached. "She was a poison. My dad, her lover, their affair. It broke my mom, tore her apart until she was a shell. I was seven, watching her cry herself hollow every night." His gaze drifted to the cave's shadows as if seeing it play out on the damp stone. "Mom hanged herself. But I was in the closet. I saw it all. Nicole came to our house, all soft words and nursery rhymes to 'comfort' me, reading 'Peter, Peter' like a twisted saint. But then she turned on Mom, coaxed her to the noose, and said if she didn't hang herself, she'd make sure I'd die slowly, painfully. Mom chose to save me. She stepped into that rope, with tears streaming down. Nicole made it look like a suicide, but it was murder. She took away the only person who could ever love me!"

My breath caught, and a sickening wave of horror and guilt crashed over me. Nicole did that? Forced a woman to die to save her son? My stomach churned; the cave's cold seeped deeper, its flickering flames blurring as tears came full force. "Nathan," I whispered, voice shaking, "I... I had no idea. I'm so sorry for what she did to your mom, to you. But I'm not her. I'd never..." I swallowed, my scraped hands trembling. "You don't have to be her pain. You're more than this."

He shook his head, gun wavering, eyes haunted. "I wanted you dead to make her pay, her blood is in you. But you're... different. It's eating me alive." His ragged breath echoed in the cave's silence.

He turned, and I followed his gaze. Sadie lay curled up against Tanner on the cave floor, her battered body marked with bruises as she watched through bloodshot eyes. "Get up!" Nathan roared. She stood shakily, the shadows of the cave deepening her wounds. My heart sank at the sight of her fragile, damaged frame.

Tanner tried to hold on to her but ended up supporting her broken body as it stood. We all stared at each other wide-eyed; the fear in our eyes bound us together as we recognized that killing was Nathan's drug, his addiction, and he was going to kill Sadie.

Nathan tapped the side of his head. "Ladybug, I am clever," he taunted, his voice sharp. "She was my pawn, my delivery man."

My mind shattered. Why? Sadie sobbed, collapsing and clawing at the sand. "Alexis, I'm sorry," she choked, her voice raw. "He said he'd kill my mom, my family, burn our house... I had to give you the costume. I tried to warn you, but he was always watching." Her pleading eyes begged for forgiveness, hands scraping the gritty floor of the cave. I wanted to reach her, to say I understood, but Nathan's gun silenced me, its barrel glinting.

A shot rang out, echoing off the cave's walls. Sadie's body crumpled, and my scream tore through, carrying every moment I'd failed her.

Tanner's anguished cry echoed, his body collapsing over Sadie's, hands trembling as he cradled her lifeless form, and blood stained his fingers. I froze, my scream caught in my throat, tears burning as guilt and horror choked me, my failure, her blood. Nathan's cold laugh sliced through, his eyes glinting with twisted satisfaction, unfazed by the life he'd stolen.

My defiance shattered her. Tears burned my eyes. I killed her. Nathan pulled the trigger, but it might as well have been me.

"You're going to watch everyone die, then I'll kill you slowly," Nathan spat, his mouth near mine, rancid breath mingling with the cave's moldy stench. He dropped me to the sand, jarring my scraped knees.

My gaze locked with Asher's as he comforted Tanner, their chains rattling against the cave's slick stone. I mouthed, "I'm sorry," but Asher shook his head, anguish etched deep. I stared at Sadie's still body, blood pooling on the cave floor, and struggled to escape this killer's trap. I'd been foolish to think I could save everyone. My defiance provoked Nathan, but his words, Mom's betrayal, and his mother's forced death shattered me. I wasn't her, but her shadow clung to me, and I had to try for the girl—I wasn't my mother.

58

Alexis

Nathan's voice sliced through the cave's salt-heavy air, a jagged edge of menace that cut deeper than the stalactites glinting overhead. He barked orders at the figures silhouetted at the entrance, Zane, Trevor—their code names—Beetle, Owl, rattling in my skull, a perverse echo of the "Peter, Peter" note scrawled in Mom's blood. The cave's shadows swallowed his exact words, but the venom in his tone was unmistakable, a predator orchestrating his trap. The fire's flicker cast their forms in distorted relief against the slick stone, their movements tense as if bound by more than Nathan's commands.

Beside me, Cooper's face, usually a mask of quiet resolve, contorted with a fierceness I'd never seen, eyes narrowed to slits, jaw locked so tight the tendons stood out like cords beneath his skin. His wrists strained against the zip ties, the plastic biting deep, cutting into flesh already slick with blood. With each painstaking pull, calculated and torturously slow, he strained as if his sheer force of will could shatter the bonds, driven by nothing but raw, unyielding defiance.

The ties didn't yield; they embedded deeper, blood welling up in thick, dark rivulets that traced paths down his forearms, pooling at his elbows before dripping onto the cave floor. The metallic tang hit my nose, sharp and nauseating, mingling with the damp rot of the cave.

I jumped when I heard Becca shout, cracking like a whip as she entered the cave. "Up against the wall!" Her gun trembled in her grip, the barrel jerking wildly. My breath hitched a shift in the air, a fracture in their control. Relief flickered in my chest, fragile and fleeting, like a candle flame in a storm.

We were saved.

The group hesitated, their eyes darting between one another, creating a ripple of uncertainty that broke their formation.

"Mom, what are you doing?" Trevor's voice splintered, raw with confusion and dread. My stomach twisted. The pieces didn't fit, but the weight of his words sank into me like lead.

"Back up!" another voice snapped, cold and authoritative, cutting through the chaos. His gun, held in his right hand, glinted in the slant of dawn sunlight piercing the cave. The other hand gripped Kaitlyn's arm tightly. He shoved her into the cave, causing her to stumble and fall onto the rocks. What's happening? Was Kaitlyn involved?

"Dad!" I cried. Hope surged through me like a tidal wave, my pulse hammering in my ears. Rescue salvation. But as he stepped into the cave, his suit pristine and badge glinting under the firelight, his face was a blank slate with no warmth, no recognition. He knelt before me, and Nathan didn't move to stop him. Confusion choked me, thick and suffocating. "Dad?" My voice wavered, and hope teetered on the edge of collapse.

He squinted, his gaze icy and piercing. "Nathan, I told you that the blindfold stays on till I'm here," he said, his voice devoid of anything human. My heart cracked, a fault line splitting wide, betrayal seeping through the fissures.

What the hell?

"Sorry, Spider," Nathan replied, his tone flippant and dismissive as he gestured toward Sadie's crumpled form in the shadows. "She figured out who I was, and she kept testing my patience."

Spider?

The word struck like a sledgehammer, shattering the last remnants of the man I'd called father. Luke was one of them. Part of Nathan's grotesque menagerie.

"What's going on, Dad?" I demanded, clinging to the title like a lifeline, desperate for it to anchor me or to wake him up.

"Stop calling me that. You know I'm not your dad!" Luke roared, the words a blade, sharp and final, the cave's echo amplifying the sting of truth. His voice shook with fury, eyes glinting with a betrayal that mirrored my own.

I flinched, my chest cracking under the weight of his rejection. "Then why, Luke?" I demanded, voice raw, tears burning my eyes. "Why are you here? What did I do?"

He stepped closer, his badge shining brightly from the firelight, a cruel reminder of someone who should be trusted. "You don't get it, Alexis," he spat, voice low and venomous. "Nicole was a poison, her lies, her affairs, forcing Samantha to hang herself, which I helped cover up. I wanted her gone, needed her erased for what she did to us, to everyone. I made a deal with Nathan to make it happen. We both felt she had to go. And you..." His gaze hardened, pinning me like a specimen. "Deep down, I've always felt like you weren't mine. The test proved you weren't mine, just like I always suspected. I tried to be your dad, the closest you'd ever have, but once I knew I wanted a real family, a fresh start with Becca. You're a reminder of Nicole's betrayal, and you kept digging, unearthing her crimes, threatening to expose me for covering them up. You had to go, too."

The cave's damp air pressed in, and his words felt like a second betrayal, cutting deeper than the first and shattering the fragile bond I had clung to. My knees trembled as the fire's crackle mocked my pain, and Sadie's blood pooled nearby—a silent echo of my failure. Luke wasn't my father by blood, but he had been my anchor, and I was a pawn for him. My identity fractured further, a mirror shattered by his cold eyes. I wasn't his daughter, but I had loved him—did that mean nothing?

His need to erase me and start anew with Becca tore every good memory I had with him, leaving me adrift in Nathan's deadly game.

"Your mother was a whore!" he spat, his voice dripping with venom, a hatred I'd never heard before. I flinched, the cave walls seeming to pulse inward, crushing the air from my lungs.

"Becca, get the three of them out of here and onto the boat," Luke ordered, his tone cold and detached. He kissed her passionately and possessively, a display that turned my stomach. She left with Trevor, Kaitlyn, and Zane, their footsteps fading into the darkness. Luke clapped his hands together, a dark smile curling his lips, his badge glinting like a cruel tease.

"Alright, Nathan, we're wasting time. I called the department after I had set up the bombs. Right before I got here, they're swarming the bridge like flies." His voice lit up with excitement, his eyes gleaming as he wrapped an arm around Nathan, a gesture grotesquely paternal that made bile rise in my throat.

"Those explosives I set up? Pure genius, son. Your idea to blow the bridge and throw the cops off our trail was brilliant. Kessler, Becca's crazy uncle, came through with the bombs. He's been tinkering in his garage for years, hoarding fertilizer and diesel from his farm, mixing in some homemade C4 with wiring from old construction sites. Said it was his finest batch yet, enough to turn that bridge to rubble and buy us time to slip away."

My chest tightened as the pieces clicked into place. Kessler Becca's uncle was the one always "cleaning up messes," their messes. But he wasn't just a fixer; he had helped create this mess, crafting those bombs in his garage, his hands as dirty as Nathan's. Now, the memory twisted into a sickening realization that his tinkering had armed this nightmare, with his loyalty to Becca binding him to Nathan's plan.

The cave's damp air pressed down harder, Nathan's predatory grin glinting like the stalactites above as if savoring the chaos they had unleashed.

Luke handed Nathan a black remote from his pocket, his smile mirroring Luke's predatory grin, full of teeth and malice. The end was drawing near, like a noose tightening.

His gaze locked onto me, his Ladybug, and he began to hum, low and deliberate, "London Bridge is falling down, falling down, falling down, London Bridge is falling down, my fair lady."

The Trips and I watched, frozen, as Nathan's voice twisted the rhyme into something sinister, each note a thread in the web he'd spun around us. His eyes gleamed with madness, a maniacal glint that reminded me of the Joker unhinged and reveling in the chaos. He toyed with the remote, his fingers dancing over it, then slammed his fist onto the red button, his off-key singing grating against the cave's stone: "London Bridge is broken down, broken down, broken down, London bridge is broken down, my fair lady."

Nathan stabbed the remote with his thumb, letting out a cynical, pleased laugh. The ground shuddered beneath us, a low growl rising from the earth. Dust poured down from the ceiling, coating us in a choking veil that clung to my skin and hair. The explosion's rumble followed seconds later, a delayed thunderclap that vibrated through my bones. We weren't far from Gold Beach. If I could just break free, there was still a chance.

"Now I can take my time. So, who wants to go first?" Nathan's voice was deceptively casual, like a predator toying with its prey. He unsheathed his hunting knife, the blade glinting in the firelight as he stepped closer to the Trips. He dragged the tip along Asher's hairline first, slow and deliberate, the skin parting beneath the steel. Blood welled up, thick and dark, spilling into Asher's eyes. He flinched, a sharp hiss escaping his lips, but Nathan moved on, unfazed, repeating the act with Tanner, then Cooper. The blood flowed freely now, staining their faces and dripping onto the sand. "Three blind mice, three blind mice," he sang softly, the rhyme a chilling undercurrent to his actions. "See how they run, see how they run…"

He paid no attention to their reactions — Asher's fists clenched, Tanner's ragged breathing, and Cooper's defiant glare burning with intensity. His gaze stayed fixed on me, watching the color fade from my face and my breath catch in my throat. I opened my mouth to protest, but he shook his head, a silent order. Tears traced hot, bitter paths down my bruised cheeks, but I bit my lip, swallowing the scream fighting to break free. He aimed to break me, and he was succeeding in shattering my spirit when he killed Sadie.

"Run, run, little mice," he taunted, twirling the knife between his fingers. "But there's no farmer's wife here, only me, and my blade's sharper than hers." He stepped closer to Tanner, pressing the knife's edge against his cheek, not cutting this time, just letting the cold metal rest there. "Tell me, mouse, do you see now? Or are you still blind? Do you want to go on living life without your precious Sadie?"

Tanner spat blood onto the sand, his voice hoarse yet steady as he clung to Sadie's still body. "You're a sick bastard."

Nathan laughed, a sound echoing off the walls, hollow and cruel. "Oh, I like you. Maybe I'll save you for last, let you watch your brother's squeal."

The scream lodged in my throat pulsed like a living thing desperate to escape. The Trips were going to die, and my anguish fueled Nathan. I tried to hide it, to bury the terror and grief, but the sight of their bloodied faces burned an unforgettable mark into my mind. I squeezed my eyes shut, trying to push the image away, but it stayed—on Asher's clenched jaw, Tanner's shuddering body, Cooper's fierce stare.

"Open your goddamn eyes, or I'll carve them like the pumpkin," Nathan snapped, his voice snapping like a branch, jolting me back.

I glanced at Luke through the flickering firelight, my eyes silently pleading for the father I'd always known to show at least a shred of mercy. His face contorted, rage igniting in his eyes like I'd never witnessed before.

"Don't look at me like that," he snarled, his voice sharp enough to cut through the tense air. "Pretending to care for you was torture and just part of his game." He extended his hand, gesturing to Nathan.

His words hit me like a fist to the chest, knocking the air out of me. Before I could even process the venom in his tone, he raised his gun, his hand as steady as stone, and fired. The shot exploded through Tanner's shoulder, blood spraying in a crimson arc across the sand. Tanner's scream tore through the cave, raw and guttural, echoing off the walls.

I stood there, frozen, my mind racing. All those years, this is why he didn't want me around, didn't fight for custody, and in that moment of realization, it dawned on me. He had always known I wasn't his daughter. He'd hated me this whole time, and I had never realized it. Did he know who my actual father was? The truth clawed at me, sharp and icy, but there was no time to dwell. Chaos erupted around me, with shouts and movement swallowing the moment whole.

Asher, hands still bound, lunged at Luke from behind, the zip tie cutting deeper into his wrists as he looped it around Luke's neck, choking him. "Drop the gun!" he snarled, legs bracing for leverage. He'd somehow freed his ankles, his movements fueled by rage. Cooper, wrists unbound, grappled with Nathan, seizing his knife hand in a desperate bid for control. They were evenly matched; Cooper's tied ankles hobbled him, but his determination burned bright, a fire that Nathan couldn't extinguish.

Time blurred into a frenzy of motion. Asher wrestled the gun from Luke, their struggle a deadly tangle. The gun fired, and Luke's body went limp, blood pooling beneath him from his stomach as he collapsed. His gaze met mine, a tear slipping down his cheek before the light faded.

"Asher!" I screamed, the zip ties cutting into my wrists as I clawed at them, desperate to break free. My scream was raw, Asher's eyes meeting mine, wide with shock and something unspoken. The smoke from the fire thickened, acrid, and suffocating.

Empty. Gone.

Nathan pushed Cooper's stunned body aside, forcing him to the ground as he pulled the blade from his leg. Then, in one swift motion, his hand clamped around my throat, yanking me to my feet and cutting off my air. I gasped, ragged and weak, staring into his murky eyes, bottomless pits of shadow. He released me, dropping me to the sand. His knife, in hand, dripped with Cooper's blood. I forced my breathing steady, hiding the fear clawing at my insides. He knelt, cutting the ties from my legs, his fingers lingering as they rubbed the raw, abraded skin beneath my jeans with a sickening intimacy.

"Don't touch her!" Asher's voice was a guttural roar, primal and protective. I wanted to shout at him to stop, that he'd only fan Nathan's cruelty, but Nathan's creepy smile silenced me, the predator savoring the hunt. His hand slid up my leg, clenching my hip, pulling me closer. The cold blade pressed against my neck, reopening the wound, blood trickling warm and sticky down my collarbone.

Nathan's eyes followed the blood, his tongue darting out to wet his lips. Then he kissed me aggressively, possessively, a violation that made my skin crawl. I pushed against him, but the knife dug deeper, pain flaring white-hot. I whimpered, and he deepened the kiss, his tongue invasive, tasting of sulfur and decayed rotten eggs. His hand groped my backside, pressing me against him, his arousal evident and revolting. I gagged, and he spun me, slamming me against the cave wall, the knife inches from my face.

His laugh was eerie, a high-pitched mockery as he taunted Asher and Cooper. "You both want her to live, don't you? Can't blame you; she's as sweet as she feels. You don't love her. I've watched you, Asher. You want her in every way possible. That's lust, not love. She's manipulated you just like her mother did with all the men she had. You won't want her when I take her first. She'll be ruined, tainted."

No! My glare screamed at Asher and Cooper to do something! The fire's heat was suffocating, their faces pale with horror and exhaustion. They were injured and bleeding, but they could still fight. I blinked away tears, scanning the cave for anything: a weapon, an escape. Nathan would have to kill me before he'd violate me.

"You don't know what love is, Nathan!" Asher's guttural, primal yell drowned out the other sounds in the cave.

A growl came from Nathan's throat. "My mom loved me, I felt her love, and I loved her. You're nothing, Asher!"

He closed the distance, his words freezing the Trips in place. "Three blind mice," he sang again, softer now, his voice a lover's caress laced with venom. "Didn't run fast enough, did you?" He tilted my chin up, his breath hot and foul against my skin. "Lay down."

I shook my head. "No."

"I'm not asking. Be a good girl, like your mother was, and do as you're told." His sneer was contemptuous, the scent of egg-breath choking me.

"Did you rape her too?" I spat, thinking of Mom.

"No. Whore, broke up families!" he roared, his face twisting with rage. "Don't you get it?"

"I do," I whispered, the weight of our shattered family crushing me, my voice trembling as I grappled with Mom's sins. "She had her own trauma; she was scarred just like you and me from childhood abuse. She had been beaten and broken, which shaped her cruelty. But no matter what pain anyone endures, it doesn't excuse killing others, not her, not YOU, not anyone."

"Ladybug," he warned, his voice a deep rasp that slithered through the dark; his eyes blackened until the pupils consumed the irises entirely. The firelight carved shadows across his face, transforming those black pits into endless voids, hungry, unhinged, showing no sign of remorse or empathy. My chest tightened, each breath a shallow stab as if the cave itself were squeezing the life out of me.

The ache on the side of my head made me dizzy, my vision swimming in sickening waves as I sank into the sand, the cave's chill biting into my bones like teeth. The grains scraped my palms, cold and unyielding, a thousand tiny needles pressing into my skin.

This is the end.

The thought clawed at me, heavy and relentless, like a drumbeat in my skull. My head slumped as the world blurred at the edges, but I fought to keep my eyes open, resisting the darkness that crept in.

Asher's gaze locked with mine across the cave, steady and fierce, a beacon through the haze. Cooper's hand gripped tightly onto his shoulder, their whispers urgent, jagged bursts of sound slicing through the fire's low roar. A plan? My pulse stuttered, a fragile thread of hope twisting in my gut. I clung to it, my focus narrowing to the two of them, their tense silhouettes, the flicker of defiance in their eyes, praying they could pull us out of this abyss.

Nathan straddled me, his weight a crushing force, pinning me to the sand like a trapped animal. The knife hovered at my throat, its steel kissing my skin with a frigid, lethal edge as warm blood seeped and fell to the dirt. I felt the pulse in my neck thud against it—each beat a countdown. He moved the knife down and snapped my zip ties off, and I rubbed the ache away from my red line wrists. My lungs burned; the air was too thin and cold. "Please," I begged, my voice trembling, splintering into shards of desperation. "I'll do whatever you want. Just put the knife down." The plea scraped my throat raw, a humiliating surrender, but fear drowned out my pride.

Asher's voice was barely audible. "Lex." I knew they couldn't watch this happen. I didn't want them to. I didn't want to be here.

His gaze softened for a heartbeat, a flicker of something human breaking through the mask, a cruel tease of mercy. My breath caught, a wild hope flaring. Could he stop? But then his eyes hardened, the monster snapping back into place as he glanced at the Trips. "It stays right here," he growled, placing the knife beside my shoulder, within reach but tauntingly distant. The blade glinted, mocking me, its cold presence a constant whisper of death.

With his unzipped jeans, a slow, nauseating tear echoed in the stillness, turning my stomach to acid. The stench of his sweat, blood, and something rotten flooded my senses, thick and suffocating. My hand crept toward a jagged rock half-buried by my hip, fingers brushing its rough, damp edge as I read the couple's names scrawled on the cave wall. They gave me a reason. My reason. Me. Now. The word pulsed in my veins, a frantic command. My skin prickled with cold sweat; every nerve screamed as I fought to keep my movements small and unseen.

Nathan shed his pants, the fabric crumpling into the sand with a dull thud. My grip tightened, the rock solid in my palm, its weight a lifeline. Our eyes locked, his stare a furnace of intent, mine a mask hiding the storm inside. The Rhyme Reaper, not the Nathan I thought I knew, loomed over me, his bulk a shadow blotting out the firelight, fumbling with my jeans. But I knew him. This was not a man. He was a monster who had taken lives and acted like he was God. His fingers were clumsy and invasive, the heat of his skin a violation against mine.

I sat up, closing the gap inch by agonizing inch, my body trembling with effort. The air thickened, time stretching thin as I moved. He flinched, a split-second falter in his control. My heart roared, a caged beast clawing to break free.

"It's okay," I whispered, leaning in, lips brushing his a baited trap woven with revulsion like Mom. The taste of bitter metallic roiled in my gut, but I maintained the act. His hand slid to my neck, possessive and greedy, as he kissed back, lost in his own hunger. His grip tightened, a vise threatening to crush my windpipe, and I felt the moment teeter on a razor's edge.

Now!

I smashed the rock into his temple, the impact reverberating up my arm like a shockwave, his grunt echoing off the walls, a raw, animal sound of shock and pain. Blood poured from his head, a dark river matting his hair, staining the sand beneath him. "Bitch!" he roared, the word slurring as he lunged, dazed but furious, his hands clawing for me through the haze of his own blood.

Asher and Cooper tackled him, their bodies slamming into his with a bone-jarring thud, pinning him to the sand. Their combined weight held him down, but he thrashed beneath them like a wounded predator spitting rage, his blood-slick hands scrabbling for purchase. Once he calmed, they hoisted him to his feet and pinned him up against the wall, he stopped fighting.

"Get help!" Asher yelled, his voice raw and fraying with panic. My legs trembled as I staggered to my feet, the ground tilting beneath me and threatening to swallow me whole.

I stumbled, kicking through the sand, each step a battle against the dizziness clawing at my skull. My eyes fixated on Luke's gun, half-buried near the fire, its metal glinting in the flickering light like a cruel promise. The heat burned my face, and the smoke stung my lungs as I lurched forward.

"Lex, go!" Asher's voice cracked, desperate and urgent, a lifeline pulling me through the chaos. I grabbed the gun, my hands shaking so violently that the weight nearly slipped from my grasp. Cocking it was a clumsy, fumbling task; the click of the hammer was a deafening snap in the suffocating silence.

I aimed at Nathan, my arms trembling, the gun feeling foreign in my grip, heavy with intent. The Trips stared wide-eyed, their blood-smeared faces taut with tension, the firelight casting hues of hell upon them. "Answers," I hissed, the fire's heat pressing in, sweat beading on my brow and dripping into my eyes. My voice was a ragged thread, barely holding together.

"You won't shoot," Nathan mocked, his voice faltering, a wet rasp as blood trickled from his temple, pooling in the hollow of his cheek. His grin was unhinged, a death 's-head leer daring me to pull the trigger.

"Bet I will," I snarled, steadying the gun with both hands, my finger twitching on the trigger, the metal cold against my skin. "Tell me, or I will. Where's my mom's body?" The question tore from me, a jagged wound laid bare, the need for truth a fire raging through the fear.

"Pull your pants up first," I commanded, my voice sharp and unyielding, cutting through the tense air. I couldn't stand him exposed like that, a sickening sight I refused to endure a second longer. My grip on the gun tightened, steadying my resolve.

Nathan hesitated, his eyes narrowing with a flicker of defiance, but then he slowly reached down and yanked up his pants. The fabric rasped against itself as he fastened them, his movements deliberate, each snap and zip a taunting delay. His gaze locked onto mine, simmering with hatred yet tinged with a grudging acknowledgment of my control.

Asher and Cooper flanked me, looking like warriors with their dried blood coating their faces. Their presence offered a silent strength, grounding me as the cave seemed to pulse and shrink; the walls closed in with every ragged breath. Nathan's eyes flicked between us, calculating and defiant, but I didn't waver. The gun was steady now; my hands were still shaking, but my will was iron. He doesn't get to win.

"I'll tell you only if you let me walk out of here. I won't come back to Gold Beach. The killings stop, and I'll let you live," Nathan bargained, the cave's echo mocking his words.

I laughed, bitter and hollow, the barrel steady. "I'm the one holding the gun."

Nathan's grin was unhinged, madness gleaming in his eyes. I needed to make a deal. "Fine, where?"

"Scattered in the Pacific. Your dad raped her. I carved her. She became shark food," he spat, his words icy, cutting deep. My stomach churned, bile rising.

"You son of a bitch! Why?" I shouted, advancing. Asher's hand on my arm held me back from lunging.

Nathan stood, staring at the gun, unfazed. "My father loved your mother more than mine. Once she was gone, my dad beat me. All I have left of my mother was her killing herself and the note she left me: '*I will always love you, Nathan.*'" His voice was flat, rehearsed, and emotionless. He stepped closer, the gun inches from his chest. "Then Nicole thought she could replace her, reading me those damn rhymes. Dad tied me down every night, forcing me to listen. He tried to erase my mom, saying Nicole was my mom. Her voice still claws at me, a monster. My mom was an angel."

Angel? I felt pity for that broken boy, twisted into a monster by my mother and Ronny—a tragedy I couldn't unsee.

He stepped again, but I held my ground. "Stop!" I yelled. He smirked. "Why them?" I nodded at the Trips.

"Just shoot him," Cooper whispered, his voice tight with urgency.

"She won't," Nathan beamed, charming and mad. "I need her; she needs me. We are more alike than you know."

I pulled the trigger *click*. My heart lurched.

Click. The cave walls seemed to laugh.

Again *click*. My breath hitched.

Click. The glow of the fire mocked me.

Nathan's triumphant laugh rang out as he jumped over Tanner and Sadie's still bodies, then shoved me into Asher and Cooper before bolting for the exit. We chased after him, the tide surging in and slowing him as the water lapped at his knees. Asher and Cooper lagged, weakened by blood loss, but I pressed on, my legs burning, driven by a fury I couldn't name.

I couldn't let him escape.

"Nathan!" I shouted over the crashing waves, my voice hoarse but fierce.

He turned, with the sea battering us both, his silhouette striking against the bright horizon.

He threw his hands up. "What? You already tried to kill me and failed."

"You're right," I said, wiping water from my face and tasting salt and blood. "I need you."

He stared, skeptical. "You're lying."

"No," I shook my head, stepping closer.

He grabbed my arm, yanking me against him as our needs hit the sand beneath the waves. I drew a wooden-handled blade, his knife I had slipped into my sleeve and drove it into his stomach. He staggered, eyes widening. I struck again, deeper. "Need you to die," I hissed, my voice steel.

"Ladybug," Nathan rasped, blood flecking his lips and spattering my cheek. "Alexis… you're not her. That's what makes you such a thrill to chase. Cats were mere practice. You're my true prize."

I recoiled as the warm blood hit my neck, a sickening mark of his obsession. Nathan crumpled into the surf, the tide seizing him, his form a fading shadow amid the churning waves. Cooper plunged in, grappling to hold the body, but the relentless current tore Nathan free, swallowing him into the abyss. I stared into the darkness, my breath ragged, catching a faint reflection bobbing northward, a distant boat, cold and indifferent to our chaos.

The roar of the sea thundered in my ears, a persistent sound that felt like a taunt against the chaos inside me. My chest heaved, each breath feeling like a jagged shard of glass, while my heart raced so fiercely I feared it might break free. I surrendered to the waves, indifferent as to whether they carried me away too.

"Lex," Asher's voice sliced through the tumult, soft but steady, a thin thread tethering me to something solid. I barely registered it over the screaming in my skull. He pulled me from the waves and cradled me against the ocean behind him.

My hands grasped the warm knife—fingers locked around the hilt as if it were part of me now. The blade gleamed, slick with blood that wasn't mine, its weight a sickening burden that dragged at my soul. My arms trembled not just from exhaustion but from the bone-deep terror that wouldn't let go. I could still feel it: the moment the metal bit into flesh, the resistance, the give. My stomach churned, bile clawing up my throat, but I swallowed it down. I couldn't let go. Not yet. If I did, I'd fall apart completely.

Cooper limped by us, and his hand moved toward mine, slow and deliberate, as if he were approaching something wild. His fingers brushed my skin gently and began to pry the knife from my grip. I flinched, a whimper escaping before I could stop it. Cooper spoke softly, "We got you. You're safe." I let him take the knife. Now, without it, I was nothing but a tangle of raw nerves, exposed and fraying.

Nathan was gone.

I forced my eyes to meet Asher's, searching for something, anything to hold onto. His gaze met mine, calm and unshaken, like a lighthouse in the storm raging inside me. I wanted to scream at him: How can you be so steady when I'm drowning? Instead, I raised an eyebrow, a pathetic attempt at normalcy that felt like a lie even as I did it. He smiled a small, reassuring curve of his lips that promised safety I couldn't feel. For a fleeting second, the knot in my chest loosened. But it wasn't enough. The storm wasn't over. It was inside me, clawing at my ribs, tearing at my mind.

Blue and red lights pierced through the darkness, their flashes cutting into my vision like blades. Sirens wailed, drowning out the waves, a piercing cacophony that made my head throb. I glanced up, dazed, as police cars lined the hill, their silhouettes stark against the night. People in FBI jackets scattered at the cave entrance as boats edged closer to the shore, engines growling amidst the chaos. Safety, they promised. Order. But the sight only tightened the vise around my lungs. It was over, they said. Over. The word rattled in my skull, hollow and meaningless.

It wasn't over, not for me. The trauma clung like damp rot, seeping into every crevice of my being. I could still smell the copper tang of blood, sharp and metallic, coating my tongue. My hands, empty now, felt sticky and stained, as if the blood had sunk into my skin. The sea's roar echoed the violence I'd endured, each wave a memory crashing against me: the struggle, the panic, the moment I'd stopped being me and become something else. Someone who could hold a knife. Someone who could use it.

Guilt gnawed at me, sharp and relentless. I shouldn't have had to. I shouldn't have wanted to. But there had been no choice, or had there been? My mind spun, replaying every second, every decision, searching for a way to escape this nightmare without blood on my hands. Fear coiled tighter, whispering that this wasn't the end and that I would never outrun what I had done. And beneath it all, a numbness crept in, cold and heavy, threatening to swallow me whole.

Asher's hand found mine, his grip firm and warm against the icy tremor of my fingers. "You're safe now," he said, his voice a steady anchor in the howling void. I nodded mechanically, but the words slid off me like rain on glass. Safe? The storm inside me laughed, a bitter, broken sound only I could hear. Safe didn't erase the weight pressing on my chest or the shadows flickering at the edges of my vision. Safe didn't stop the shaking, the memories, or the dread that this was who I was now.

But when I looked into Asher's eyes, those infuriatingly calm, unwavering eyes, I sensed a flicker—faint and fragile. Hope, maybe. Or just exhaustion disguised as something softer. He didn't flinch at the wreck I had become, didn't pull away from the blood I couldn't wash off. Perhaps, over time, the storm would settle down. Maybe, with him by my side, I could start to piece myself back together.

For now, I let the lights and sirens wash over me, a chaotic lullaby promising an end I couldn't yet believe. They said the worst was over. But I wasn't alone. And that shaky, uncertain, and small as it was had to be enough.

59

Alexis

Several police cars from Curry County were gathered nearby. Officers from Coos and Josephine Counties arrived in Gold Beach to assist after the tragic accident. Asher and I huddled together in the back of a Coos County ambulance, watching people sob hysterically as we waited for a boat to take us to the other side for medical care. Rubble from the bridge was strewn around and in the Rogue River. Blankets, clothes, and anything people could find covered the bodies of the brave police officers and some fishermen.

The air hung heavy with salt and smoke, Curry County cruisers flashing red and blue against the Rogue River's churn, their sirens muted now, drowned by grief's wail. Officers from Coos and Josephine swarmed, "Multi-jurisdictional response," their radios crackled, assisting Gold Beach after the "catastrophic structural failure" of the bridge's collapse, Nathan's final act.

The ambulance antiseptic tang was sharp, and the blankets felt rough against my bandaged neck. We watched mourners sob, their faces twisted with grief. Bridge rubble littered the river, jagged chunks bobbing and catching the sunlight, while tarps and jackets, whatever was at hand, draped over the fallen: officers, fishermen, lives snuffed out by Nathan's bombs. My pulse echoed the water's lap; each beat was heavy, Sadie, Luke, Ranger guilt creeping like fog over the cliffs.

The ambulance door creaked open, letting in a gust of salty air and the distant wail of a mourner. Detective Jacobs stood there, his weathered face etched deeper from all the chaos, with his detective jacket smeared with ash and river mud. His eyes, usually as sharp as a hawk's, softened with what looked like regret as they settled on me and Asher, huddled under the ambulance's harsh lights.

"Alexis, Asher," he said, his voice low, as if he were afraid the river itself might overhear. "I need a word." He climbed in, the bench groaning under his weight, and shut the door with a thud that felt final. The antiseptic smell mingled with his damp wool scent, and I clutched the blanket tighter, my neck throbbing beneath the bandages.

Asher's hand found mine, his fingers cold yet steady. "What is it, Jacobs?" he asked, his voice rough from smoke and shouting over the chaos.

Jacobs rubbed his jaw, the stubble rasping against his palm, and leaned forward with his elbows resting on his knees. "I talked to Ronny." He glanced at where the wreckage of the bridge glinted like broken teeth in the moonlight. "A few weeks ago, he tried reaching out to me and left a voicemail, scared out of his mind, before he vanished. He said he found something in the forest behind his and Nathan's place, a burn barrel, hidden deep in the pines. Gutted cats, half-charred, were piled inside. And pictures, Alexis. Semi-burned photos of you and Nicole, with faces scratched out."

My stomach lurched, the image searing into my mind of those cats, their lifeless eyes defaced in flame.

Asher's grip tightened, his knuckles white. "Why the hell didn't he say anything to us?" he growled.

"He tried," Jacobs said, his voice heavy. "Ronny was piecing it together, sneaking around to gather more proof. But Nathan caught him out there, watching from the shadows. Ronny didn't realize he'd been seen. He wanted to confront Nathan himself but got spooked when Nathan threatened to kill him in his sleep. Nathan was always one step ahead. By the time Ronny came to me, Nathan had already flipped the story and planted just enough evidence to make it look like Ronny was the one burning those pictures, killing those animals. The cops searched the barrel after Ronny tipped me off, but it was cleaned out. Nothing left but ash and a few of Ronny's own tools, conveniently placed. He knew about Nathan's plan but didn't know when,"

I swallowed hard, my throat raw. "So Nathan was telling the truth. He framed him," I whispered, the truth sinking like a stone. "And we didn't see it."

Jacobs nodded, his eyes dropping to the floor, heavy with regret. "I should've seen it sooner," he said softly. "Should've pushed harder when Ronny came to me, begging for help. But Gold Beach was stretched thin, and I was chasing dead-end leads up in Coos. By the time I got back, Nathan had his plan locked in too far gone to stop." He lifted his gaze, meeting mine with a piercing intensity that made my breath catch. "I'm sorry, Alexis. I didn't get to him in time."

He cleared his throat, his shoulders hunching as if retreating into himself. "It's worse than you know," he continued voice barely above a whisper. "Ronny admitted to abusing Nathan after Samantha died. But that's not all. Nicole was the one who killed Samantha. Ronny and Luke both knew and covered it up, all because they loved her. Buried the truth to protect her, even as it tore Nathan apart."

The revelation hit like a punch; Nathan was telling the truth, guilt and rage twisting in my chest until I could barely breathe. But Nicole's betrayal, along with Ronny and Luke's involvement, was pretty messed up—a tangled web of loyalty and lies that had poisoned everything. Nathan's trauma, his abuse, and his mother's murder had driven his downward spiral, turning him into a monster. I wanted to scream, to reject the truth, but it sank in, heavy and undeniable. His cruelty wasn't just madness; it was a wildfire born from years of buried wounds, consuming everyone in its path. My mind reeled, picturing Nathan as a boy, broken by those meant to protect him. How could I hate him and pity him at once?

Outside, the river churned, its roar a grim echo of the chaos within me. Fragments of the shattered bridge and the lives we'd lost swirled in the dark current, carried away into the night.

Jacobs patted my hand and then left to attend to other areas of the crime scene, assuring me that we would talk more later.

"Not your fault," Asher murmured, his breath warm against my ear, his chin resting like a tether amid the chaos, his voice remaining steady.

"It's not?" I leaned into him, my head against his. Asher's warmth anchored me, keeping me safe.

"You can't control others' minds," he said, the temple kiss soft and grounding, reminiscent of Dr. Finn's calm in therapy. "You're stronger than you know."

The image of Sadie's body wouldn't leave me–limp and broken on the cave floor, blood spreading like ink from the gunshot that ended her life. Luke was gone, too, his lifeless eyes fixed on nothing, blood trailing from the wounds he'd sustained in the chaos he unleashed. Tanner had been shot in the shoulder by Luke while just trying to survive; he'd been flown out in critical condition, the helicopter's echo now long gone. Cooper had been stabbed in the leg and airlifted as well, both men now locked in battles they might not win. Beneath tarps laid officers and fishermen, casualties of my mother's unraveling, their deaths stained by the trauma she passed down. Everything pressed on my chest.

I grazed the bandage, neck pulsing, Nathan's knife.

"Wish you'd gone," Asher said, his eyes on my bandage, worry sharp he'd pushed for the chopper.

"I'm okay," I said, shrugging. Pain flared, not okay, my wince hidden, river's cold seeping,

His snort sparked my laughter sharp, pain spiking, alive, the ambulance's hum steady.

Asher's shoulder brushed against mine, a quiet anchor in the storm. His jaw was clenched, and his eyes were red-rimmed from holding back what he refused to let spill. Sadie had been his cousin in every way but blood. Now, he stared at the floor, hands clenched as if he were wrestling with grief itself. I pulled our hands together, my fingers wrapping around his to ease the tension. He didn't pull away; he just exhaled, a shaky sound that said more than words ever could.

"You holding up?" I asked, my voice hoarse, barely above the hum of the river outside. It wasn't the right question, but it was all I had.

His gaze flicked to mine, a flicker of his usual defiance shining through the sorrow. "Not really. You?" His voice cracked on the last word, and it struck me how much he was carrying Sadie's absence, the guilt of not stopping Nathan and the same questions about family that gnawed at me.

I shook my head, leaning into him; the faint warmth of his jacket anchored me. "Feels like… I'm underwater. Everything's muffled. Like I should feel more, but I can't." The admission slipped out, raw and unguarded. I had always been the one to push forward, to stitch myself together after every bruise, every betrayal. But Sadie's death had fractured something in me, and I didn't know how to rebuild this time.

Asher's arm slid around my shoulders, tentative at first and then firm as if he feared I'd slip away too. "She'd hate this," he said, a bitter laugh breaking free. "Sadie would've kicked our asses for sitting here, moping."

I snorted, the sound catching in my throat. "Yeah. She'd call us soft." The memory of her grin flashed sharp, fearless, and it stung, but it also tethered me to her, to us. I pressed closer to Asher, his heartbeat steady against my side. "I keep thinking… I should've been faster. Should've seen Nathan coming. If I'd… "

"Stop." his voice was low, fierce. "Don't do that. It's not on you." He turned to face me, his hand touching my cheek. "We both missed it. But Sadie… she wouldn't want you tearing yourself apart. She'd want you to keep fighting. Like you always do."

His words hit hard, stirring something inside the fog of my mind. Fighting. It's what I've done my whole life through Mom's darkness, the scars she bore from her past, and the secrets that left me questioning who I was. But this fight felt different. It wasn't just about surviving anymore; it was about carrying Sadie with me, honoring the light she saw in me, even when I felt like I was drowning in shadows.

"I missed you."

He glanced at me, our eyes locked, conveying emotions that couldn't be expressed right now. "I missed you, too." His hand touched my neck gently, brushing against the bandage. He was, and always had been, my constant.

Dr. Finn hovered nearby, his face etched with worry, the same expression he'd worn after pulling me from the pit. He'd always been there, stitching my wounds and calling me 'Angel' with a tenderness that felt like more than a doctor's care. But now, after hearing Nathan call his mom an 'Angel,' I couldn't shake the feeling that there was more to it. Were they linked somehow? I used to think it was because he saw me as a light born from Mom's chaos, but now I wasn't so sure.

"You both okay?" he asked, his voice soft and searching. "I'm sorry about...Luke." I was happy he didn't call him my dad. He seemed awkward, like he was fighting an internal battle or holding back unspoken words.

I met his eyes, seeing the weight he carried— grief for Sadie and fear for me. "Don't be. I need time," I said, my voice small but steady. I tightened my grip on Asher's hand, feeling the calluses on his palm and the warmth that reminded me I wasn't alone. "We all do."

Asher nodded, pulling me closer with a silent promise. The dim ambulance light cast shadows over us, but his presence was a shield against the haze threatening to pull me under. Sadie was gone, and the truth about my father was still a tangled mystery I couldn't yet unravel. Still, with Asher, I felt a faint stir of something new—a resolve to keep going, not just for myself but for her. For us.

Epilogue

Alexis

The Oregon rain fell in a hushed cadence, wrapping Gold Beach in a gray veil that felt more like home than California's blistering sun ever could, despite everything bad that had happened here. Three months had passed since the Rogue River claimed Nathan's body, and his bombs shattered the old bridge, leaving scars on the town and on me. I stood at the edge of the rebuilt bridge, my boots scuffing the fresh asphalt while the river below churned secrets it would never yield. The knife mark on my neck, now a faded scar, itched a reminder that survival meant shedding old wings and forging new ones. I was still learning to fly, but the weight felt lighter.

Asher's footsteps crunched behind me, his presence a warmth against the drizzle. He stood close, red hoodie unzipped, hair wind-tousled, ice-blue eyes softer than ever. "You're quiet today, Lex," he said, voice low, pulling me back. "Thinking about Sadie? Or… everything?"

I turned to meet his gaze, the river's rush fading away. "All of it. Nathan, Luke, Sadie… I killed him, Ash. I'm free, but I'm not." My voice cracked, trauma's claws tightening. "You're leaving soon, going back to Princeton. I don't know how to do this without you."

He moved closer, his hand lightly touching mine, hesitant. I didn't pull back. "You're stronger than you realize," he whispered. "I saw it in that cave, every step since. I don't want to be Dad, fixing people. I want to fight for kids like us who were adopted or abused. You're the reason I'm chasing that, Lex."

My heart raced, his words unraveling my defenses. "Me? Ash, I'm… broken. Why stay? Why care?" My fingers curled around his, the ladybug's sting fading away.

His gaze held mine, intense yet gentle. "You're not broken. You mean everything to me." He cradled my face, his thumb lightly brushing my cheek, our breaths intertwining. "Can I...?"

I nodded, a tear slipping down my cheek as his lips met mine, soft, warm, a promise forged in survival. The kiss deepened, salty and heated, my hands clutching his hoodie while his arms pulled me close. It was a refuge, a vow against the Rhyme Reaper's shadow. I felt whole, if only for a moment.

We separated, foreheads touching, breaths unsteady. "I'm not letting you go, Lex," Asher whispered. "Princeton can wait. You're my home."

I smiled, shaky but real. "Good. I need you, Ash. More than I can say." I leaned into him—the river's whisper was steady.

Nathan was gone, his body lost to the depths of the Atlantic, just as he had scattered Mom's. The Coast Guard called off the search after ten days. Dr. Finn referred to him as a ghost, but Nathan's shadow lingered in my nightmares—his knife, his nursery rhymes. He had named me Ladybug, his twisted muse, but I wasn't the delicate insect he envisioned. I had outlived his rhymes, though the cost haunted me.

Tanner survived, his defiance outlasting the bullet that scarred his shoulder. At the bridge's memorial, he grinned. "Takes more than a psycho to ground me," he said, fist-bumping Asher and Cooper. Cooper's leg was healing, his spirit dubbing us "the Four Blind Mice" for our shared trauma. We found each other where ladybugs go to die; not a grave, but a crucible, tougher together. Tanner's laughter anchored me when the past grew heavy. Sadie's absence hurt; her laughter became a ghost I could not outrun.

Gold Beach was healing, stitches visible. The bridge's collapse claimed twelve lives: officers, fishermen, and a father whose name caught in my throat. A granite plaque bore their names, glinting under the drizzle, while Ray's banner read "Gold Beach Strong." The words rang hollow to those locking doors at dusk, whispering of the Rhyme Reaper's ghost. The FBI's vans lingered outside the sheriff's office, chasing leads.

Kessler's lot lay deserted, his '66 Pontiac GTO towed, but his shadow loomed. The FBI found bomb-making remnants in his garage: fertilizer, diesel, wiring linking him to the bridge explosives, and his connection to Becca through her maiden name. His muttering about "cleaning messes," shovel in hand, now echoed with the intent of shielding Becca's secrets. No trace of their flight remained, but the hunt continued.

Luke's betrayal hurt, but I had stopped mourning him. He had chosen his path; I chose mine, stepping into the light I was learning to trust. The ache of Luke's truth—that I wasn't his daughter—still lingered, a quiet pain beneath my scars. The shock of that test result had unraveled me, leaving questions about who I was without his name. I'd built my life on his love, only to find it hollow, tainted by Nicole's lies. Yet, standing on this bridge, I realized I didn't need his blood to define me. Asher, Cooper, Tanner—they were my family now, their loyalty stitching me whole. Still, the shadow of my real father loomed, a mystery I wasn't ready to chase but couldn't ignore.

The FBI's theory about Kessler chilled me. Becca was out there, and I knew the nursery rhymes might hum again. I pushed the thought down, the river's lap steady.

I refused fear's grip. Ladybugs thrived in tempests, their shells unyielding. My pulse beat, no longer a requiem but my own rhythm. Kessler's secrets might breathe, but I was done chasing ghosts. I was alive.

Kate approached, her face drawn and eyes vacant, holding wildflowers. "Alexis," she said, her voice breaking. "I didn't expect you here."

"I come sometimes," I said, feeling uncertain.

She set the flowers by the plaque. "She loved this town, you know. Even with everything."

I swallowed, guilt welling up. "I'm sorry, Kate. If I had"

"Stop," she cut in sharply. "Don't. It's not your fault." Her eyes flickered with pain beyond grief, and her trembling hands betrayed her words.

Tami appeared somber. "Kate," she said softly. "How are you holding up?"

Kate's strained smile wavered. "As well as can be expected."

Tami glanced at me. "If you need anything, we're here."

Kate nodded, gaze drifting to the river. "I just need time."

As Tami walked away, she sighed. "She's struggling. The loss... It's overwhelming."

I watched as Tami caught up to Kate, vanishing into mist, unease stirring. Something about Kate felt off, deeper than grief.

I turned to leave and spotted a folded piece of paper in the sand. I brushed it off and unfolded it, my breath catching. I crumpled it while scanning the shore. The wind carried a faint, chilling hum that mocked me. This wasn't over.

Raindrops dotted my hoodie as I climbed into the Shelby. Asher's gaze was fixed on Tami and Kate, who grew smaller in the distance. He kept the knife I'd used, Nathan's knife, locked in the glove box, honoring our unspoken vow. "Ready?" he called, his smile unwavering.

"Yeah," I said, climbing in. The engine roared, taking us to Finn's, Cooper's bad jokes, and Tanner's steady presence. The rain blurred the windshield, but I didn't need clarity—I'd survived the Rhyme Reaper.

I discovered my stitched-up family where ladybugs meet their end—not a grave, but a forge where I shed my fears and forged wings of steel.